James Edwin Thorold Rogers

Eight Chapters on the History of Work and Wages

Fourth Edition

James Edwin Thorold Rogers

Eight Chapters on the History of Work and Wages
Fourth Edition

ISBN/EAN: 9783337252984

Printed in Europe, USA, Canada, Australia, Japan

Cover: Foto ©Thomas Meinert / pixelio.de

More available books at **www.hansebooks.com**

EIGHT CHAPTERS

ON THE HISTORY OF

WORK AND WAGES

BEING A REPRINT OF CHAPTERS VIII., XII., XIV., XV., XVII.,
XVIII., XIX., XX., OF

"SIX CENTURIES OF WORK AND WAGES"

BY

JAMES E. THOROLD ROGERS, M.P.

AUTHOR OF
"SIX CENTURIES OF WORK AND WAGES."

FOURTH   EDITION

LONDON
SWAN SONNENSCHEIN & CO.
NEW YORK: CHARLES SCRIBNER'S SONS
1893

PREFACE.

THE following chapters, extracted from my larger work, and printed in a cheap form, have been published separately in order that they may reach those who might be deterred by larger volumes, and especially by those portions of them which deal with political history and bygone social conditions. I have, therefore, printed those chapters only which deal with comparatively modern facts.

It is significant and instructive, that at present persons are beginning to take a novel but profound interest in the condition and the history of those who live on wages, and to consider the narrative of their fortunes to be as interesting and important as constitutional antiquities, to be more important than military and diplomatic annals.

It is still more significant, that the political economist appears to be returning to his proper and ancient function, that of interpreting the causes which hinder the just and adequate distribution of wealth, and that he is putting into the background those airy and unreal speculations which have, during the last three-quarters of a century, been made his main business, to the serious injury of the practical lessons which he might have inculcated.

JAMES E. THOROLD ROGERS.

Oxford.

CONTENTS.

on looking at the course of the wheat markets, that information as to the aggregate crop was very widely diffused, and that corn was sent to very considerable distances for sale. There were horses and carts in plenty, the rate of carriage was low, and the bailiff could easily reach a market where there was a demand. Beyond question, the surplus produce of country places was taken to the nearest towns, and sometimes to those which were at a distance.

The cause of bad harvests is always excessive rain. In the years 1315-16, we are told that the wet was incessant, and much of the corn never ripened. Contemporary writers tell us that the poorer classes were constrained to live on unwholesome or disgusting food, and that numbers of them perished from famine. An attempt was made to procure corn from the Continent, and ordinances were published fixing maximum prices—of course without avail—and prohibiting the consumption of beer, as was done in 1800 with the distilleries. To add to the distress, a pestilential murrain broke out among the cattle, and the bailiff's rolls bear testimony to the universality of the disease, and the magnitude of the losses. It is said by chroniclers, that in the universal scarcity, numbers of servants and domestics were discharged; that, made desperate, these people became banditti; and that the country folk were constrained to associate themselves in arms, in order to check the depredations of those starving outlaws.

That the famines of this unfortunate period led to a considerable loss of life is proved by the unquestionable rise in the rate of agricultural wages after their occurrence. This is visible in the payments made for threshing corn, and still more markedly in those for reaping, where the rise is fully a penny an acre, the exaltation in the rates for oats and rye, previously the lowest paid, being the most considerable. The same rise is seen in payments for mowing, for thatching, and for women's labour. Now it is generally the case that, unless the labourer is paid at a rate which leaves him no margin over his necessary subsistence, an increase in the price of his food is not followed by an increase in the rate of wages, this result being arrived at only when there is a scarcity of hands. We shall see, when we come to deal with the wages of the sixteenth century, how slight was the rise in their amount compared with that of other values. Now the exigencies of the weather put certain opportunities within the reach of the labourers which, as their numbers had now become scantier, they could easily use.   The immediate rise in the wages of labour after the famine of Edward the Second's reign is as much as from 23 to 30 per cent., and a considerable amount of this becomes a permanent charge on the costs of agriculture.   That part which is permanent amounts to 20 per cent. on an average.

The habit of cutting corn high up on the straw, and therefore of avoiding weeds, must have materially shortened the drying process, and subsequently that of threshing out the grain.   Hence I conclude, if the corn only ripened, the mere presence of rain was not so injurious as it came to be, when, at a later period, the corn was cut low with the weeds.   That this change took place is proved by the statement of Fitzberbert, who advises that corn used for home consumption should not be screened too carefully, as the seeds of many weeds in corn supply a notable quantity of meal which might well be saved for flour.   In Arthur Young's times, it is again clear that wheat was cut high on the stalk.

During the reign of Edward II., the practice became increasingly general to accept money compensations in lieu of labour rents, and by the end of the first quarter of the century the rule had become almost universal.   It was to the interest of both parties that these commutations should be effected.   It was a vexation to the tenant that he should be called away from the work of his own holding to do the lord's labour.   It is plain, from Walter de Henley's statement, quoted above, that the bailiff had no little trouble in getting the due quota of work from the tenant, some three roods of first ploughing a day, or an acre of second stirring.   Hence, if the lord could get a fair money compensation for the labour, he could spare the cost of the bailiff's supervision over unwilling labourers.   And as money was more useful than the work he got, as well as perhaps more profitable in the end, he would be induced to make liberal terms with his tenants in villeinage, even if he were not morally constrained to take the alternative in money, which was prescribed as an alternative in case the labourer, for any cause, made default in the field.   At the same time he could, unless he made a special bargain, save the allowances which he made of bread and beer, and the license of every day taking as large a sheaf as the serf could lift on his sickle from the corn crops. These commutations would be entered on the manor rental, and would tend to assimilate the tenure of the surf, now increasingly called a tenant by copy or custom, with that of the freeholder who sat at a fee farm rent, besides familiarising all parties with the redemption of those contingencies which affected the status of a serf. Ultimately the money payments would be deemed to be fixed and determinate liabilities, the satisfaction of which was a discharge of all the old labour rents, and the proffer of which was a tender which the steward was bound to accept. I do not mean to say that the change was invariable, for there is evidence that the monasteries clung to the old system longer than lay lords did, and it is alleged that, while the regular clergy urged on these lords the expediency and humanity of enfranchising their serfs, they failed to practise in their own persons the moderation which they commended to their patrons and their penitents.

The period which intervened between the last of three bad harvests and the great event to which I shall next advert was one of exceptional prosperity. The harvests were generally abundant, the wages of labour had been permanently improved, and all kinds of produce were cheap, The early days of the great war did not impair the general well-being of the English people. The supremacy of England on the sea was assured, and the famous battle of Crecy was fought, less considerable in its immediate consequences than in the exalted reputation which it conferred on English arms. But this country, and all Europe with it, was on the verge of a great calamity, the most extensive in its immediate incidence, and the most significant in its ultimate effects, of all events which have happened in the history of this country, and, indeed, of all Europe.

The Black Death is alleged to have had its origin in the centre of China, in or about the year 1333, and is reported to have been accompanied by various phenomena in the earth and atmosphere of a very novel and destructive character, such, indeed, as were noticed as long ago as in the plagues of Athens and the simultaneous visitations at Rome, or the mortality which prevailed in northern Europe near three centuries before our era, and at the terrible pestilence which visited the known world in the age of Justinian. So in later times the cholera and the influenza were traced to particular spots in India or China, which had been desolated by earthquakes, as Justinian's plague was said to have had its origin at Pelusium. Nearly every infectious or contagious disease which has desolated mankind appears to have had its origin in the farthest East, and to have travelled along thence to Europe, though the yellow fever is said to be a product of the West. It is alleged, that before it reached the West, the Black Death exhausted itself in the place of its origin. Like most other plagues, it was infinitely more destructive at the commencement of its career, than after it had endured for a time. This is not to be accounted for by the fact that the weakest members of the community naturally succumbed the first, for we are told that it killed the strong, and that, just as with the Asiatic cholera, when it is most virulent, many of those attacked perished speedily, and before the disease had developed its most characteristic symptoms. It appears, indeed, and the impression is confirmed by scientific research, that when some new infection or contagion is developed, the whole population is specially liable to the assaults of the disease, and that sometimes it may totally perish, as in all likelihood the ancient occupants of the ruined cities in Central America have disappeared without leaving any sign, other than their stupendous buildings, of their existence. So also diseases familiar to us in England, and now become mild, are specially deadly to those races into which they have been for the first time introduced. In course of time, either the original virus of the disease is weakened, or those who are most susceptible of it are removed by death, or remedial measures are discovered which check or extinguish it. For more than three centuries the plague wasted England, though at no time, it seems, so seriously as at its first and last visitations.

The Black Death, as our forefathers called it, from the dark purple blotches which appeared on the skin, when the blood and tissues had become wholly disorganized through the virulence of the disorder, still lingers in the East, under the name of the Levant, or Oriental, plague. Even now we are occasionally informed of some outbreak in an Eastern plague spot, where the hateful **Turk** has reduced every one to squalid poverty and misery, and whence Europe is again threatened. But the progress of sanitary science has probably put an end to the worst ravages of a disease which was so terrible more than five centuries ago. In England it does not seem to have been assisted by any prevalent distress among the people, as the Athenian plague was by over-crowding, as that of Cadiz was in 1800, or as the last visitation of small-pox was by the miseries of the Franco-German war. The period just before the plague was one of prosperity and abundance; and though our forefathers were immeasurably unclean in their habits and surroundings, and remained unclean for centuries afterwards, the best conditions of life do not appear to have given an immunity from the plague. Among the victims of the first year were one of Edward's daughters and three Archbishops of Canterbury. So the narrative given us by Boccacio proves that all classes were equally affected, for the ladies and gentlemen who retire in the Decameron to tell each other stories in a country house on the road to Fiesole had all of them lost relations by the plague. The Black Death visited Christ Church, Canterbury, very lightly, for a century before the prior had laid on pure water from the hills to the monastery.

The Black Death first attacked Europe in Cyprus at about the end of the year 1347, and was accompanied by great convulsions of the earth, and by atmospheric disturbances. Many persons who were seized with the disorder died instantly. The plague seemed not only to the frightened imagination of the people, but even to the more sober observation of such men of science as lived at the time, to be moving forward with slow progress from the desolated East, under the form of a dark and fœtid mist, which settled on the garden of the Lord, and left it a howling wilderness. On January 25th, 1348, an earthquake had laid waste great part of the peninsulas of Italy and Greece. Meanwhile the mischief was steadily progressing along the basin of the Mediterranean, for the caravan traffic was carrying it everywhere, as the pilgrimages to and from Mecca disseminate disease in the homes and cities of returning devotees. The Black Death appeared at Avignon in January 1348, was in Florence by the middle of April, and had thoroughly penetrated France and

Germany by August. It entered Poland in 1349, reached Sweden in the winter of the same year, and Norway, by infection from England, at about the same time. It spread even to Iceland and Greenland,—the former, a well-wooded country and fairly flourishing Colony of Norse origin; the latter a region with which communications had been kept up for centuries. We are told that, among the physical changes which ensued from the Black Death, or preceded and aided it, vast icebergs were formed on the eastern side of Iceland and on the whole coast of Greenland, and effectually cut off all communication between the Old World and those parts of the New which heretofore had been familiarly visited. In 1351 it reached Russia, after having inflicted its first severities on the rest of Europe, and having taken the circuit of the Mediterranean. It is probable that the caravan trade through Russia had been at this time suspended, and that the natural spread of the disease had been checked by the barrier of the Caucasus.

On the 1st of August, 1348, the disease made its appearance in the seaport towns of Dorsetshire, and travelled slowly westwards and northwards, through Devon and Somerset, to Bristol. In order to arrest the progress of the mortality, the authorities of Gloucestershire prohibited all intercourse with the citizens of Bristol. It was in vain; the plague spread to Oxford, where it was terribly destructive, and travelling slowly in the same measured way, reached London by the 1st of November. It appeared in Norwich on the 1st of January, and thence spread northwards. Later in the year 1349, the Scotch made one of their customary raids into England, and, as they ravaged the north, invented an oath, " By the foul death of the English." On their retreat they were attacked by the pestilence in the forest of Selkirk, and the northern part of the island suffered as seriously as the more populous south.

The mortality was no doubt enormous and appalling. It is probable that one-third of the population perished. To be sure, panic always exaggerates numbers. One chronicler says that nine out of ten died. Similar amplifications, which have been heedlessly accepted by writers who are inexperienced in possibilities, are found in all the chroniclers. We are told that sixty thousand persons perished in Norwich between January and July, 1349.

Norwich was probably the second city in the kingdom at the time, and Norfolk was certainly the richest county; but the number is twice as much as the population of both city and county at the time. Joshua Barnes, the author of a diffuse life of Edward III., pretends to give exact information as to the persons who died in the principal English cities. His numbers are undoubtedly untrustworthy. The nearest estimate to likelihood which I have seen is that of Knighton. He was a canon of Leicester, and lived a short time after the events. He tells us that the deaths in the three parishes of Leicester town were 1,480. Even this number I believe to be exaggerated, for there is reason to conclude that at this time the population of Leicester was under 3,500.

Every town had its plague-pit. That of London was a spot afterwards occupied by the Charterhouse, and purchased for the purpose of sepulture by Sir Walter Manny, one of Edward's captains. Some years ago, being at Cambridge while the foundations of the new Divinity School were being laid, I saw that the ground was full of skeletons, thrown in without any attempt at order, and I divined that this must have been a Cambridge plague-pit. I have no doubt that the principal place of burial for the Oxford victims was at some part of New College garden, for when Wykeham bought the site, it appears to have been one which had been previously populous, but was deserted some thirty years before during the plague, and apparently made a burial-ground by the survivors of the calamity. Hecker estimates the loss of population in Europe at twenty-five millions, a moderate and probable calculation.

No doubt the ravages of the pestilence were more general among the poorer classes. But, as I have already stated, the more opulent were not unaffected by it. The disease made havoc among the secular and regular clergy, and we are told that a notable decline of learning and morals was thenceforward observed among the clergy, many persons of mean acquirements and low character stepping into the vacant benefices. Even now the cloister of Westminster Abbey is said to contain a monument in the great flat stone, which we are told was laid over the remains of the many monks who perished in the great death. The novelist

Boccacio dwells on the effect which the mortality caused in the character of the survivors, and how panic or despair made men callous, reckless, superstitious, heartless, cruel, and licentious ; and Sismondi, in his great history of the French people, and of the Italian Republics, has collected contemporaneous evidence to the same effect.

The Black Death formed an epoch, and, for many years afterwards, facts were computed according to their nearness from the great pestilence. A century after the event, Gascoigne makes it the era of the new departure in Oxford, after which learning, morality, and the adequate discharge of duties began to wane ; the universities were, relatively speaking, deserted, and the whole spirit of society was changed. It is said by Sir Harris Nicolas that of the three years, 1349, 1361, and 1369, in which note was made of the extraordinary virulence of a disease now become sporadic, the first pestilence was said to have lasted four months ; the second through the winter, for eight months and nineteen days; the third for nearly three months. These dates of duration, given centuries after the event, cannot be accepted as authentic, but they are indirect testimony of the singular impression which the calamity left on the mind of England. I have been struck with the fact, from more trustworthy sources, when I have noted certain entries made in the records of several Hertfordshire manors, where the plague appears to have been specially deadly. In these manors it was the practice for thirty years to head the schedule of expenditure with an enumeration of the lives which were lost and the tenancies which were vacated after the great death of 1348. Nor have I any doubt, if some antiquary were to have the patience to peruse and tabulate the taxing rolls of Edward I., and compare the names of residents in the several manors with the entries of tax-paying inhabitants resident in the same manors after the great plague, he would find that thousands of names perish from the manor registers, as that of the Oldhams did from Cuxham. It may be noted that the foundation of colleges in Oxford, which was rapidly proceeding before this stupendous event, ceased for many years, when it was taken up with renewed vigour.

At first, as is constantly the case in times of panic, there was a suspicion that the disease was the work of human agencies. As usual, the Jews were credited with having contrived the calamity. They were charged with poisoning the wells, and throughout France, Switzerland, and Germany, thousands of these unhappy people were destroyed on evidence derived from confessions obtained under torture, or even from the fact of their religion and origin. They were protected as far as possible by the Emperor, Charles IV., whose own influence in Germany was very circumscribed. They escaped persecution, too, in the dominions of Albrecht of Austria. It is said that the large Jewish population of Poland is due to the fact that Casimir the Great was induced, by the entreaties of Esther, a favourite Jewish mistress, to give them harbour and shelter in his kingdom. The story is curiously corroborated by the respect which is still paid by the Podolian Jews at the present time to the memory of this second Esther, who, being taken into the harem of another king, also alien to the race of Israel, remembered her kindred in the day of their trouble, and to the generosity of the Polish monarch who yielded to her wish. It ought to be added that Clement VI. forbad the persecution of the Jews at Avignon, where the pope was still residing. The English people was saved from being tempted to the crime of murdering the Jews, because the king's grandfather had expelled the whole race from England. And yet, in this our own day, one sometimes wonders whether we have really escaped from the contingency, even in countries calling themselves civilised, of witnessing again the bigotry, the malignity, the spirit of hatred which accepts impossible lies, for which there was the excuse of ignorance in the Middle Ages, but not the shadow of an excuse now.

We learn from contemporary accounts, and here we can trust them, that a rapid growth of population followed on the destruction of the Black Death. It is said that after this event, double and triple births were frequent; that marriages were singularly fertile; and that, in a short time, the void made by the pestilence was no longer visible. The repressive check of a high standard of living was removed by the ease with which the survivors could obtain that standard, and accumulate from a considerable margin beyond it. The physiologists of the time, however, averred that

the human race suffered a permanent diminution in the number
of teeth, which had been always possessed by those who were born
before the visitation of the Black Death. I make no doubt that
the population speedily righted itself, as it has done on many
other occasions when a sudden or abnormal destruction of human life
has occurred in a people and the people has a recuperative power.
That they had this power is proved by the events which followed.

Probably a third of the population perished. Froissart made
the same estimate a generation later, when fear had ceased to dis-
turb the judgment; and, as I have said, it is described as having
been peculiarly deadly to persons in the vigour of life. It is certain that the immediate consequence of the plague was a dearth
of labour, an excessive enhancement of wages, and a serious difficulty in collecting the harvests of those landowners who depended
on a supply of hired labour for the purpose of getting in their
crops. We are told that these crops were often suffered to rot in
the fields for want of hands; that cattle and sheep roamed at
large over the country for lack of herdsmen; that land went out
of cultivation; and that the grandees were utterly impoverished.
I have referred already to the collateral evidence of an extraordinary falling off in the assessments under customary taxes. Many
of the lords excused their tenants' rents lest they should quit their
holdings from a want of labour and the increasing and excessive
cost of materials; the omission of rent sometimes extending to
a half, sometimes for a term of years, as the landowner could
arrange with the tenant. So, says Knighton, "they who had let
lands on labour-rents to tenants, such rents as are customary in
villeinage, were compelled to relieve and remit such labour, and
either to utterly excuse them or to rehabilitate their tenants on
easier terms and less payments, lest the loss and ruins should
become irreparable and the land lie utterly uncultivated." It
appears, therefore, that in the panic, the confusion, and the loss
which ensued on the Great Plague, that process which, as I said
before, was going on already, the commutation of labour-rents for
money payments, was precipitated; that the lords readily gave
in to compositions; and that even less than had hitherto been
demanded in exchange for the service was arranged for the future.
The plague, in short, had almost emancipated the surviving serfs

I shall point out below what were the actual effects of this great and sudden scarcity of labour. At present I merely continue the narrative. Parliament was broken up when the plague was raging. The king, however, issued a proclamation, which he addressed to William, the primate, and circulated among the sheriffs of the different counties, in which he directed all officials that no higher than customary wages should be paid, under the penalties of amercement. The king's mandate, however, was universally disobeyed, for the farmers were compelled to leave their crops ungathered, or to comply with the demands of the labourers. When the king found that his proclamation was unavailing, he laid, we are told, heavy penalties on abbots, priors, barons, crown tenants, and those who held land under mesne lords, if they paid more than customary rates. But the labourers remained masters of the situation. Many were said to have been thrown into prison for disobedience; many, to avoid punishment or restraint, fled into forests, where they were occasionally captured. The captives were fined, and obliged to disavow under oath that they would take higher than customary wages for the future. But the expedients were vain, labour remained scarce, and wages, according to all previous experience, excessive.

As soon as Parliament could meet, the proclamation was reduced to the form of a statute, which remained, with the proclamation, a law, till both were formally repealed by 5 Elizabeth, Cap. 4. The statute contained eight clauses :—(1) No person under sixty years of age, whether serf or free, shall decline to undertake farm labour at the wages which had been customary in the king's twentieth year (1347), except they lived by merchandize, were regularly engaged in some mechanical craft, were possessed of private means, or were occupiers of land. The lord was to have the first claim to the labour of his serfs, and those who declined to work for him or for others are to be sent to the common gaol. (2) Imprisonment is decreed againt all persons who may quit service before the time which is fixed in their agreements. (3) No other than the old wages are to be given, and the remedy against those who seek to get more is to be sought in the lord's court. (4) Lords of manors paying more than the customary amount are to be liable to treble damages. (5) Artificers are to be liable to the same conditions, the artificers enumerated being saddlers, tanners, farriers, shoemakers, tailors, smiths, carpenters, masons, tilers, pargeters, carters, and others. (6) Food must be sold at reasonable prices. (7) Alms are strictly forbidden to able-bodied labourers. (8) Any excess of wages taken or paid can be seized for the king's use towards the payment of a fifteenth and tenth lately granted. The statute provides for the difference between summer and winter wages, and guards against the emigration of the town population to country places in summer. In answer to complaints from the employers of labour, the Statute of Labourers is constantly re-enacted, with accumulated penalties and precautions,—penalties sometimes laid on the labourer only, sometimes or the employer, sometimes on both. An attempt, which was, I believe, premature, was made to enforce apprenticeship in handicrafts at the beginning of the fifteenth century, with the view of making the agricultural labourers an ever-increasing residuum, and thereby securing cheap labour for the tenant and the lord.

The statute of Labourers may have induced some slight effect on the wages of farm labourers. The peasantry were under the eye of the lord's steward or bailiff, and might have been denounced and punished if they claimed more than the law allowed them. But they had great power of combination,—a power which they used, perhaps, in a manner which made it very difficult to enforce the statute, for the enforcement of it is given to the manor court, where the goodwill of the tenants was essential to harmonious action between lord and tenants. This combination the statute called the "malice of servants in husbandry." But there was the pretence of submission to the statute in the bailiff's rolls, which might have been taken in evidence. After the Black Death, payments are frequently entered in these rolls, at a particular rate, and this a very exalted one. These payments are drawn through with a pen, and a less sum substituted. Thus, in 1349, on one estate, the bailiff enters 5*d*. as the price at which wheat was threshed. A line is drawn through the figure and 3*d*. substituted. In the next year, wheat, rye, peas, and vetches are threshed at 6*d*., barley at 3*d*., oats at 2*d*. But a pen is drawn through these rates, and 2½*d*., 1½*d*., and 1*d*. are substituted. In the same year, barley is reaped at 1*s.* 2*d.* at first, but the sum is altered to 1*s.* Very many of these instances could be quoted. Occasionally, but rarely, the hirer of labour makes similar changes in artizans' labour, as though to show obedience to the statute.

I cannot help thinking that these transparent erasures are simulated, and that they point to evasions of the statute. The labourer, if he did not receive his full money wages, was compensated in some covert way to the full extent of the previous entry, and by some means which would not come under the penalties of the law, and the process by which these penalties might be enforced. There might be larger allowances at harvest time, a more liberal concession of common rights, or, as I have often seen, a license given to a shepherd to turn his own sheep into the lord's pasture, or some analogous equivalent to a necessary, but, under the statute, an illegal money payment. Even though we take the substituted entries, we shall find that a great rise in the wages of labour was effected. We know that this rise was in direct contravention of the law,—a law created in the interest of those who employed labour, and, therefore, who wished to have it cheap, and who might be within the risk of the penalties imposed on employers for violating that law which they had probably been instrumental in enacting, but were compelled to incur. Besides, the wages of many kinds of labourers whose callings were enumerated in the statute were not affected by the law at all. These men took their full increase. It was no marvel that Parliament constantly complained that the Statute of Labourers was not kept. The marvel is that they did not see that it could not possibly be kept. But the straits in which the capitalist landowner found himself were sufficiently serious for any one; and the landowner might be pardoned for believing, that if he could fix, as he thought he could, the price of provisions and materials, he could also fix the price of labour. He clung to this delusion for centuries, and at one time he seemed to have achieved what he desired. But he paid for his remedy in a far more ruinous way than that of giving what would have been in the end cheaper labour than he actually procured.

I mentioned in a previous chapter that the rate of profit

derived from agricultural operations, after all charges had been deducted and an average allowance had been made for rent, when the occupier was also lord, was about 20 per cent. on the capital invested, about 2 per cent. being represented by the rents of assize and manorial receipts. This estimate has been taken from an actual balance-sheet, in a year of average, or rather more than average, fertility, but when the price of stock was, on the other hand, rather high, and so returned more than the ordinary profit to the farmer. Still, it will be remembered that the superintendence by the bailiff was a heavy charge on the owner's profits, or, at least, was a charge from which the small proprietor was free. It will be obvious that, with such a rate of profit before them, landowners, who possessed by inheritance a large amount of live and dead stock, would naturally cultivate their land themselves. There was, indeed, no way in which they could use their property to equal advantage.

In the year which I have taken, 1332-3, the outlay, though in some particulars large, is, on the whole, very much an average. The charges which come under the head of necessary expenses are rather high, but the bad debts are very low, and the cost of labour is so small as to suggest that some part of the regular cost of farm labour must have been omitted or put under another head. In another year we shall find a large cost incurred for fittings to the mill; in a second, a serious loss in customary or ordinary rents; in a third, a heavy loss of stock, and the consequent necessity of large purchases. An enormous quantity of cider was this year produced from the orchard, and, therefore, the spring must have been mild and the summer genial. On the whole I cannot but think that the year was in no way exceptional, and that the rate of profit on agricultural operations was neither unduly exalted nor unduly depressed.

Now if we take the balance-sheet of the same estate in the year 1350-1, we shall see the full effects of the loss of life and the scarcity of hands which ensued from the plague. The whole family of the bailiff, as I have more than once said, had perished. The rents of assize have sunk to one-third their former amount. The fulling-mill is abandoned; there is no tenant for it. No one will give more than 22s. for the corn-mill—the previous rent

having been 50*s.*; and next year there is no tenant to be found at
all. The exits of the manor are a little more than a fourth of the
sum previously received, and the profit of the court is not a tenth.
The harvest had been poor, for notwithstanding the loss of
population, the price of wheat was 50 per cent. above the average,
and the crop was small, the sales being less than two-thirds of the
earlier year. The profits of the dairy are about three-fifths of
those in 1332, and about half the amount of stock is sold. On
the other hand, the expenses are very heavy. The outlay is cut
down; but little is spent on repairs, nothing but what is absolutely necessary in order that farm operations should be carried
on is bought. Labour in harvest time and in the manor house
costs three times what it did in 1332. There is a great increase
in the cost of all services, and of such articles as depend mainly
on labour for their manufactured value.

The expenses exceeded the receipts. The new bailiff, however,
possesses a quantity of wool, the accumulations of two years. He
had no doubt kept it in hand in the hopes of more remunerative
prices. He had good reason for this caution, for wool had been
sold at little more than three-fifths the money value which it
realised in 1332. Then there were some of the chattels of the
deceased bailiff and his family, which could hardly be reckoned
among the profits of the farm, but an accidential escheat. Without them the profit for the year is only 4 per cent., with them it
is 5½. In all these calculations I have taken corn and stock at
their average prices for the year, when the actual value of any
item is not given, as is of course the case with anything except
what is actually bought and sold. In the next year the owners
of the estate did not lose heart, they sowed a larger breadth of
corn than usual, and strove to carry on their operations, only
to meet with a second failure. Four years later, in 1354, there
were lower prices and greater plenty. But the old rates of
profit on such farming operations as had been carried on by the
capitalist landowner had entirely passed away, never to be recovered, at least to their full amount. Sooner or later, labour must
be hired at the old prices, or a new system must be adopted.

Although I am by no means convinced that the erased figures
were not paid to the labourer, and that the substituted amounts

were, I have always assumed that the after-thought was the
real payment. Even under these circumstances the rise in agricultural labour was enormous; and if, as we are told, the
young and healthy were the principal victims of the disease, the
quality of the labour must have been considerably deteriorated.

In the autumn of the year 1349, the fullest effect is induced
on the price of agricultural labour, in the Eastern, Midland, and
Southern Counties. The cost of threshing wheat is nearly
doubled in the first division, that of barley and oats considerably
more than doubled. In the Midland and Southern Counties the
rise is even greater for wheat and barley, but oats, in the south,
are still threshed at the old rates. The price in the west is raised,
but in a far less degree, and, indeed, it appears that Western
England did not suffer so much from the disease and the consequent paucity of hands as the greater part of the rest of the
country did. But the prices of this year are panic rates. Even
if the Statute of Labourers had not been passed, a fall would have
ensued, though the price of labour, proclamations and statutes
notwithstanding, did not ever fall to its old rates.

If we take the whole period from 1350 to 1400, when the
prices paid for labour had been steadied by custom, and examine
the divisions of England which it will be convenient to take, we
shall find that the final rise in the prices of threshing, taking the
three principal kinds of grain together, is 60 per cent. in the
Eastern Counties, 73 in the Midland, 48 in the Southern, 37 in
the Western, and 59 in the Northern. The most notable rise is
that in the payment for threshing oats. But the prices paid for
this service had been very low, and, as may be expected, the
dearth of hands told far more on low-priced labour than it did on
high-priced. This is strikingly illustrated in the price of women's
labour. Before the plague, women were employed in field work,
as in reaping straw after the corn was cut, in hoeing, in planting
beans, in washing sheep, and sometimes in serving the thatcher
and tiler. Generally they are paid at the rate of a penny a day,
but sometimes less. After the plague, women's labour is rarely
recorded, but they are seldom paid less than twopence, sometimes
as much as threepence, a day. The same facts are observed in
boys' labour, which becomes much dearer.

The rise in the wages of harvest work is equally suggestive. Naturally the increase should be less as the rate in the old time was higher. But against this is to be set the opportunity which the labourer had of pressing his claim in a time of urgency. In the first place, the rate is equalized, or nearly so. Before this event, the highest price was paid for barley, the lowest for rye and oats. Now the same, or nearly the same, rate is secured for all. The price, too, is constantly rising. The old average was about 5½d. an acre. It rises at once to 7d. and 7½d., and soon is much more, so that it is evident that the Statute of Labourers was from the first entirely inoperative as regards harvest work. For the ten years, 1371-80, it is more than double what it was before the plague. We shall see hereafter how serious were the consequences which ensued from this progressive exaltation in the price of harvest labour. About 1770, as Young tells us in his "Eastern Tour," vol. iii., the rate for reaping wheat, the only corn reaped, was 5s. an acre ; for mowing other corn, 1s. In the decade I am referring to it is 10d. all round, though nearly every kind of grain was below the average price. With corn of all kinds at an average of 3s. 8½d., and reaping at 10d. the acre, the peasant in Young's time got a little more than one-tenth of the price of a quarter of wheat for his labour, and the fourteenth century peasant about two-ninths of the value of the whole produce.

The general rise of harvest work, however, if we omit the exceptional period 1371-90, is 59½ per cent., the reaping of the acre of wheat and barley rising by 51, bigg by 44, rye by 47, beans, peas, and vetches by 59, and oats by 69 per cent. But after the plague, the cultivation of bigg and rye becomes increasingly rare. Had this not occurred, I am convinced that the invariable rule in prices, whether of labour or food,—that in a general rise of anything in demand, what was paid for or purchased at the lowest rate previously gets the largest increase subsequently—would have been again exhibited. The rise effected in the labour of mowing grass is not so considerable. But it is found to be 34 per cent. above the old rates. I should not expect that so notable an increase would be effected in the rate at which grass was mowed by the acre, as in ordinary harvest work. The mower is hired at a time when—I am speaking of the fourteenth

century, when early summer ploughing for root-crops was
unknown—agricultural labour is least in demand, and, therefore,
better bargains could be made for it.   But at the same time, if
we refer to the parallel already cited, the prices paid for labour
in the middle of the third quarter of the eighteenth century, the
facts when compared are very striking.   The ratepaid for mowing
grass, on the authority of this writer, Arthur Young, was a maximum of 2*s.* 6*d.* an acre, but was ordinarily 2*s.*   At the latter rate
the labourer received no more than the equivalent of a twenty-
fourth part of a quarter of wheat ; at the former rate it was about
a nineteenth ; whereas before the plague the rate was about a
thirteenth of the quarter ; and in the latter part, *i.e.*, after the
plague, it rose to one-tenth.   I have already observed that in the
eighteenth century the price paid for mowing an acre of corn is
far less than that given for mowing an acre of grass.

The price paid for the thatcher's labour is equally suggestive.
He was practically a farm-servant, employed to keep buildings
in repair, when the thatch was worn out or imperfect, as occasion
required, but constantly to cover stacks after harvest, and hay-
ricks before harvest.   His labour attains a slight and permanent
rise after the great famines of 1315-21, but a far greater rise
afterwards.   He is always accompanied by a help or *homo.*
This assistant is ordinarily a woman, and the wages are frequently
paid conjointly, though sometimes separately.   This is explained
by the fact that the help was very often the thatcher's wife
or daughter, or perhaps young son.   When the wages are paid
separately before the plague, the rate is about a penny a day :
afterwards it rises to 2½*d.*, or by an increase of 125 per cent.

Now we might expect that a thatcher's employment was
influenced generally by the two causes which affected or moderated
labour prices.   His services were occasionally needed when the
roofing of houses and barns was to be done, and if his wages
were over high, this demand might be economized.   But no such
economy was possible in the roofing of ricks and haystacks.
Hence we should expect that the rise in his wages would not
equal that of other kinds of farm labour.   It is actually 48 per
cent.   But if we take the payments made to himself and his help
together, the proportion is sure to be enhanced by the extra-

ordinary increase made for the helper's services. It is found to amount to 79 per cent. Even this is less than the amount paid for the two services taken separately. I conclude, that if the help was, as I have said, his wife, daughter, or young son, a slightly lower rate of remuneration would be agreed on than that demanded or paid when the bailiff or employer was hiring two persons whose bargains with him were independent.

It is necessary to follow out the facts in the wages of artizans. These are chiefly the carpenter, the mason, the tiler, the tiler and help, the slater, the slater and help, and the sawyer, either by the day and the couple, or by the hundred feet of plank; this latter, the only kind of piece work which can be conveniently handled, being taken as almost identical with the day's work of a pair of sawyers. The others are paid by the day.

There are two kinds of carpenters regularly employed. The one is engaged on ordinary farm work, and was in frequent requisition. The other was employed for the more difficult business of house building, and the more delicate business of joinery, for which there was plenty of occupation in the domestic buildings of the more opulent classes. The best paid carpenter gets about 25 per cent. above the average paid to common carpenters, though, in taking a general average, I have thought it fair to include the former's wages with those of all others, as he may have been engaged at lower rates, or even the same rate if he were a good workman, on commoner kinds of employment. Here the same facts appear. He gets a slight permanent rise after the great famines, and a large one after the great plague. The common carpenter's wages experience an enhancement of 48 per cent., and, exactly in accordance with the rule laid down as the regulator of prices, the highest kind of carpenter's work gets a rise of only 42 per cent. Masons, however, are more fortunate. The rise in their wages is 60 per cent. It is very probable that the combination which these artizans were able to effect, the regulations by which they might govern their trade, and the manner in which they were certainly associated together under the title of free masons (as is proved by the fact that these combinations were made felony by 3 Hen. VI., cap. 1), would have enabled them to take full advantage of the situation. The

tilers' wages rose only 34 per cent. But the joint wages of the
tiler and help rose 90 per cent. The evidence of the slaters'
wages is less clear. The calling was confined to some of the
Midland Counties, where fissile oolite had long been used for
roofing, and, as we have seen, the general rise in the rate of
wages was very great. It would seem that the increase is 60
per cent. in this kind of labour The rise in the wages of the
pair of sawyers is 70 per cent., and that of sawing by the
hundred feet is nearly the same amount.

The rise in agricultural labour is, all kinds of men's work being
taken together, about 50 per cent. ; and of women's work, fully
100 per cent. When taken together, the rise in the wages of
artizans' labour is almost exactly the same as that effected in the
case of the husbandmen. The result is marked, universal, permanent, and conclusive, even if we had not on record the
complaints of the landowners in Parliament that the Statute
of Labourers was entirely inoperative.

The peculiarity of the situation is that, while every kind of
agricultural produce experiences no rise, everything to which labour
adds its principal value is exalted proportionately. Thus the price
of wool, though temporarily depressed, recovers, though only to its
old rate. There is no appreciable alteration in the market value
of cheese, butter, and eggs, in the price of the different kinds of fat
and candles. The price of wax and cider remain the same ; and so
does that of firewood, except during the very height of the plague.
But there is a rise of 50 per cent. in the price of charcoal.

The price of salt is nearly doubled, that of lime and iron more
than doubled. The price of laths rises 60 per cent., of tiles
75. Crests, *i.e.*, ridge tiles, are three times as dear as they were
before the plague ; and the different kinds of nails, such as were
fashioned by the town smith, and sold by retail to his customers,
are proportionately enhanced. Quite as great is the exaltation
in the price of millstones, articles which the lord was constrained
to buy if he were to get the profits of his most lucrative franchise,
the manor mill. The price of hurdles, which are generally
purchased, is exactly doubled : of horse-shoes more than doubled,
as are also horse-shoe nails and plough gear. The share and the
shoe are almost doubled. The iron clouts, by which the frame

and axles of a cart are strengthened, are nearly trebled in cost; and the nails by which they were fastened rose as other nails did. Plain wheels—that is, wheels formed from the trunk of a tree, with holes bored through them for the axles to run on—are more than doubled in price. Wheelwrights' wheels are nearly trebled; and the iron framework of a pair of cart-wheels, one of the most costly parts of agricultural furniture, rose by 130 per cent. There was scarce an article needed for agricultural operations, the cost of which was not doubled instantly after the calamity occurred, and which did not remain at these exalted and ruinous rates. Even the coarse canvas, which was employed for fans, mill-sails, and sacks, was nearly doubled in price. The hair-cloth used for drying malt was more than doubled, as was linen for shirts and sheets, and that which was used for table, with most of which probably, if not with all of which, the peasant dispensed. The least rise was effected in woollen cloth, one of the indirect illustrations of the fact that the domestic manufacture of woollen goods was a very general, and also what is called a bye industry. Lead, again, a metal used very frequently and generally in the Middle Ages, was more than doubled in price. Tin, pewter, or solder articles, substantially the same, rose 50 per cent.; while little increase occurred in the price of brass and copper vessels. They were probably economized, and, lasting a long time, few purchases were made of them.

I have stated before that in the face of these serious changes in the value of these articles, on the regular and cheap supply of which the success of capitalist agriculture in the fourteenth century so largely depended, there was no corresponding rise in the price of provisions. The different kinds of grain are not appreciably dearer, beyond what is occasionally due to the unfavourable character of the seasons. Oxen and cows are a little dearer, but in no such degree as to suggest that there was any rise of general prices to account for the change. The price of horses is absolutely stationary. There is no change in the price of sheep or in that of pigs. . Poultry, too, is similarly unchanged in money value. The loss of the agriculturist was confined to the cost of labour and the products of labour, and the only thing which could have been sacrificed was rent, or rather, under the circumstances which prevailed at the time, the profits of capitalist husbandry. The fact that these profits had to bear the first shock of the crisis, and therefore that a little time intervened in which the landowner could look round him, and probably take some new departure, and so keep his fixed rents, probably saved English society from a severer shock than it would have otherwise experienced. No doubt, as we indeed have seen, these fixed rents were at first reduced and generally imperilled. In many cases, where the landowner had leased his land, and had abandoned cultivation on his own account, he was constrained to remit a portion, or even, as Knighton says, to effect a new and permanent composition with his old tenants; for just as rent, when agriculture improves and a country progresses, is a constantly increasing quantity, so when a serious reverse takes place, when labour is dearer and deteriorates, or capital is lost or scanty, or agricultural profits are otherwise depressed, it is natural, nay, inevitable, that rent should have its reverses, and decline in value and quantity, even for a time to a vanishing point. We shall see hereafter how the English landowners of the fourteenth and fifteenth centuries applied themselves, when they found that parliamentary regulations were futile and misleading, to the solution of the great problem which lay before them.

One article of food rose greatly in price, was, in fact, doubled in amount. This was fish, especially herrings, an article which derives all its value from human labour, the raw material, so to speak, being free to all. The consumption of herrings was all but universal, even in the inland counties of England, large numbers of them being salted and smoked, or pickled without being smoked, and called in the former case red, in the latter white, herring. It would seem that the barrel or cade of smoked herring was marketed earlier than the barrel of white herring; for the former is found in the purchases long before the latter. But in the thirteenth and fourteenth centuries the art of the fish-curer had not reached that amount of skill and variety which was common in the fifteenth, and we know from various sources that much capital and enterprise were devoted to deep-sea fishing in many of the eastern ports and at Bristol during the reigns of the House of Lancaster.

All at once, then, and as by a stroke, the labourer, both peasant and artizan, became the master of the situation in England. The change was as universal as it was sudden. The lord found on all sides a stationary and retrograde market for every kind of produce, in which he dealt as a seller, and a rapidly advancing market for everything he needed as a buyer. Even if he should succeed, after making desperate efforts, in recovering labour at the old prices; if the old but deep-seated delusion that law can regulate prices should turn out in the end to be possible as regards the wages of farm hands; should the police of the manor be only armed with sufficient power for the purpose, he was still confronted with the difficulty that everything he wished to buy, beyond the labour employed on his own fields, had risen by 50 or 100 or even 200 per cent. Even on his estate nearly one-half of the charges of cultivation set down to the credit side of the bailiff's account are derived from outlay, over the amount of which no proclamation, statute, or ordinance could have had any influence whatever, and the exaltation of price on these items alone would reduce his profits to a minimum. If the value of his own produce had risen to an equivalent, the void would be filled, but no Act of Parliament could be devised by which the producer should be able to compel the consumer to pay 50 or 100 or 200 per cent. more for bread and beer, beef and mutton, pork and poultry. Besides, he was not the only dealer. A number of industrious and prosperous tenants were settled round his manor house, who tilled their own lands, from which they could not be evicted ; on the profits and improvements of which he could not, as long as they paid their dues, lay his clutches, and it was certain that if he strove to force an enhanced price for what his bailiff had to sell, they would undersell him. They were protected against him, as he was against the king, by custom,—a custom which he dared not break if he could, and could not if he dared. No position could be more unsatisfactory. If he left matters as they were, ruin to all appearance was imminent. If he strove to remedy the mischief by violent or unusual means, the danger was serious. We shall see, by-and-by, that he tried the remedy of force, and signally failed.

The peasant farmer shared the new charges which were put on

his calling, but not in the same degree. The costs of the harvest to the lord amounted to £3 13s. 9d. before the plague, they are swelled to £12 19s. 10d. in the year following it. From this charge the surviving peasant farmer was free. He found his own labour on his own holding, and hired none. Besides, he could, after his work was over, hire himself and his children out at the enhanced rates ; or, if he had thriven and saved, he could double his own holding, and that on easy terms, for the lord was seeking tenants, not tenants seeking lords. Perhaps the household of the miller was desolate and without inhabitants, and he was one of those who offered less than half the old rent for it ; or, maybe, he aspired to the bailiff's vacant place, for the lord was not going to desert his old calling without an effort. Only he could now save his wife and daughter from field labour, and set them to spinning and weaving for the household ; perhaps do better at that than they did at the drudgery of the field. The tools had decome dear, the sickle and scythe were doubled in price, and the shares and plough-shoes were going the same way. But he would patch up his stock of husbandry tools in the winter, and rub along for a time with the old, as his lord did.

The free labourer, and for the matter of that, the serf, was, in his way, still better off. Everything he needed was as cheap as ever, and his labour was daily rising in value. He had bargained for his labour rent, and was free to seek his market. If the bailiff would give him his price, well ; if not, there were plenty of hands wanted in the next village, or a short distance off. If an attempt was made to restrain him, the Chiltern Hills and the woods were near, and he could soon get into another county. There was no fear in these times that the lord could spare to follow him, or that they who wanted his service would freely give him up. He had slaved and laboured at the farm, and now his chance was come, and he intended to use it. So the peasant farmer and the labourer were to try conclusions with the landlord. We shall see how the struggle was fought out. The machinery which the former used had been long in preparation, though no one guessed its efficiency.

CHAPTER II.

LABOUR AND WAGES.

The Fifteenth Century the best Time for the Labourer—The Working Hours of the Day, and Yearly Wages—The Labourers' Board—Spread of Piece-work—The Wages of the Agricultural Labourer—The Impressment of Labourers, and Journey Allowances—Prices of Food do not increase, while Labourers' Wages are increasing—The Great Plague—The Civil War—The Effect of the latter on Husbandry and Wages imperceptible, and the People indifferent—The Lollards probably friendly to the House of York—The Sweating Sickness—The Capitalist Artizan in the Fifteenth Century—The Decay of Towns—The Increase of Sheep Feeding in the Sixteenth Century—The Debasement of the Currency—Its Effects on Wages—The Confiscation of the Guild Lands—The Origin and Uses of their Property—The Guilds like the Oxford Colleges—Induced Weakness of the English Labourer—No Rise in Rents, and the Reason—The Statute of Apprenticeship—The Result of these Changes, Pauperism—The Cost of maintaining Labour illustrated—Elizabeth's Expedient of making the Coin only Two-thirds its nominal Value.

I FIND that the fifteenth century and the first quarter of the sixteenth were the golden age of the English labourer, if we are to interpret the wages which he earned by the cost of the necessaries of life. At no time were wages, relatively speaking, so high, and at no time was food so cheap. Attempts were constantly made to reduce these wages by Act of Parliament, the legislature frequently insisting that the Statute of Labourers should be kept. But these efforts were futile; the rate keeps steadily high, and finally becomes customary, and was recognised by Parliament. It is possible, that as the distribution of land became more general, and the tenancy of land for terms of years became habitual, the phenomenon which has often been noticed as characteristic of peasant proprietorship, a high rate of wages paid to the free labourer, may have been exhibited in the period on which I am commenting.

The wages of the artizan during the period to which I refer

were generally, and through the year, about 6*d.* a day. Those of the agricultural labourer were about 4*d.* I am referring to ordinary artizans and ordinary labourers. Persons who plied a craft in which greater skill was needed, perhaps one which was rarely procurable except from a distance, received more. Thus, the carpenter, taken generally, gets a little under—it is a very small fraction—6*d.* He was constantly employed in agricultural operations and for domestic business. But the plumber, who might not be so regularly employed or was hired from a distance, gets 6½*d.* on an average. The mason, whose labour was likely to be suspended during winter time or in very bad weather, gets the full average. The joiner, who is employed in finer carpentry, is better paid than the average carpenter. It should be noted, too, that as the century goes on, the wages of labour tend decidedly upwards. Nor is there any material difference, with one notable exception, in the payments made for labour all over England. It is equally well paid throughout the whole country. The exception is London, where the wages were from twenty-five to thirty per cent. over the rates paid in other places. This increase may be due either to the cause that the guilds made labour in London comparatively scarce, or to the greater cost of living in London, for general prices are, as a rule, higher in or near the metropolis ; or to the fact that the best craftsmen sought London as a place of employment, and were better paid, because worth more than elsewhere.

There is no reason to think that these labourers were paid well because their employment was precarious. Men got just as good wages in the fifteenth century, whether they were employed for a day or a year. Nor, as I have already observed, were the hours long. It is plain that the day was one of eight hours. Nor was the period of winter wages, when the pay was lessened, considerable, for the short-pay season is, when such a period is specified, only the months of December and January. Sometimes the labourer is paid for every day in the year, though it is certain that he did not work on Sundays and the principal holidays. Thus, at Windsor, in 1408, four carpenters got 6*d.* a day, and six got 5*d.*, for 365 days in the year, *i.e.*, the former receive £9 2*s.* 6*d.* for their year's wages, the latter £7 12*s.* 1*d.*, the rate per day and the amount for the year being specified in each case. These men were no doubt in the service of the king, and the king, as I shall show presently, was a very good paymaster; but he is not the only person who hires labour on these liberal terms. At York cathedral, six masons got £8 8s. a year each; six others £7 16s.; six more, £6 3s.; and one carpenter gets £7 5s. 4d. This is in 1415, when the prices of labour had not risen to their full amount.

Very often the labourer is fed. In this case, the cost of maintenance is put down at from 6d. to 8d. a week. Sometimes the labourer is paid as though he were fed, and a further allowance for his board is given him, this probably being paid to some person who has contracted to feed him at a rate. Sometimes the food is given in, and the labourer's wages are paid at the full average. This is especially the case when the workman is hired by opulent corporations and on their premises. There was always a servants' table in these establishments, and the workman is bidden to it without stint or grudging. I find, for example, at some of the Oxford colleges that ordinary rates are paid, and the workman is fed into the bargain. Food was so abundant and cheap that it was no great matter to throw it in with wages.

Piece work becomes more common in artizans' labour. In the earlier time, for instance, the pair of sawyers were generally paid by the day, occasionally by the hundred feet, *i.e.*, the long hundred of 120, the pair evidently being understood to be competent to get through such a quantity in a day. In the earlier time the piece price is a little less than the day price. In the fifteenth century it is a little more. This is evidence of an upward tendency. When the reaction, on which I shall hereafter comment, begins, the former state of things is reversed in an exaggerated form, piece work falling below the remuneration of day work. So laying tiles and slates by the thousand, splitting laths by the hundred, walling by the yard, casting and rolling lead, by the hundredweight, making plate by the ounce, and doing ceiling work by the yard, are found, and are generally well paid.

The agricultural labour gets about 4d. a day for his work; but in harvest time 6d. The practice of paying this person by the day instead of by the piece becomes commoner than it was. But piece payments are progressively higher than they were in the dearest period of the fourteenth century. The man (*homo*) who is employed as a help to the thatcher or tiler, and often to the mason, later on to the bricklayer, is paid at the rate of agricultural labourers in ordinary times, or a little less. This help was sometimes a woman, as was generally the case in the earlier period ; and thus it is seen that women's work, when of what we may call an unskilled kind, was equally well paid with that of men. Piece work in the harvest field was paid at even higher rates than during the famous years of the fourteenth century, in which the labourer's combinations were so effectual and so alarming to employers. The full price of a labourer's board was a shilling a week, often considerably less ; his wages were twice or three times the cost of his maintenance under contract. In 1467, two girls are hired to work, and are paid 2*d.* a day. They are also boarded, and this is put at 2*d.* a day more. In the same year, at Selborne Priory, in Hampshire, the board of men is put at 2*d.*, of women at 1½*d.*

The king, who pressed labour at his pleasure, and from all parts of England, for he sends for workmen from distances of 150 miles, paid his agent in the business handsomely. This official sometimes also got a handsel for not taking workmen who were employed by private individuals and on works where despatch and convenience were important. But he cannot succeed in misusing the king's press, as Falstaff does, for he is paid by results, and would no doubt run considerable risks if he sent inefficient workmen. The men are also well paid. They are frequently boarded on contract, and we shall see presently how important is the information which these contracts give. They were also paid a *viaticum* on coming to and going from their work, at so much per mile of distance. One reads, too, of free-masons who get a slightly higher pay than ordinary craftsmen do ; of principal masons, who receive an annual fee, besides their daily wages ; and of master masons, like that one at York in 1423, who was paid £10 a year.

From 1260 to 1400 inclusive, the price of wheat is 5*s.* 10¾*d.* a quarter. From 1401 to 1540 inclusive, it is 5*s.* 11¾*d.*, and this slight increase of a penny a quarter is due to the dearer years of the period, 1521-1540. Had it not been for the rise induced on the general average, the price would have been 5s. 8¾d., or 3d. a quarter less. But, including these dearer years in the average, every kind of grain, except wheat and peas, is cheaper in the fifteenth and part of the sixteenth centuries than it was in the thirteenth and fourteenth. Now, notwithstanding the extraordinary cheapness of provisions (a fact to which public men turned their attention in the sixteenth century, by comparing the prices of the past with current experiences), there is no evidence that the wages of labour were depressed, or that the payment for service was the least affected by the low price of food. I do not, indeed, imagine that the economist who duly corrects his inferences from a wide range of facts, would be under the impression that such a result would necessarily ensue, or, indeed, unless there were other causes at work, conclude that the tendency of population would be to grow up to the limits of subsistence, as it grew for special causes in the seventeenth and eighteenth centuries. We shall see in the course of this inquiry that an excess of population is quite compatible with no increase in numbers, and that the misery of the working classes can be frequently ascribed to other causes besides their own improvidence and recklessness.

There occurred during this long period from the accession of Henry IV. to the dissolution of the great monasteries a number of social facts to which one should refer. And, in the first place, to the waste of human life by pestilence and other causes.

The Great Plague was said to have visited England twice in the fourteenth century after its first appearance, in 1361 and in 1369. But there is no information of a contemporary kind as to its ravages on these subsequent occasions, and though it is exceedingly likely that the disease remained endemic, it does not appear to have recurred with alarming severity. The farm accounts of the time make reference abundantly to the losses of 1348, but none speak of the return of the disease at the later dates, though we are told that the summer of 1361-2 was exceedingly hot and dry, and we know that though the price of wheat was low, that of other kinds of grain was abnormally high. But in 1369-70, all kinds of grain were very dear,—dearer than at any time since the great famine of 1315 and 1316, a convincing proof that the summer and autumn were cold and wet, and that, therefore, the temperature was unfavourable to the spread of contagion ; and I, therefore, set little store by the computation given by Sir Harris Nicolas, on the authority of a King-at-arms in the reign of Charles I., as to the duration, and even as to the occurrence, of these visitations. The notes I find of plagues in the fifteenth century are in 1477, 1478, and 1479, when unusual mortality seems to have prevailed in the Eastern Counties ; and during the sixteenth, in 1521, in 1538, in 1545 and 1546, when it was at Cambridge and Oxford ; in 1555 and 1556, in 1570 and in 1579. All these are reappearances of the Levant plague ; for another disease, which occurred for the first time in the fifteenth century, will be treated separately. In some of these cases, the note is of precautions taken against a possible visitation ; but in 1579, the Norwich register expressly states that 4,918 people died, a loss of life which must have been as serious as that in the first attack. But I cannot discover that the wages of labour were affected by any of these occurrences of the fifteenth century, nor in those of the sixteenth, until the general change in money values puts it out of one's power to infer anything from such events. I conclude, therefore, that the steadiness with which high relative wages were secured was in no sense due to the losses which labour suffered from pestilence. The existence of this formidable disease may have checked the growth of population ; but if abundant evidence as to the rate of wages and silence as to the loss of life are to go for anything, it did not create a sensible void in the number of labourers.

From 1455 to 1485, the country suffered from civil war. I doubt the statements made in chronicles as to the number of combatants engaged in the struggle. In the first battle of St. Albans we have been told that five thousand persons were slain. It is almost certain that not much more than half that number were in action. It was an accidental skirmish, provoked, as is alleged by contemporary writers and even eye-witnesses, by the king's party. Henry had liberated Somerset from the Tower, and York felt, or professed to feel, that his life was in danger. Nor do I doubt that, if we could arrive at the actual facts of the case, the combatants in the other battles were far fewer than the narrative affirms.

There was abundance of wealth in England possessed by the partizans, especially by the Duke of York's party, which was strong in London and the Eastern Counties. In the first period of the war, indeed till after the battle of Wakefield and the second fight at St. Albans, the sole purpose of the Yorkist party seems to have been the reform of abuses in the administration. It is true that the unfortunate murder of Tresham, and the development of violent partizan feeling in the Commons, made men, I conclude, despair of constitutional remedies against misgovernment. Matters were further complicated by the fact that, after Parliament had appointed York Protector, and had continued his office till he should be discharged of it by Parliament, Margaret contrived to create such a diversion in favour of the royal party that York surrendered his authority little more than two months after he had it granted him, and the queen went off with her husband and son into the county of Chester,—by which I believe is meant the city of Coventry,—the stronghold of the Lancastrian party, and there undertook the management of affairs. I make no doubt that during this period the Yorkist faction settled their differences and consolidated their plans.

The soldiers of fortune, who had long been familiar with partizan warfare in France and had now returned to England, were numerous enough for the armies of the rivals. In this the Yorkist party had an advantage, for Warwick was in command of the fleet and was governor of Calais—offices which he would certainly not have retained if the king's party had at all suspected the direction to which affairs were tending. When they were discovered, Margaret took the decisive step of summoning the Coventry Parliament, which was said to have been packed, and in which Tresham's son was Speaker, and of passing a sweeping bill of attainder by which York and all his partizans were pro scribed.

We are told that house was divided against house, that families were rent by factions, and that partizanship invaded even monasteries and colleges. Our great dramatist, as is well known, has illustrated the passions of the day with tragic incidents in his plays of Henry VI. But in this I suspect there is the special pleading of the Tudor writers, who wished to represent in the strongest way how great were the blessings which came in with the accession of the family under which they lived, and how healing had been the pacific policy of the first Tudor prince. I can only say, that though I have read hundreds of private documents compiled for private inspection only during the whole of this period, I have never met with any significant allusion to the troubles which were impending or the scenes which were enacted. It is true, that, in the summer of 1460, between June 26th and July 8th, just before the battle of Northampton, where Grey de Ruthin, the murderer of Tresham, deserted to the Yorkist party, and so insured the defeat of the king's troops, the provost and fellows of King's College, Cambridge, who had despatched two of their number to Coventry the year before, and had induced the University of Cambridge to celebrate the obsequies of the king's warrior father, were exceedingly anxious for news, and sent no less than eight times in the twelve days to obtain information as to the king's affairs and his doings. It was natural enough; the college was Henry's favourite foundation, which a year before had received its last statutes from the king, in which all disciples of the heretics Wiklif and Pecok were proscribed. Besides, the chapel was unfinished, and the king was making an annual grant for its completion.

During the struggle between the rival houses, it seems to me that the people were absolutely indifferent. It was not a war of sieges but of battles, in which the combatants appear to have sought out some secluded spot, and to have fought out the combat. I have never seen or read of any injury done to neutrals, except the outrages of Margaret's northern army in the beginning of 1461,—deeds which led to the instant deposition of Henry and the coronation of Edward. The war, as I believe, was as distant from the great mass of English people, and was as little injurious in its immediate effects, as summer lightning is. If it was followed by the destruction of human life, the loss did not fall on the working men of England, but on the nobles and professional *condottieri.* It had no bearing on work and wages. At the same time it is not wonderful if the partizans on either side believed that the rest of the country took sides in their struggles. One of the commonest and most persistent delusions into which parties fall is that of imagining that the rest of the world has as keen an interest in their affairs as they have themselves. A strong upheaval of national feeling is a rare event. Its continuity beyond the occasion of its first activity is rarer still. The farmer and workman, during the last half of the fifteenth century, must have had only a transient and languid interest in the faction fight which was going on around them.

It is exceedingly likely that the Lollards were active enemies of the House of Lancaster when the issue was fairly before them. John of Gaunt had been the friend and the patron of Wiklif ; and the reforming party, who finally overthrew the Government and put an end to the reign of Richard II., was identified with those who had been willing to strip the Church of its overgrown wealth. But Henry Bolingbroke had made his peace with the persecutors, and compelled, in deference to them, the civil authorities to execute the sentences of ecclesiastical tribunals. The Lollards pit at Norwich always had its stake and faggots ready, and we may be pretty sure that the Norwich weavers had no love for their persecutors, whom they identified with Henry and his bishops. So I can quite understand that the authorities of the city were doing no unpopular act when they clothed and paid forty hired soldiers to join the king at Tewkesbury fight, and aid in the final discomfiture of the House of Lancaster and its chiefs, as they had sheltered the queen and her daughter a short time before the king's triumphant return. So the same citizens the year following gave a handsome present to the Duke of Gloucester in a gilded purse, fed his actors, and put in prison those who spoke evil of the duke and the king.

After the battle of Bosworth, a new and fatal disease occurred in England. It is remarkable that for a long period it was confined to this country, or to Englishmen, though at last it broke out in Germany and the Low Countries. Its appearance was at special and well-defined periods, its duration being on each occasion brief. While it lasted, it was specially destructive, especially in the towns. So local was it that it did not reach Scotland or Ireland. The Sweating Sickness broke out in

Henry's army during its march to London.   It appears to have
had its origin, according to the chroniclers of the time, in the
Welsh mountains, and to have been primarily due to the privations which Henry's army underwent before he reached his foe
and gained the timely treason of the Stanleys.   The disease was
a violent inflammatory fever, accompanied by great prostration,
general disorder of the viscera, great oppression of the brain,
a lethargic sleep, and a profuse fetid perspiration, which flowed
from the patient in streams.   " So deadly was it," says Holinshed,
copying the exaggerated language of the older annalists, " that
not one in a hundred recovered."   The course of the disease was
very brief, the crisis being always over in a day and a night.
Men who had been quite well at evening were often dead in the
morning.   It attacked robust and vigorous people more frequently than the weak, and went from east to west through the
kingdom.   Two lord mayors and six aldermen were victims to
the disease in a week.

It visited the country again in 1506, though on this occasion
the malady was not so severe.   As before, its ravages were confined to England.   In 1517, it appeared for a third time, when
it was as destructive as it had been thirty years before, and was
particularly deadly in the Universities.   It also attacked Calais,
but it was noticed that it affected only the English inhabitants
of the town.   The fourth visitation was in 1528 and 1529.   It
was so destructive that the time was known afterwards as the
Great Mortality.   The period was one of scarcity, almost of
famine, and it was noticed that the " smut " first appeared in
wheat in this year.   On this occasion it attacked Northern Germany, beginning at Hamburg, where it is said that 1,100 persons
died in twenty-two days.   Thence it spread to Dantzic, Cologne,
and the Low Countries, and afterwards to Amsterdam, Copen-
hagen, and Stockholm.   The last visitation of the disease was in
1551, when it was described by Dr. Keyes, or Caius, the founder
of a well-known and distinguished Cambridge college.   Since that
time it has not re-appeared in England, though epidemics closely
resembling the described symptoms of the sweating sickness have
occurred in modern times, especially in Northern Germany and
North-eastern France.

The sweating sickness, though alarming for its virulence and the rapidity of its course, was not so destructive of human life as the plague had been and still was. Still it is desirable to give a brief account of it, because not only are the effects of pestilence marked on the social condition and moral character of nations, but the many economical consequences of plagues are more lasting and more significant than those of famines. Famine, indeed, has rarely occurred in England, for a reason which I have frequently given. But the habits of the people were favourable to pestilence. Every writer during the fifteenth and sixteenth centuries who makes his comments on the customs and practices of English life, adverts to the profuseness of their diet and the extraordinary uncleanliness of their habits and their persons. The floor of an ordinary Englishman's house, as Erasmus describes it, was inconceivably filthy, in London filthier than elsewhere, for centuries after these events. The streets and open ditches of the towns were polluted and noisome beyond measure. The Englishman disdained all the conditions of health, and in the large towns the deaths, to judge from the returns up to the eighteenth century, greatly exceeded the births. When pestilence was abroad, the town folk, not always welcome visitors, hurried into the country; the students of colleges sought their country seats, generally provided by the foundation against those occasional risks of town life, and there perhaps encountered nothing much more serious than a dunghill heaped with all sorts of festering offal at their doors. But the residence was only temporary, the townsman and the student had no love for country life, and when the danger was over, the shop-keeper and artizan returned to their guild houses, the student and the monk to common hall and refectory.

I cannot, therefore, conclude that either the civil disturbances of the fifteenth century or the visitation of disease, sporadic from the re-appearance of the old pestilence, or endemic at times from the occurrence of the new, materially affected the population of England during the period before me. It must not be imagined that the outbreak of a new disease such as the sweating sickness is evidence by itself of a low vitality among the people. We are expressly told that the victims of this disease were constantly tho strong and healthy, not the weakly, the infirm, or the young. The disease, it is supposed, sprung from the privations to which Henry Tudor's army were exposed. But it is constantly the case that an epidemic which has its origin in the privations of one set of people, or even in a foreign nation, may seriously affect those who have not been brought under the conditions to which the first outbreak of the disorder is due. It is, I think, admitted that the severe and destructive outbreak of small-pox which passed through many parts of Europe, and our own country in particular, some ten years ago, was directly traceable to the sufferings which the French and German armies underwent in the war of 1870, just as it is probable that the ravages of the same disease at the conclusion of the seventeenth century were not obscurely connected with the wars of Louis XIV.

One notable fact in the economy of the fifteenth century is the development of the capitalist artizan. At a previous period of social history in England, this personage has scarcely an existence. The farmer, landowner, or noble, the monastery, or lay corporation, when it wants products on which the craftsman's labour is required, buys the material in a raw state, and hires the smith or other artizan to fashion it. Thus iron and steel, lead and copper, or brass, stone, and lime are either purchased raw and in bulk, or, as in the case of the latter articles named, are manufactured from chalk or limestone, or quarried by the person who requires to use them. There are always, indeed, some articles which the purchaser buys ready made. Such, for instance, are lath nails, and, in certain parts of England, particularly the Eastern Counties, other nails, these being, I am convinced, manufactured by the local smith, when he is not being engaged in regular employment by others. But other iron articles were, at the commencement of the century, regularly manufactured from the employer's material. In course of time finished articles were more and more purchased from what is evidently the stock of the craftsman. Take, for instance, a farmer's waggon. In early times, every part of this is constantly fashioned on the spot as I have described. In course of time, the farmer buys the cart frame from one person, the wheels from another, and the ironwork, the most costly part of the whole, from a third. Later on he purchases the whole article complete from the wheelwright. The same is the case with ordinary ironwork. First he hires the smith to fashion it from his stock; then he buys the article from the smith by weight; then he bargains for the article he needs at a price, without reference to weight. The special department in which the custom of buying materials lasts the longest is in building. In the Midland Counties the purchase of bricks and tiles, stone and lime, is continued, though often with special contracts for particular work, in which the items are not given, till the epoch of the Parliamentary wars. In the Eastern Counties, the old system lasted longer. But in the middle of the fifteenth century, small repairs were often done by craftsmen, who send in their charges with a bill of particulars. Now the growth of this system proves that the artizan was beginning to accumulate such capital as would enable him to wait for and deal with customers, and therefore is indirect evidence that wealth was growing.

I have referred before to the fact, that in the first half of the fifteenth century, grants of fifteenths and tenths were made with a fixed deduction from the total, afterwards increased, for the relief of towns which were decayed or temporarily impoverished, and that generally certain towns were named. It is highly probable that some of this decay is due to the spread of woollen and linen manufactories into country places, where the charges of the town dues and the restrictions of the guilds did not apply. But in the year 1515 (by 6 Henry VIII., cap. vi.), complaint is made of the decay of towns and the growth of pastures. The Act states that, in " places where there used to be two hundred persons, men, women, and children, who used to be occupied and also lived by the growing of corn and other grain, and the herding of cattle, and the increase of man's sustenance, the number is lessened, and the husbandry, which is the greatest commodity of the realm for the sustenance of man, is greatly decayed, that churches are destroyed, divine offices neglected or suspended, and that public health and safety are endangered, by various causes," pointing to urban depopulation. The owners of these houses are bidden to rebuild them under pain of forfeiture to the king or the lord, and the pasture lands are to be restored to tillage. The statute is re-enacted in the following year.

Acts of Parliament in the sixteenth century complain that enclosures of arable and common fields are made for the purpose of laying them down in pasture, and that there is a serious increase in sheep breeding, accompanied by a great enhancement in the price of sheep and wool. The complaint about enclosures is as old as the fifteenth century, when the land hunger of the age led to encroachment on common pastures, and the forcible extinction of rights over common land. I do not, indeed, find that the price of sheep has risen generally as high as the Act of 1533 asserts it to have been, but wool was undoubtedly dear, being in some places nearly 8s. the tod,—a price, however, which was frequently reached as early as the beginning of the fifteenth century. The preamble to the Act states that some persons keep as many as 24,000 sheep, and some from 20,000 to 5,000, and the statute enacts that hereafter no one shall keep more than 2,000, and in order to avoid the ambiguity in the number implied by a hundred, which sometimes means the long hundred of six-score, the sum shall be five-score only, and any breach of the Act shall be followed by a penalty of 3s. 4d. on every head above the legal number, to be recovered by any informer, who shall receive half the penalty, the other moiety going to the king. The adoption of sheep farming in lieu of ordinary tillage was due to the greater profit gained by sheep raising, especially as the importation of wheat and rye from the Baltic had already attracted the notice of the legislature.

Twenty years afterwards, in 1536, in order to prevent the decay of agriculture, a new statute orders that the owners of land taken by tenants to farm shall provide proper farm buildings for every holding from fifty to thirty acres which were so let. The Act is made to apply principally to the Midland Counties, twelve of which are specified, to Lincolnshire, and to the Isle of Wight. These counties had been, in the assessments made at different times, among the most prosperous in the country. In the same year, and in divers Acts of Parliament between this year and 1545, lists of towns are given which are said to be greatly decayed. There is scarcely a town in England which is not in a declining condition, if we can rely on the statements contained in these Acts. Complaints are made that the decay of some of these towns is due to the fact that the country people have set up the business for themselves which had hitherto been the staple of the town, and the practice is forbidden. Thus the town of Bridport is protected in rope making, and the towns of Worcestershire in cloth weaving. But I do not discover that the rate of wages falls, though the price of wheat keeps continually, though slightly, rising. Complaint is made by the city of London that foreign manufactures are injuriously imported, and that English agricultural produce is extensively exported, and that remedy should be supplied.

It would have been well for the English labourer and artizan if no worse fortune had been before them than was apprehended in these several Acts of Parliament, and provided for, on paper at least, by these regulations. Henry had spent his own substance and that of his people. The treasures of the religious houses had been squandered in an incredibly short time, hurled away in the wanton waste of his boundless extravagance. In the short remainder of his life he inflicted two wrongs on his people, the mischief of which was incalculable, the effects of which lasted for centuries. They were the debasement of the currency and the confiscation of the guild revenues. It is possible that the king did not understand the mischief which he was doing, for his apologist certainly does not.

It has been stated before that at various periods of English history the English sovereigns lessened the weight of the unit, the silver penny, till, in the year 1464, the penny of Edward IV. was almost exactly half the weight of the penny of Edward I. It is remarkable, that notwithstanding these successive diminutions, no effect is traceable in the price of commodities, and no discontent is expressed of the action of the Crown. If anything, after the last change, commodities became cheaper, and yet all those persons who were receiving fee farm or fixed rents, the amount of which had not varied from the thirteenth century, were receiving contentedly, and without the consciousness of change, about half the money in the fifteenth which their ancestor received in the thirteenth century. The king, too, whose fif-

teenths and tenths, whose dues and aids, had long been a fixed
sum, had deliberately, and for the sake of a temporary gain, from
time to time deprived himself of half his income. Now Adam
Smith, imperfect as his materials were for the interpretation of
prices, saw that when the weight of the coin was diminished no
appreciable rise of prices ensued, and he came to the conclusion
that silver, measured in commodities, was becoming increasingly
dearer in the fifteenth and earlier part of the sixteenth century.
But it is difficult to understand why it was that the increase of
value and immobility of prices corresponded with chronological
precision to the several changes which were made by the inden-
tures of the mint, and how the issue of new light money was not
followed by the immediate disappearance of all the old heavy
money. And if it be alleged that the force of Government is constantly able, provided the country is not affected by the foreign
exchanges, to give a nominal value to a legal currency, it may be
answered that the commercial transactions of England in the
fifteenth century were considerable, especially with Antwerp, at
that time the principal centre of trade, and that every effort was
made by Government to regulate the exchanges, as was supposed,
in the English interest.

I cannot explain the facts given above, except on the hypothesis
already stated, that payments were ordinarily made by weight.
This appears to be confirmed by the price paid for silver plate.
In the very year in which the penny is reduced to one-half the
amount it stood at in the thirteenth century, plate is bought at
3*s.* and 2*s.* 11*d.* the ounce.   In 1493, an Oxford college purchases
a quantity of new plate, some of it gilt (and mediæval gilding
was very substantial), at 2*s.* 9½*d.* the ounce.   But it is difficult to
understand how raw silver could be purchased at anything like
these prices, and the cost of manufacturing plate, when the goldsmith was on the premises and had his commons, was not less
than 8*d.* an ounce, and gilding assuredly doubled the cost of work-
manship at least, and, on many occasions, more than trebled it.
Such low prices are inconsistent with a payment by tale, but are
perfectly intelligible if they are estimates by weight.

In 1543, Henry put out his first debased money.   Hitherto the
coin had contained eighteen pennyweights of alloy in the twelve

ounces of metal, and the pound was coined into forty-five shillings. In the issue of 1543, the debasement was two ounces in twelve; in 1545, it was six ounces in twelve; in 1546, it was eight ounces in twelve. This vile mixture was coined into forty-eight pieces. The process was continued by the guardians of Edward VI. In 1549, the alloy was six ounces, and in 1551 nine ounces, the pieces now being seventy-two in the pound, and the nominal shilling possessing less than $5\frac{1}{2}d$. worth of silver in the one, and less than $2\frac{3}{4}d$. worth in the other. In the last year of Edward's reign, 1552, an issue was put out of nearly the standard fineness, and nearly the weight of the latter currency. But there is no doubt that this coinage was made in order to enable Edward to negotiate for the payment of his debts at Antwerp, through the agency of Gresham, who was his factor there.

When Elizabeth reformed the currency in 1560, restoring the old standard, and coining the pound Troy into sixty shillings, the amount of base money by weight received at the Mint was nearly 632,000 lbs. Its nominal value is said to have been a little more than £638,000, which gives an additional illustration to my theory that payments were made by weight and not by tale. The actual amount of sterling silver contained in the mixture was 244,416 lbs., and the average debasement was therefore 60 per cent., or a little more than seven ounces in twelve. Elizabeth coined £733,248 in the new coinage out of the silver she refined. She was supposed to have made a profit on the transaction. I shall show hereafter that the difference between the actual and the reputed value of the old base currency was almost exactly the ratio between the price of provisions and the general necessaries of life, before the debasement occurred, and after it had taken full effect.

Now it is clear that prices were rising, though slowly and moderately, during the first forty years of the sixteenth century. In the first decade the money value of the principal necessaries of life, corn and wheat, were at the rates, speaking generally, at which they had stood for two centuries. In the last decade they had risen by twenty to forty per cent.; and the rise was recognised and wondered at, being set down to the changes which had been made, as I have already stated, in agriculture. But the knowledge of the fact should have stayed Henry's hand, when he contemplated the great fraud which he practised on his people. Silver, probably owing to the conquest of Mexico, was getting progressively cheaper ; and had Henry not taken the step he did in 1543, the rise in prices, inevitable after the discovery of the New World, would have been as slow and regular as it was during the period to which I have referred, as foreign trade gradually distributed the fruits of the Spanish conquests over Europe.

It is not possible, I believe, to determine the precise extent to which a government may exact a seigniorage on a metallic currency, or issue an inconvertible paper, which it professes that it will afterwards redeem, without seriously disturbing internal prices. It may easily render its paper vauleless, as the French did with their assignats and mandats at the time of the Revolution. It may lower the actual value of its metallic currency while it gives it a nominal value, till it stimulates private coining, either at home or abroad. In the interval, however, it may give an appearance of prosperity to a country where such a policy is adopted, for the price of exports may be raised, while the money value of products in the home market may remain unaltered. It is very likely that the operation of Henry's issues was disguised for a time at home, and it is remarkable that corn was very cheap in 1547, and not dear, as matters now ruled, in 1546 and 1548, perhaps owing to very plentiful harvests. The monetary history of all countries is full of instances which illustrate the rapidity with which people fall into the delusion that high prices, due to over issues of paper, the coinage of an overvalued metal, or to excessive speculation, are evidence of prosperity. Our English Parliament in the present century endorsed the follies of Vansittart and repudiated the truths which were announced by the Bullion Committee and Lord King. But the issue of base money is rapidly and irremediably mischievous. It affects all, except those who are quick at measuring the exact extent of the fraud, and, by turning the base coin into an article of traffic, can trade on the knowledge and skill which they possess. To the poor, and, indeed, to all who live by wages and fixed salaries, it is speedily ruinous. The effect of Henry's and Edward's base money, though it lasted only sixteen years, was potent enough to dominate in the history of labour and wages from the sixteenth century to the present time, so enduring are the causes which influence the economical history of a nation. Whether payments were made by weight or not before the debasement, they were certainly made by tale speedily afterwards, and when Elizabeth reformed the currency, the new system, to her evident disappointment, was permanently adopted.

The proportionate money value of meat is nearly three times the old rates, that of corn nearly two and a half times, that of dairy produce, two and a half times. But the rise in wages is a little more than one and a half times. In other words, if a labourer's wages rose from 6*d.* a day to 9*d.*, he had to pay 3*s.* for meat, 2*s.* 5*d.* for bread, and 2*s.* 6*d.* for butter or cheese, where he paid 1*s.* before. And the same facts are visible in those products whose value depends almost entirely on the labour which renders them fit for the market. The price of fish, of prepared fuel, of building materials, rises but a little above the rate at which labour rises. The producer of animal food, grain, and other agricultural necessaries commanded a better market than the dealer in any other article of value did, while labour, and those products the value of which is principally derived from the outlay of labour, partook in the least degree in the rise of prices. Henry and his son had at last, though unwittingly, given effect to the Statute of Labourers.

Had the offence of issuing base money not been committed, and had prices risen through the distribution of the precious metals over the civilized world, the condition of the labourer would have still been impaired, for when prices are raised without there being any increased demand for labour, wages very slowly follow the rise. The general inflation of prices which I have pointed out as taking place in the forty years which followed Henry's base money have their particular explanation. But between the middle of Elizabeth's reign and the breaking out of the Parliamentary War, a period of sixty years, general prices were more than doubled, while a very miserable percentage of increase is effected in the wages of labour, certainly not more than twenty per cent. Wages are raised first by an increased demand for labour; secondly, by a limitation of those who compete for employment, and, thirdly, by the regulative action of labour partnerships, or trade unions as they are commonly called. Wages may rise when profits are stagnant or even declining.

The second injury which Henry put on his people was the destruction of the guilds and the confiscation of their property. The sums he had received from the monasteries, and the profits which he made by debasing the currency, were still insufficient for his wants, and he resolved on confiscating the rest of the corporate revenues which still survived. In the last year but one of his reign a Bill was actually passed by both Houses for the dissolution of all colleges, chantries, hospitals, free chapels, etc.; and it is probable that the universities, the colleges, and the public schools would have been swept away into the all-devouring exchequer, had not Henry died before the Act was carried out.

The corporate existence of the town long preceded that of the guild. It is possible that associations of traders, voluntarily united or recognised by some external authority, were active from very remote times, from the merely gregarious instinct of human beings. They are traced to a period before the Conquest. It is probable, for instance, that the guild of goldsmiths in London was an association at a date earlier than the earliest extant charter of the city, just as it is probable that in the town of Oxford associations of students preceded the foundation of the University. But the chartered town or city was antecedent to the chartered guild. In course of time the associations of traders obtained charters, but were obscure and feeble societies, though rallying places for the burghers against the urban aristocracy. In time they united in a guild-hall; in time they constrained all the inhabitants of the city to enter in one or the other of the companies, and ultimately obtained the exclusive franchise. But the relics of an older constituency remained in the residential electorate of the wards. In just the same way the Oxford and Cambridge colleges, which were in the first instance tolerated excrescences on the academical system, became finally the monopolists of education and academical authority.

The guilds gradually acquired property, sometimes entirely for their own ends, more generally as interested in the remainder of

a trust. A brother of the craft would give house and lands to
better the annual feast, which the craft always held; or he
might found a school, an hospital, or an alms-house, and after
defining the amount of his benefaction, would leave the surplus,
if any, to the discretion of the guild. Or he would make the
guild the trustees of the fund from which the mass priest should
receive his stipend for spiritual offices, the residue being left to
the guild as remuneration for management. Occasionally the
corporation bargained for the amount of the spiritual service, and
refused to agree to a proposal which might be too costly for the
fund to bear. They exacted fees for apprenticeship, for taking
up freedom by inheritance or servitude, and more lately for
admission into the guild by purchase. Like prudent men, who
might be liable to occasional charges, they saved and invested
these funds, as also gifts for lending without usury to poorer
citizens, for apprenticing poor boys or girls, or for marriage
portions, or for widows' pensions, or for the relief of the destitute
members of the craft, the first and the most enduring duty of the
guild. The guild estates, the chest of the company, its revenues
and rents, were, like the endowments of an academical college, at
once the support of the fraternity and the means by which the
discipline of the order or craft was maintained. The analogy
between the guild and the college was close, and perhaps this was
fully understood. Two guilds in the town of Cambridge founded
out of their resources one of the older colleges in that University.
Sometimes the permanent revenues of the guild or college were
scraped together from the savings of the fees which bygone
generations of applicants had paid, and the college or guild
had hoarded.

Somerset, Edward the Sixth's uncle, procured the Act by which
these guild lands were confiscated, on the plea of the " superstitious use " with which they were generally associated. He did
not, indeed, venture on appropriating the estates of the London
guilds, for London had it in its power to make revolutions, and
they were spared, after ransom paid, under the plea that the
guild did service to trade. Similarly the chantries annexed to
the Oxford and Cambridge colleges were not reft from these
institutions. but allowed, discharged of the duty. I conceive

that most of the outlying bits of land in the urban boundaries of Oxford and Cambridge which were possessed by the pre-Reformation colleges are mainly chantry lands. These guild lands were in the aggregate considerable, and the confiscation made Somerset and the Reformation unpopular. After Somerset's execution, the rapacity of Northumberland made the Reformation still more odious; and when this schemer attempted to set Jane Grey on the throne, the most Protestant district of England rose against the new order of things, protected Mary, who trusted herself to them, and made her queen, to be repaid by fire and faggot. For anything which Northumberland, the son of Henry the Seventh's hateful instrument, the father of Elizabeth's worthless favourite, had touched, was tainted. He had secured, in the last year of Edward's reign, the surrender of the see of Durham, with the regalian rights of the County Palatine. He intended to appropriate this to himself, and to dismember northern England by making an independent principality, which should include the Northern Counties, and probably York, to ally with the Scots, and to procure the hand of Mary Stuart for his son Robert. In this case he would be able to defy all attempts to dispossess him. But Edward's death disconcerted his plans, and the hatred of all parties cowed him.

The issue of the base money was recognised to be the cause of dearth in the realm. Latimer preached before the king and lamented that the silver had become dross. All the good money disappeared, of course, and the king's credit with it. Pauperism began to show itself, and the people were exhorted to charity and almsgiving by proclamations which issued from a gang of coiners and smashers. In Mary's days the rich who declined to give were to be denounced to the ordinary as heretics. It may be doubted whether, even if she had reformed the currency in her reign, the old prices would have been restored. Elizabeth effected the reformation, but the facts were too strong for her, the wages of labour possessed less and less purchasing power, and pauperism increased. The great queen's government strove to stay it by insisting on the creation of peasant holdings, or by supplementing wages with land allotments of four acres to each cottage. But the evil was too far gone for the remedies of legislation, and a poor law, under which the relief of destitution was guaranteed, was the only expedient before her government when it was left face to face with the irremediable poverty of labour.

The English labourer, then, in the sixteenth century was almost simultaneously assailed on two sides. The money which he received for his wages was debased, and the assistance which his benefit society gave him in times of difficulty, which allowed him loans without interest, apprenticed his son, or pensioned his widow, was confiscated. All the necessaries of life, as I have already stated, rose in value in the proportion generally of 1 to $2\frac{1}{2}$, while the wages of labour rose to little more than from 1 to $1\frac{1}{2}$. His ordinary means of life were curtailed. The considerable advantage which the London labourer and artizan had over his country fellow in the calling disappeared, and the wages of country and London hands were nearly equalised. This was indeed to be expected, for in the virtual decline of wages, the advantage of the better paid or selected hands would certainly be lost. But the deterioration of his condition was not confined to the loss of money wages. He lost his insurance also, the fund destined to support him and his during the period of youth and age, when work is not open to the imperfect powers of youth, and has become impossible to the enfeebled powers of age. Nor is the extent of the loss which the working classes suffered by the confiscation of the guild lands to be estimated by the value which was set upon the capital fund, as we may see from the enormous amount to which those funds have increased in London, where they were spared, for it is admitted that most of the guild or corporate estates of the city companies are of pre-Reformation origin. The estates of the guilds in country towns might not have nearly reached the value of the London property belonging to the companies, but they would hardly have been so entirely perverted from their original objects as they have been in the city, and would have remained, in some degree at least, to fulfil the original purposes of the donors. The country guilds, though not formally suppressed after being plundered, were practically superseded by the corporate action of the burgesses, who appropriated such income as was left, from fees and fines, to the common purse of· the freemen.

4

The purpose which the legislature had before it for two
centuries had now become possible. The Statute of Labourers
had been passed, re-enacted, invoked, and put into execution in
vain. There is hardly a trace in the history of English labour
and wages that the passionate desire of the employers of labour
that workmen should be constrained to accept reasonable wages
had been satisfied. The rise in wages, and what was even more
significant, of articles the price of which no law could pretend
to control, had changed the form of English husbandry from
capitalist cultivation on a large scale to the stock and land lease,
and thence to tenancies of the ordinary farm kind on short lease,
or to tenancies at will. But though there was a formidable
increase in prices after the full effect of the debased currency was
reached, there was no rise in rents. The landowner was paying
nearly three times as much in the first years of Elizabeth's reign
as he paid in the first years of her father's reign, and receiving no
more rent in the latter than he did in the earlier period. This is
proved by the evidence given of corporate income at the two
periods when the income is the source of the corporation's
existence. For a long time the revenues of King's College,
Cambridge, and New College, All Souls, or Merton, Oxford,
show no increase in amount. The Cambridge College, it is true,
tries to remedy the loss by demanding its rents in kind, but the
Oxford societies either did not attempt the expedient or found
that their tenants could resist it. The bishoprics were opulent
before the Reformation, but poor after it, not so much because
they had generally been shorn of their possessions by the greedy
courtiers of the later Tudor princes, though this took place, as
because rents had remained stationary while prices had been
rising. Nor is the cause far to seek. Rents do not rise because
prices rise, for the power of the tenant to pay an enhanced rent
which the rise in the price of farm produce will give him may
be entirely neutralized by the rise in the price of that which he
must purchase in order to carry on his industry. This is made
clear at the present time. The high price of meat and dairy
products is more than a compensation for the low price of
corn, if one is to interpret the power of a tenant to pay rent
by the price of agricultural produce. But all farmers will tell

us that, owing to the great price of lean stock, no profit, or little profit beyond manure, attends stock keeping. Nor would the difference between high and low wages materially diminish or increase the power of paying rent, apart from other causes. Wages may be high, and profits may remain high, because demand is great and supply indefinite. This is the common case when there is great activity in manufactures, and it arises from the fact that business has become more brisk, that the industry is for the time capable of indefinite extension, or that a great and notable economy has been induced on the process of production. Wages may be high and profits low, not because, as some economists have absurdly argued, wages trench on profits, but because an increasing number of persons compete for an inelastic or stationary amount of business, and therefore at once overbuy each other in the wages market and undersell each other in the produce market.

In mediæval agriculture the greatest outlay, as I have frequently said, was on stock, live and dead. It is not easy, in the old system of capitalist farming, to precisely figure the wages of labour, because the tenants of the manor frequently paid the rents for their small holdings in labour, and an estimate of this would have to be given in any interpretation of the cost of labour in the earlier husbandry. But in the small tenancies which followed, this kind of labour is extinguished, and it is not easy, in the absence of direct evidence, to determine what additional cost the tenant would be at. Still the farmer gave, as in older times, his own labour and that of his household to his holding, and would not be as likely to employ independent labour as the capitalist farmer was, except in harvest time and under urgency. And it will be clear, that unless hired labour formed a considerable item in the cost of the tenant farmer, a fall in wages would not of itself render him, under such altered circumstances, able and willing to pay an enhanced rent. There is only one cause for a rise in rent, and this cause has manifested itself at well-defined periods in the history of English agricultural industry.

This is an economy in the process of production due to improvements in the process of agriculture. From the days of

Henry III. to those of James I., no such economy or improvement occurred. It is probable that some processes by which land was tilled were neglected or forgotten. It is not unlikely that the care which had been taken to improve breeds of sheep had been remitted. Only one new kind of agricultural industry had been introduced,—the cultivation of the hop ; and this was suspected and even denounced. But from the time of James I., especially after the middle of his reign, large and important improvements are made in agriculture, great economies discovered, and a rapid rise in rent ensues. These will be subsequently commented on. It is to be regretted, though it is not to be wondered at, that these improvements and economies had no beneficial effect on the wages of labour.

The government of Elizabeth was, however, convinced that the legal restraint of wages was a necessity or a benefit, or both. Hence the Statute 5 Eliz., cap. 4 (which enacts that no person shall, under a penalty of forty shillings a month, use or occupy any art, mystery, or manual occupation without a previous seven years' apprenticeship), seems to favour traders and artizans at the expense of labourers in husbandry, by limiting the number of the former and making the latter the residuum of all non-apprenticed labour. But the favour is more apparent than real in the case of the artizan ; for what the statute gives with one hand it takes away with another. The justices in Quarter Sessions are empowered to fix the rate of wages in husbandry and in handicrafts, and they do not let their powers lie idle. The great collection of Elizabeth's proclamations now in the Bodleian Library, a volume which probably once belonged to Cecil, gives two of these exhaustive assessments,—one for the county of Rutland, which seems to have been published as a type for the southern counties, and one for that of Lancashire, which is probably a guide for the northern counties. There are others in existence.

This expedient was at last successful, and was the third in the set of causes from which pauperism was the inevitable effect. The two former, the base money and the confiscation of the benefit societies' funds, are economical, and can be so interpreted. The third is capable of historical proof. The wages of labour do conform, notwithstanding the continual increase in the price of the necessaries of life, to the assessments of the Quarter Sessions, and the system is continued under legal sanction till 1812, and by a sufficient understanding for long after that date. It seems that as long as the practice remained, under which the wages of the peasant were eked out by land allowances and commonable rights, he continued to subsist, though but poorly, under the system; but that when the enclosures of the eighteenth century began, and the full influence of the corn laws was felt, during the fourth quarter of that century and the first quarter of the nineteenth, it became necessary to supplement his wages by an allowance from the parish fund, and thus to indirectly qualify the assessment which the magistrates had established.

Had, however, the first two acts to which I have so often referred not been committed, the third would have, I am persuaded, been nugatory. It was nothing more than had been enacted in the reign of Henry IV., and had been wholly inoperative, at any rate in the direction which it was intended to take—the reduction of agricultural wages; for these, as we have seen, improve after the enactment. But it was a very different thing when the workman had been weakened, and he had been constrained for half a generation to submit to a base currency and to undergo other losses.

The altered condition of the labourers is further illustrated by the rise in the price of their maintenance. In the early part of the fifteenth century the average cost of a labourer's board is 9d. a week. In the famine year of the fifteenth century, 1348-9, it rose to an average of 1s. 6d., a proof that the rates which I have given were contract prices. Nor is there much variation in the rate till after the issue of the base money. In 1542, board and lodging are put at 1s. a week; but in ten years from this time it rises to an average of 3s. a week. In 1562, 1563, and 1570, Elizabeth makes quarterly contracts for victualling her workmen in her dockyards at Deptford and Portsmouth. In the first year the contract is at an average of 4s. 0½d.; in the second, at 4s. 6d.; in the third, at 3s. 11d.; the first and third being a cheap, the second a dear year. The Queen also rents lodgings at 2d. a week, the contract being that the men should have feather beds, that two should lie in a bed, and that the queen should find sheets and pay for washing them at 1d. the pair. Similar contracts are made at 4s. in 1573; at 4s. 8$\frac{1}{2}d$. in 1577; at 4s 3d. in 1578. These prices represent the highest increases of any, for I find that in 1562 the average price of labour was 4s. 9$\frac{1}{2}d$. the week; in 1563, 4s. 0$\frac{1}{2}d$.; in 1570, 4s. 7d.; in 1573, 4s. 11$\frac{1}{2}d$.; in 1577 4s. 10$\frac{3}{4}d$.; and in 1578, 4s. 8d.; these average rates of wages, taken from eight different kinds of labour, five artizans and three ordinary or unskilled, being only a very little in excess of the amounts for which Elizabeth contracted in the same years to board her artizans at the docks.

Elizabeth soon discovered that one of the causes which was impoverishing her people was making her also poor. The rents and dues of the Crown, the subsidies, tenths and fifteenths, all the revenues of the Crown, except, perhaps, customs, were fixed in amount. The purchasing power of the revenue had fallen to about one-third of its ancient capacity, and the Queen strove to meet the difficulty by declaring that the new currency should run at only two-thirds its nominal value—$i.\ e.$, that the shilling should be current at 8d., and so on. But the proclamation, though drafted, was not issued, probably because the Queen's advisers feared that the step would be unpopular, and would suggest that the Crown was trying arbitrarily to enhance its right against its debtors.

The enactment and development of the English poor law, unique among legislative enactments, must be treated in a separate chapter. But I must remind my reader that it by no means follows that population had increased because there was a virtual decline in wages. Low wages may be the concomitant of a scanty population, high wages of an abundant one. Nay, unhappily, society may make notable progress in wealth, and wages may remain low, misery may be general, and discontent may be imminent. The mass of English workmen are far better off now than they were two generations ago, though population has greatly increased. But relatively speaking, the working man of to-day is not so well off as he was in the fifteenth century, when the population was not one-tenth of it what it is now.

CHAPTER III

Corn Prices should be Estimated over a wide Area—Bad Harvests in the Sixteenth, Seventeenth, and Eighteenth Centuries—Estimate of a Labourer's Real Wages in 1495, 1533, 1563, 1593, 1597, 1610, 1651, 1661, 1682, 1684, 1725—The Consequence of the Assessment of Wages System—the Extension of Conspiracy to Workmen's Combinations—Principles of a Trade Union—Mr. Mill on Unions—The Artizan from 1725 to 1750—Arthur Young's Notes on Wages—The Rise from 1750 to 1770—Wages of Manufactures—The Dear Years from 1780 to 1820—The Speenhamland Act of Parliament—Tooke on Prices, from 1800 to 1815—The Rise in 1853—Concluding Remarks on Trade Unions.

ON examination of the rise which was effected in the price of all articles of consumption during the last sixty years of the sixteenth century enables us to see clearly what was now become the condition of those who lived by wages. If we look at the money value of most articles, we shall see that, with very few exceptions, it keeps steadily increasing during each successive decade. This is not, it is true, precisely the fact with regard to wheat and other kinds of grain, for the money value of this produce is affected in each decade by the occasion of years of special scarcity and plenty. Hence in the case of wheat or similar kinds of grain, it becomes necessary, if we would exactly interpret the change which had come over money values, to take a longer period, during which cheap and dear years neutralize each other. But the course of the seasons during the period which intervenes before prices have reached their true level and go on steadily rising, on the whole, for half a century, is striking and exceptional.

The issues of base money put into circulation by Henry were in the years 1545 and 1546. Those of Edward's guardians were in 1549 and 1551. In 1560 the currency was restored. It is important to remember these dates in estimating prices, and the immediate effect of the issue on them. There must have been, I conclude, some general impression at first that these moneys would be redeemed, and, under these circumstances, it appears that they did not produce the immediate effect which such a proceeding invariably does sooner or later. Now the harvest of 1545 must have been a very bad one, for the price of wheat was higher than it had been in any year since 1316, the great famine of Edward the Second's reign, though it was soon to be surpassed. But for the next three years wheat is decidedly cheap; in 1547 very cheap, the price being lower than it had been since 1510. Then follow three dear years and two comparatively cheap ones, Mary Tudor having come to the throne in the last year. Then follow three dear years, the third being dearer than in all previous experience, wheat being nearly five times the average price for the 280 years, 1261-1540, and standing, during the spring, at a price which must have indicated the worst anticipations of famine. In the next two years it is cheap again, a cheap year being now about double the old price. The years 1563 and 1573 are also dear. After the latter year, the ordinary price becomes about three times the old rate. The next dear year is 1586, when the price again goes beyond previous experience. But the harvest of 1588, the Armada year, was very abundant. Five years successively, 1594-98, are very dear, the last but one, 1597, being a veritable famine, the price being ten times what it was in the early period and not being paralleled till 1648 and 1649. By this time, however, the average price had reached from five to seven times that at which it had previously stood for more than two centuries and a half. The price of wheat in 1649 was reached again in 1674, in 1661-2, in 1709, and 1710, and not again till 1767, 1774, and 1795.

Now up to the year 1540, the average wages of an artizan in the country were 3s. a week; of a labourer in husbandry, working by the day, 2s. a week. Such wages, in some cases rather more, are allowed by 11 Hen. VII., cap. 22 (1495), to which I shall presently refer. The labourer in harvest time, when working by the day, received the same wages as the artizan; and, in harvest time, the wages of the women labourers were only a little less than those of men. It should be remembered that this Act of Henry VII. is one which was intended to carry out the Statute of Labourers, and that therefore the minimum rate would be pre-scribed and, as far as possible, enforced. The price of wheat in 1495 was 4s. 0¾d. ; of malt, 2s. 4½d. ; of oats, 1s. 7½d. ; and of oatmeal, 5s. 4d. a quarter. An artizan, therefore, earned nearly a bushel of wheat by a day's labour, and an ordinary labourer three-quarters of a bushel. A week's work would enable an artizan to purchase more than a quarter of malt, and a little more than seven days' work would supply the farm labourer with a quarter of malt. In so cheap a year as this, the peasant could provision his family for a twelvemonth with three quarters of wheat, three of malt, and two of oatmeal, by fifteen weeks of ordinary work ; an artizan could achieve the same result in ten weeks. Such wages were regularly paid, and even more, par-ticularly in London.

In 1533, a large proportion of Henry's artizans got 4s. a week even during the winter months, the labourers earning, as before, 2s. In 1533, the price of wheat was, relatively speaking, high, 7s. 8d. a quarter, while malt was 5s. 5¼d., oatmeal 8s., and oats 2s. 9½d. the quarter. In this case, then, the farm labourer would have had to give nearly double the labour in wheat and oats, and more than double in the case of malt, though a good deal less than double in that of oatmeal, to make such a provision as his ancestor did in 1459 ; while the artisan at 3s., would have had to give between fourteen and fifteen weeks' work for a similar store. The first-named year is an exceedingly cheap one ; the latter, though less advantageous to the labourer, is one in which he might still be able, as we see, to maintain his family, and lay by a considerable margin from the charges of his house-hold, from a fourth to a half of his earnings.

In June 1564, the Rutlandshire magistrates met in order to carry out the provisions of the Act to which I have several times referred, and which had just been passed. The schedule of wages to which I am about to refer is printed by the royal authority among the proclamations of the Queen, and is preserved in the great collection of Elizabeth's instruments which was begun by Burleigh and continued by Cecil. It is without doubt a typica

list, intended by the fact of the publication to be a guide to the
other Quarter Sessions throughout the country.   The list is
drawn up " on consideration of the great prices of linen, woollen,
leather, corn, and other victuals."   The ordinary artizan is to
have 9*d.* a day in summer, 8*d.* in winter ; the heads of the craft,
who are to be competent draughtsmen of plans, to have 1*s.*   The
labourers are to have 7*d.* in summer, except in harvest time, when
they have 8*d.* to 10*d.*, and in winter 6*d.*   The summer is from
Easter to Michaelmas, the winter from Michaelmas to Easter.
In 1563-4, wheat was 19*s.* 9¾*d.* a quarter ; oats, 7*s.*, malt, 10*s.* 8*d.*
The price of oatmeal has not been found, but it could not have
been less than 25*s.* the quarter.   The Rutlandshire schedule is
a little lower than the prices actually paid in Cambridge and
Oxford, as far as regards artizans' labour, for the artizan is paid,
as a rule, not less than 1*s.* or 10*d.* a day.   The wages of ordinary
labour are those of the magistrates' schedule.   Now the price
of food is more than three times the old average, though malt,
as we might expect, when wheat was at a scarcity price, is less
than the corresponding price, being actually cheaper than barley.
Now if we suppose the ordinary labourer to get 3*s.* 6*d.* a week
through the year, by adding his harvest allowance to his winter
wages, it would have taken him more than forty weeks to earn
the provisions which in 1495 he could have got with fifteen,
while the artizan would be obliged to have given thirty-two weeks'
work for the same result.

In 1593, the magistrates of the East Riding of York met on
April 26th, and fixed the wages of artizans and labourers in
husbandry.   The mower is to have 10*d.*, the reaper 8*d.* a day,
or by the acre 10*d.* for meadow and 8*d.* for corn, it being clear
that a man was supposed to mow an acre of corn or grass in a
day.   The winter wages of labourers are to be 4*d.*, in summer 5*d.*
Ordinary artizans are to have 8*d.* and 7*d.*   The price of wheat
in 1593 is 18*s.* 4½*d.* ; of oatmeal, 29*s.* 4*d.* ; of malt, 12*s.* 3½*d.*
The work of a whole year would not supply the labourer with the
quantity which in 1495 the labourer earned with fifteen weeks'
labour.   The artizan could procure it with forty weeks' labour.

In the same year, the mayor and others in the city of Chester
fixed the wages of artizans and labourers who dwelt within their

jurisdiction. The roll is unfortunately mutilated, and the day payments of artizan and labourer, without meat and drink, are torn off. But it is clear that the workmen here are even worse paid than in the East Riding,—that the wages of artizans were not more than 6*d.*, those of labourers than 4*d.*, and that there was actually no rise here from the older prices.

The year 1597 was one of fearful famine. The price of wheat was 56*s.* 10½*d.*; of oats, 13*s.* 9½*d.* (I do not find that of oatmeal, but it appears to have been 64*s.*); malt, 28*s.* 9½*d.* It is said by the Mayor of Chester in his assessment to be a time of dearth and scarcity. The schedule is again unluckily mutilated; but the extra allowance for the dearness of this year, the price being generally almost three times that of the year 1593, is only 10*s.* more for wages by the year without food than in the earlier year. The wages of artizans are from £5 10*s.* the year to £4 10*s.*; those of husbandmen, £3 10*s.* It is not easy to see how they could have lived through the famine.

In 1610, the Rutland magistrates met at Oakham on April 28th, and made their assessment. The day wages of a mower are 10*d.*; of a reaper, 8*d.*, if a man; if a woman 6*d.*, of ordinary labour from Easter to Michaelmas, 7*d.*; from Michaelmas to Easter, 6*d.* Artizans are to have from 10*d.* to 9*d.* in the summer, 8*d.* in the winter. Master artizans, with skill as draughtsmen, are to receive 1*s.* a day in summer, 10*d.* in winter; and it appears from the register of hirings that these rates were maintained till at least 1634. The price of wheat in this year was 40*s.* 4*d.*, of malt 15*s.* 4⅓*d*; and it therefore appears that a Rutland artizan with 9*d.* a day wages, supposing oatmeal were worth, as its natural price should be, about 43*s.* 4*d.* a quarter, would have to work forty-three weeks in order to earn that which an artizan in 1495 obtained with ten weeks' labour; while the wages of the peasant, who got this supply by fifteen weeks' labour 115 years before, would be insufficient, even if he worked for fifty-two weeks in the year, and every day except Sunday, by 24*s.* 9½*d.*, to win that quantity of provisions. Even the extra payments in harvest would not make up the deficiency.

In 1651, the Essex magistrates met at Chelmsford on April 8th, and fixed the wages for the county. Wages had now risen.

The artizan had from 1*s*. 5*d*. a day in summer and 1*s*. 2*d*. in winter to 1*s*. 6*d*. and 1*s*. 4*d*., the latter prices being paid as usual to foremen or heads of gangs. Ordinary labourers had from 1*s*. 2*d*. to 1*s*. except in harvest time, when mowing was paid at 1*s*. 6*d*., reaping at 1*s*. 10*d*. the day. Women in the harvest field had 1*s*. 2*d*.; in the hay-field 10*d*. Piece-work is paid at 1*s*. 8*d*. an acre for mowing, 2*s*. for making and cocking. The reaping of wheat, rye, beans, and maslyn is 3*s*. 4*d*.; of barley and oats, 2*s*. 6*d*., this including binding and shocking. Mowing and binding barley and oats is 2*s*. 2*d*. Threshing and winnowing are, for the quarter of wheat and rye, 1*s*. 10*d*.; barley, oats, and other kinds of grain, 10*d*. Sawing planks is paid at 2*s*. 6*d*. the hundred of six-score feet. The advent of the Commonwealth had induced some beneficial change on the workman's labour, at least in appearance. In 1651, the price of wheat was 51*s*. 4*d*.; of malt, 22*s*. 7*d*.; oats were dearer than malt, being 23*s*. 10*d*.; and oatmeal was from 64*s*. to 48*s*. the quarter. The artizan on an average could earn from 7*s*. 9*d*. to 8*s*. 6*d*. a week; ordinary workmen an average of 6*s*. 9*d*., excepting hay and harvest time, when they could get from 9*s*. to 11*s*. a week; and the women reapers, 7*s*. Piece-work in the harvest field is calculated at a little less than an acre of grass a day, and a little more than half an acre of grain if the reaper bound and stacked the sheaves. The sawing a hundred of planks, always estimated from early times as a day's work, is paid at the rate of 15*s*. a week between the two workmen, the upper and under sawyers being estimated at the rate of 8*s*. to 7*s*.

The cost of the stock of wheat, malt, and oatmeal is now in the aggregate £16 13*s*. 9*d*. If the artizan worked fifty-two weeks in the year, he could earn £20 3*s*.; and therefore it would still take him about forty-three weeks to earn his stock of provisions. The peasant, however, apart from his harvest earnings, could, with the same unbroken and continuous diligence, earn £17 11*s*.; and perhaps the sum could be made up to £18 by his extra wages in the hay and corn field. He is therefore distinctly better off than he was forty years before, at least in Essex.

The rate paid for mowing grass by the acre is a little in excess of that paid at Oxford in the latter part of the sixteenth century, where the price is 1s. 3¾d. for mowing, 1s. 7¼d. for making and cocking. But during this period, the average price of wheat was 14s. 2¼d.; of malt, 10s. 5d.; of oatmeal, 20s. 10¾d. To such rates of wages the corresponding price of wheat should be 18s.; of malt, 13s. 2¾d.; of oatmeal, 26s. 6½d., in order to equalize the real wages of mowing in the sixteenth and seventeenth centuries and a similar proportionate increase for the labour of tedding and cocking. The price of threshing is relatively high, being about four times the rate which prevailed in the period before the rise in prices began. The same difference characterises the prices given for reaping, binding, and stacking an acre of wheat; but the rate paid for cutting barley and oats is less. Already much of the two latter kinds of grain is mown. On the whole, then, though the wages of labour in 1651 are infinitely below what they were in the old times, and contrast unfavourably even with the rates paid immediately after the passing of Elizabeth's Quarter Sessions Act, they represent better rates than those which were prescribed under the same machinery forty years before, and as we see actually paid, as is proved by the register of hirings.

At the Easter Sessions of 1661, the Essex magistrates again revised the wages of labourers. The summer wages are still 1s. 2d., the winter 1s. a day. The woman gets 10d.; mowing is 1s. 6d., whether it be grass or corn; reaping by men, 1s. 10d.; by women, 1s. 2d. Mowing grass is raised to 1s. 10d.; reaping wheat, rye, and maslyn is 4s.; oats, 2s. 6d.; beans, 3s. 6d.; mowing barley and oats by the acre is 1s. 6d., the price of threshing and winnowing being unchanged. But in 1661 the price of wheat is 70s. 6d. a quarter; of malt, 34s. 6d. The purchasing power of wages is, therefore, considerably reduced.

In Suffolk, 1682, the magistrates at Bury St. Edmund's fixed the day wages of haymakers—men at 10d., women at 6d.; of male reapers in harvest at 1s. 8d., of women at 1s.; and the regular wages at 1s. in summer and 10d. in winter. The wages of artizans are not given, but from other sources we may learn that they were from 1s. 6d. to 1s. 4d. In 1682, the price of wheat was 43s. 8d.; of malt, 26s. 8d.; and the natural price of oatmeal, about 48s. Either the wages were reduced as corn became cheaper, or the price of labour was ordinarily lower in Suffolk than it was in Essex. We shall see reason to arrive at the former conclusion.

On April 9th, 1684, the magistrates of Warwick met at the county town and assessed the wages for the year under the Act of Elizabeth. The assessment is said to have special regard and consideration to the prices at this time of victuals and apparel. The price of wheat was 42*s.* 0½*d.* a quarter; of malt, 24*s.* 5½*d.*; and the analogous price of oatmeal, 46*s.* 6*d.*

The artizans' wages are here 1*s.* a day, with the exception of the free mason, who has 1*s.* 4*d.*, the only man of the class who gets this rate. The plasterer is to have only 8*d.*; common labourers, except in harvest time, are to have 8*d.*; the mower of grass and corn, 1*s.*; the reaper, 1*s.*; while the haymaker, if a man, has only 8*d.*, the women 4*d.*, and the woman reaper 8*d.* These are summer wages; the winter pay is a penny a day less. The hours of labour are defined between March and September to be from five in the morning till between seven and eight at night, *i.e.*, fourteen-and-a-half hours, from which two-and-a-half hours are to be allowed for meals. Of these half an hour is given for breakfast, an hour for dinner, an hour for " drinkings," and between the middle of May and the middle of August, half an hour for sleep. From the middle of September till the middle of March he is to work from daybreak till night, and is to forfeit a penny an hour, that is at the rate of 50 per cent. above his earnings, for absence. Persons who give more wages than the prescribed assessment are to be imprisoned ten days and be fined £5; persons taking more than the assessment are to be imprisoned twenty-one days; and any retainer, promise, gift, or payment of wages in contravention is to be void and of no effect. The document is signed by eight magistrates, among whom we find the names of Mordaunt, Clopton, and Fielding, the last at this time knowing, it seems, how to spell his name.

The wages fixed by these Warwickshire magistrates are decidedly less than those allowed in Essex thirty-three years before. It is fair to them to state that the Lady-day prices of wheat and malt were lower than those which prevailed for the real hiring time (that from some date after Lady-day to a similar period in the following year), for wheat was 34*s.* 4*d.*, barley 22*s.* 7*d.* a quarter on Lady-day 1684, when the justices met. It should also be remembered that these daily payments were for regular, not for occasional service, and that the master was as much bound to pay his man as the man was to stay in the service of his master during the term of his engagement. It is to this practice that we must ascribe, in part at least, the higher wages of harvest time, and, occasionally, of piece work.

If we take the allowances of wheat, malt, and oatmeal employed for our calculations before, and fix that of oatmeal hypothetically at a low amount, say 46s. 6d. a quarter, we shall find that the cost of the stock of provisions in this year amounted to £14 11s. 6d., that the yearly wages of the artizan are £15 13s., and those of the farm labourer, exclusive of his earnings in the hay and corn fields, are £10 8s. 8d., *i.e.*, insufficient in their aggregate, whatever addition may be made for harvest work, to purchase the stock which his ancestor was able to procure on such easy terms. I have always, throughout these investigations into the labourers' wages, taken his earnings only, without allowing for what his wife or his children might earn for him, and, in the case of an artizan, perhaps his apprentices. But in a contrast established between money values and payments at different epochs, it is above all things important to take the simplest elements of calculation and comparison. I am not discussing what might have been the aggregate earnings of a family, but what were the resources on which an individual labourer could rely for procuring the means of life for a family, when those means of life were confined to what, according to the fashions of the age, were the simplest materials of customary existence.

The magistrates of Lancashire met at Manchester on May 22nd, 1725, when certain " discreet and grave men of the county, having held conference respecting the plenty of the time and other necessary circumstances " (words costing nothing in a preamble, and, it is to be hoped, deceiving no one), determined on certain rates of wages for the county, and issued them, under the authority of George and Thomas Cheetham.

The best husbandry labourer is to receive, from March to September, 1s. a day ; ordinary ones, 10d.; and during the other six months the payment is to be 10d. and 9d. Haymakers are to have—men, 10*d.* a day, women 7*d.*; mowers, 1*s.* 3*d.*; shearers, *i.e.*, reapers—1*s.* men, and 10*d.* women; taskwork in husbandry being 10*d.* a day. All artizans are to receive a maximum of 1*s.* a day, and a pair of sawyers, 2*s.* It may be observed that the maintenance of labourers is generally put at 3*s.* a week. Piecework is paid by a double kind of acre, one said to be seven yards to the rood, the other eight yards. For oats, the payments are 5*s.* for the former, 6*s.* for the latter; in barley, peas, and beans, the quantities paid are 6*s.* and 7*s.*; for wheat and rye (a proof by the way that wheat was cultivated in Lancashire in the eighteenth century), 7*s.* and 8*s.* Threshing and winnowing oats are paid at 1*s.* a quarter; barley, beans, and peas at 1*s.* 6*d.*; wheat and rye at 2*s.* It is interesting to note that colliers were paid 1*s.* a ton for getting coal in a low delf, 1*s.* 3*d.* for the same labour in a high one. The master workman in the various handicrafts is to have 1*s.* 2*d.* a day, except the tailor, who is to be content with 1*s.* The plenty of the time is not very conspicuous in 1725, as the price of corn is higher than it had been since 1713, being 46*s.* 1*d.* for wheat, 24*s.* for malt. Oatmeal should be 54*s.*

If one can arrive at a judgment from the language of the Lancashire magistrates' proclamation, these authorities appear to be alarmed at symptoms of combination and disaffection among the workmen. They order that these wages should not be exceeded in the county, though they think that they are a little too liberal for the northern part thereof, but they direct, that they should be proclaimed in every market town of the county by the authority of the sheriff, and that on market days, when business is at its height, proclamation should be solemnly made, and a legible copy should be set up and fixed in some open public place in each of the market towns, and that the rates decided on should be continued till an amended list be proclaimed. The justices then proceed to publish the penalties which are denounced by divers Acts of Parliament on offenders under the several statutes which are made to regulate the wages of labour.

They cite a statute of Edward VI., 2 and 3, cap. 15, under which a combination of workmen "concerning their work or wages" is to be followed by a penalty on conviction of ten pounds, or twenty days' imprisonment on bread and water for the first offence, a fine of twenty pounds or the pillory for the second, and a fine of forty pounds, the pillory, the loss of one of his ears, and judicial infamy for the third. This statute was confirmed by 22-23 Charles II., and was in force till the general repeal of all such prohibitions on the combinations of workmen which took effect under 6 George IV., cap. 129. The rest of the warnings are those derived from the statute of Elizabeth, and recited by the Warwickshire magistrates in 1684.

The best servants in husbandry, who must have been of a very exceptional character, are to receive 1s. a day for six months, and 10d. for the other six months, i.e., taking every working day into the pay-days, £14 7s. a year. The ordinary peasant is to receive £12 7s. 10d. These persons, however, might increase their wages by harvest work, and probably did, so as to raise the total to £15 and £13. Artizans are to be paid at the rate of £15 13s. a year, if they are at work during the whole year. Now taking the test which has been supplied so many times, and putting oatmeal (for which I have not at present a price, but shall probably be not far wrong in my estimate) at 54s. a quarter, the aggregate sum is £16 2s. 3d., and as I repeat for the last time, what a husbandman earned with fifteen weeks' work, and an artizan with ten weeks' work in 1495, a whole year's labour would not supply artizan or labourer with in the year 1725, throughout Lancashire.

I have protested before against that complacent optimism which concludes, because the health of the upper classes has been greatly improved, because that of the working classes has been bettered, and appliances, unknown before, have become familiar and cheap, that therefore the country in which these improvements have been effected must be considered to have made, for all its people, regular and continuous progress. I contend that from 1563 to 1824, a conspiracy, concocted by the law and carried out by parties interested in its success, was entered into, to cheat the English workman of his wages, to tie him to the soil, to deprive him of hope, and to degrade him into irremediable poverty. In a subsequent chapter I shall dwell on the palliatives which were adopted in order to mitigate the worst and most intolerable burdens of his life—palliatives which were rendered necessary by no fault of his, but by the deliberate malignity of Governments and

5

Parliaments. For more than two centuries and a half, the English law, and those who administered the law, were engaged in grinding the English workman down to the lowest pittance, in stamping out every expression or act which indicated any organised discontent, and in multiplying penalties upon him when he thought of his natural rights. I am not deceived by the hypocrisy which the preamble of an Act of Parliament habitually contains, and the assertions which are as habitually contradicted by the details of the measure. The Act of Elizabeth declares that "the wages of labourers are too small, and not answerable to these times;" and speaks of the "grief and burden of the poor labourer and hired man," and thereupon enacts a law which effectually makes the wages small and multiplies the labourers' grief and burden, by allowing those who are interested in keeping him poor to fix the wages on which he shall subsist, and to exact a testimonial from his past employers and the overseers or church-wardens when he quitted a service, which he had to show before he entered another.

By construction of law, the offence of conspiracy (which was originally a combination for the purpose of bringing false evidence against others, or for the purpose of subsequently committing a crime); was extended to those associations of workmen, whose purpose it was to raise the rate of wages by such a combination, for the whole basis of the practice on the subject appears to be inferential from the statute of Edward VI., under which penalties are inflicted on those who combine not to do work, except at a certain price and for a certain time, and for implied violations of the 18th, 19th, and 20th clauses of the Act of Elizabeth, which must be forced in order to bear such a construction. But at the conclusion of the eighteenth century an Act of Parliment was carried, which declares all contracts, except ·between master and man, for obtaining advances of wages, altering the usual time of working, decreasing the quantity of work, and the like, illegal. Workmen who enter into such illegal combinations are punishable by imprisonment, and a similar punishment is inflicted on those who enter into combinations to procure an advance of wages, or seek to prevent other workmen from hiring themselves, or procuring them to quit their em-

ployment. Meetings and combinations for effecting such purposes
are punishable in like manner, and offenders who inform against
their associates are to be indemnified. This Act, it may be
remembered, was passed when wheat was at famine prices,
ranging from 100*s.* to 150*s.* a quarter, and the magistrates were
beginning to confess the atrocious cruelty of the Quarter Sessions
assessment of wages by adopting that system of Poor Law allowances which I shall comment on hereafter.

The imaginary offence which employers and lawyers invented
for the purpose of keeping wages low is on a par with the crime
of witchcraft. That no end, however excellent in itself, should
be, indeed can be, aided by violence, is a commonplace in the law
of all civilization. It is equally true that the pretence to a
supernatural power of working mischief on others by a mysterious
process which its victim cannot foresee, resist, or escape, is an
offence against even a more rudimentary civilization. But the
ordinary forces of law and police ought to be, and under a proper
administration always are, sufficient against ruffians and cheats,
though the phenomena of ruffianism and knavery ought to direct
the attention of government to their causes, and to guide legisla-
tures to preventive remedies.

A trade union conducted on legal and peaceful principles, by
which I mean moral forces only, and with an entire abstention
from violence, both in its inception and its administration, does
not economically differ from any other joint stock partnership.
When a number of persons combine their capitals, their energies,
and their experiences in constituting a commercial undertaking,
when they carry it on with integrity, and gain all the advantage,
they can by interpreting demand and regulating supply, so as to
secure the greatest possible profit to themselves, the business is
welcomed as legitimate, and the managers and agents of it are ap-
plauded. If the undertaking is greatly successful, the promoters
of it are styled merchant princes, pioneers of industry, creators of
public wealth, benefactors of their country, and guarantors of its
progress. They are presumed to be peculiarly fit for offices and
titles of honour, to merit places in Parliament, occasionally to be
even qualified to transmit hereditary fortune, rank, and authority.
Examine into the process by which individual or joint stock wealth

is created, and you will always find that it has been developed from the practice of buying or producing judiciously, and by selling at as high a price as the market will consent to give. There is, indeed, no other process by which wealth can be accumulated or capital increased. The phrase may be varied as one wills, but it always means the same thing, that profits can be obtained only by selling at a better price than one has bought or made, whatever one may have obtained and is bringing into the market.

Now this is precisely what a trade union, or labour partnership as I prefer to call it, does for that which workmen possess,—their labour. They have something to sell in their strength and their skill. Like the capitalist, they wish to sell their property to the best advantage, that is, at a charge which will leave them something above, as much as possible above, the cost at which they are put in keeping themselves in an effective condition for their labour, and which exactly corresponds to the cost of production in the case of the manufacturer, and to the cost of acquisition in the case of the merchant or trader. They also know perfectly well that if they are constrained to sell their labour to the first comer or at a moment's notice, they sell at a disadvantage, and they are as much in their right in withholding their goods from the market till they can get their price, or, in other words, in refusing to work till they get satisfactory wages, as a shop-keeper is who will not sell his goods except at his price, or a manufacturer who will not bring his produce to market unless he gets his profit. In one particular, indeed, they are worse off than merchant and manufacturer. The goods in which they deal are very costly to keep, and therefore they have to be very circumspect in refusing to sell, because to withhold from the market is in their case a serious loss. In order to make this loss as light as possible, though at the best it is exceedingly heavy, they require to adopt the joint stock principle of mutual insurance against the loss of keeping their goods from the market, and on the widest possible scale. They seek to enlist the largest possible number of workmen in their association, to include all in the same trade if they can, to include all in a corporation of trades in the end, so that they may be able to strengthen, as far as possible, the exceptional weakness of their position. Now to do this successfully they should develop the most important of the social virtues. They should have consideration for the rights of others, in their own fellowship necessarily; in that of others, that they may not destroy the common agency by the harmony of which they can procure the greatest advantage : patience, and forbearance : shrewd foresight as to the condition, present and future, of the craft by which they live ; and intelligence in proving that the machinery which they employ is for the common benefit of all, workmen, producers, and consumers alike. If they take their measures rightly, they can demonstrate all this. I confess that I look forward to the international union of labour partnerships as the best prospect the world has of coercing those hateful instincts of governments, all alike irresponsible and indifferent, by which nations are perpetually armed against each other, to the infinite detriment, loss, and demoralization of all.

Mr. Mill, misled by two positions which he takes to be fundamental, but both of which are equally baseless; the first that the amount payable in wages is a fixed and inelastic quantity ; the second, that an increase of wages must necessarily be effected at the cost of the employer or consumer, or both ; has entirely ignored trade unions in his estimate of the popular remedies for low wages, and speaks doubtfully or slightingly about the machinery of trade unions in bettering labour generally, though he does, as might be expected, condemn in becoming terms the spirit which dictated the Statute of Labourers. But in point of fact, if trade unions do or can raise wages, they may do so to the ultimate benefit of producers and consumers. It is very possible, late experience proves it to be a fact, that aggregate profits may be abnormally high and individual profits small, owing to the competition of capitalists in the same employment, and a tacit or avowed understanding that competition shall be directed not to selling cheaply, but to getting custom. Now if the operation of a trade union takes the form of reducing the number of competing capitalists or traders, the workmen may be better off, the survivors of the reduction better off, and the consumers better off, too. There is an

unproductive consumption of a marked character in the presence
of a number of persons engaged in the same calling who cannot
all live well by the calling, but who do contrive in the scramble
to load the charge of the goods produced by their presence and
their profits. Men are beginning to find out that persons who
were once conceived to be a beneficial class, the intermediaries of
trade and production, are engaged in destroying profits to an
infinitely greater extent than higher wages do ; that they have
become customary in many callings, do mischief instead of service,
are parasites, and not, in any sense, producers. There is, of
course, a fixed quantity of merchantable wealth produced in any
given time. It may be distributed among an excessive number
of persons, many of whom are useless, many of whom, though in
their degree serviceable, could be spared, and by the excision of
both, profits and wages might be greatly enhanced for those who
are essential to the operation, and the public be, after all,
considerably benefited.

I do not defend the tactics which trade unions have sometimes adopted. They have, indeed, the poor excuse that they
are imitative of practices which are sanctioned by custom or
success in others. A strike, seldom, I believe, successful, though
the contingency of it may be, is, to an economist, no way
different from a speculative purchase by which the projector
hopes to control the market by shortening supply. The violence
which has characterized the action of workmen against those who
abstain from their policy, compete against them for employment
in a crisis, and, as they believe, selfishly profit by a process which
they are too mean to assist, but from which they suck no small
advantage, is indefensible and suicidal. But it has its parallel in
the attitude taken by joint stock companies of trade to interlopers,
and in the devices by which traders have over and over again
striven to ruin rivals who will not abide by trade customs, or
even seek to be independent competitors against powerful
agencies. I see no difference, beyond the fact that law allows
them, between the fattening of a Sheffield saw grinder and the
expedients by which, in the Committee-rooms of the House of
Commons, railway directors seek to extinguish competitive
schemes. Men who have not had the refinements of education

and who are not practised in the arts of polite malignity, may be coarse and rude in the expedients which they adopt, but when the process is essentially the same, when the motive is practically identical, and the result is precisely equal, the manner is of no importance to the analyst of motives and conduct.

There is but little alteration in the material condition of the artizan and labourer in husbandry up to the end of the second quarter of the eighteenth century. The wages of the former were generally 1s. 6d. to 2s. a day, those of the latter 1s. to 1s. 6d., though they are sometimes more, for the employer seems to have not infrequently disregarded the assessments of quarter sessions. In 1767 and onwards Arthur Young began and continued his tours through rural England, and constantly gives an account of the wages paid in different parts of the country. Thus, in Hertfordshire he reckons that the amount of a labourer's annual earnings is £18, of which his board, washing, and lodging amount to £12. This amounts to a little less than 7s. a week. In Northamptonshire it is £17 a year, and Young notes that day labour in that part of the country used to be only 4s. a week in winter, or even 3s., and that this was the rule ten years before. At Kettering, he tells us that labour has risen by one-third during the twenty years preceding his visit. In Derbyshire, he tells us that the price of labour (the annual earnings are set at £17) has increased 50 per cent. during the last twenty years; in Yorkshire, a fourth within the same period. In the fourth volume of his "Eastern Tour" he sets down the average wages of husbandmen at 7s. 10d. a week, this quantity being made up by the extra allowances of the hay and corn harvest; and he notes that in many places the wages had risen 50 per cent. within the last twenty years, and taking all places together, 25. This gives £20 3s. 4d. a year on an average. The house rent of the labourer is at an average of £2, his fuel at £1 6s. Bread, which he supposes to be wheaten, is 1¼d. the lb.; butter, 6½d.; cheese, 3¾d.; meat of all kinds, mutton, beef, pork, and veal, 3½d. Young comments on the equality of the price of bread throughout England as a singular and instructive fact. He also holds that such a rate of wages ought to nearly exclude parish assistance, adding that "sound and spirited husbandry while products bear a fair price, will very well pay a high price of labour, and that thorough good farmers who are alive to their business do not complain of the rates of labour, provided men can be got." Wages, too, had again become higher in the neighbourhood of London.

Such a result is to be expected. Unless the rate of wages be artificially lowered, the cheaper products are, the higher wages are, provided, of course, that the cheapness is due to progressive industry. Now this is precisely what occurred about the middle of the eighteenth century. Agriculture made a prodigious start, and though population was evidently increasing with great rapidity, prices fell. Inclosures were general, and still prices fell; a bounty was granted on the exportation of grain, and prices were still declining. Now if prices fall with an increasing population, with a greater breadth of land enclosed and under cultivation, and even under the stimulus of a payment made by the State to such persons as would export grain, the natural inference would be that rents would fall. But, on the contrary, rents rose as prices fell. The value of land, according to Arthur Young, and on this point he was not likely to be deceived, was on an average thirty-three-and-a-half years' purchase; and the owner had, at least ordinarily, to do repairs to the homestead and buildings, to run the risk of vacant farms and bankrupt tenants. Now it is impossible that so high a price should be paid for land, unless the purchaser contemplated a prospective advantage in his acquisition, was convinced, in short, that what he expected to get 3 per cent. from as an investment to-day he could get a constantly increasing percentage from shortly after he had acquired it. The country was constantly producing more vendible commodities at less cost, and the advantage was shared by the labourer, the farmer, the landowner, and the consumer. And though much that Arthur Young says is crude, and not a little even foolish, as when he ascribes the progress of agriculture to the Corn Laws and the Bounty, much that he says about the necessary, the inevitable, progress of opulence is true. The workman, it is true, got less of the profit than others did—less than the farmer, the landlord, and the general consumer, because his previous margin had been so low, but he did share in the advantage—the advantage of lower prices and higher wages. In 1768, when Young began his tour, prices to be sure were high, and the cheapness of the preceding forty years was beginning to give way to a series of harvests which were almost famine years; but it well might have been that these exalted prices were considered exceptional and likely to be reversed, and that at the most they would have afforded an additional impetus to the rise in the value of land.

In addition to the information which Young gives so copiously about the price of agricultural labour, his tours supply us with the wages paid at various manufactories in different parts of England. The highest are those earned by colliers, which at Newcastle were 15s. a week, and at Wakefield 11s. The next are those in the iron and cutlery works, which are 10s. at Rotherham, and 13s. 6d. at Sheffield. The next highest paid are the workmen in porcelain at Liverpool, Burslem, and Worcester, who get respectively 8s. 11d., 9s. 6d., and 9s. The average payment for spinning and weaving is 8s. 7d., the lowest wages out of seven localities being paid at Manchester, for fustians, 7s. 1d.; the highest at Wakefield, for cloth, 10s. The average wages of women in textile manufactures is 4s. 2½d.; of boys, 2s. 11¾d.; of girls 2s. 7d. The earnings, therefore, of the manufacturing population were already, as far as the men are concerned, greater than those of the hind; and, besides, the former calling gave a more regular and highly paid wage to women and children. The effect of the attraction to manufacturing districts may have been, indeed must have been, injurious to the health and vigour of the people who were drawn into these employments, but the fact of the attraction is plain. Again, the drugget weavers of Braintree earn about 9s.; the woolcombers, 12s.; the Wilton carpet weavers from 10s. to 12s.; the Gloucester pinmakers from 10s. to 15s.; the woollen manufacturers of Henningham 7s.; the combers from 12s. to 14s.; the steel polishers of Woodstock, from 15s. to 42s.; the blanket weavers of Witney, from 10s. to 12s. The manufacturers of Woodstock, now extinct, were the best paid of any.

The best paid workmen in textile fabrics were the wool-combers, who earned on an average, wherever they were, about 13s. a week; the lowest the say and calimanco weavers of Lavenham at 5s. 9d. The best paid agricultural labourers were those in Kent and Middlesex, with a weekly payment of 11s. 4d. The worst are those of Gloucestershire and Wiltshire, at 5s. 2½d. The wages of the manufacturing labourer, says Young, are, on an average, 8d. a week beyond those of agricultural labourers, some of whom, in the West of England, get no more than 5s. and 6s. all the year round. Young, who is an ardent advocate of high rents and high prices, informs us that the rioting which had latterly disturbed England had been invariably got up by those labourers who earned the best wages. He evidently does not see that discontent and disaffection are frequently the outcome of tolerable well-doing, rarely of penury and despair.

The old days of cheapness and abundance were now over, and dear times succeeded. In 1744 and 1745, when the upward movement of wages commenced, wheat was between 21s. and 22s. the quarter; after 1780, it was rarely below 50s. ; and towards the end of the century it rose to double that price. It is possible that the deficiency in the English harvests, prices being also elevated by the rapid growth of population, and this being due to the growing demand for hands in the factories, and especially for the labour of the young, could not have been supplemented by foreign importation in the generally disturbed state of Europe at the outbreak of the continental war. But even if the supply had been possible, the corn laws were a sufficient discouragement to foreign trade in food. If the foreign producer had known that the English people would buy corn in emergencies, he could not tell when the emergency would arise, and at what time he should make preparation for it. Trade rests upon the anticipation of a market, and the legislation, which makes a market uncertain, adopts the most effectual means for destroying the market altogether. The scarcity which now became chronic for a quarter of a century in England, developed besides that detestable interest in the mind of the farmer and landowner, and keeps it still alive in that of the former, that the best profit which they can hope lies in the calamities, the miseries, the misfortunes, the losses, the impoverishment of their fellow-countrymen. Thanks to the efforts of those who established free trade in food, the farmer and the landlord are now deprived of the pleasure which they once felt when unpropitious seasons raised the price of food in so rapid

and increasing a proportion, that a scanty harvest was bringing
enormously increased gain to the agriculturist and the receiver of
rents, and their satisfaction is limited to the prospect of interrup-
tion between the trade of this country and those regions from
which food supplies are derived.

On May 6th, 1795, a meeting of the Berkshire magistrates was
held at Speenhamland, after a public advertisement had been
made of the intended meeting, when it was unanimously affirmed
that the state of the poor required larger assistance than had been
given them generally. The meeting also decided that it was not
expedient for the magistrates to grant that assistance by regulating wages according to the Statute of Elizabeth, but that the
magistrates should earnestly recommend the farmers and others
to increase the pay of their labourers according to the price of
provisions. They thereupon put out a scale, in which they calcu
lated what should be the wages of workmen, according to the rise
or fall in the price of bread, the scale being based on the same
principle as the assize of bread. Thus when the gallon loaf should
cost 1s., they reckoned that the labourer should receive, either by
his own earnings or by an allowance from the poor rates, 3s.
weekly for himself and 1s. 6d. for each of his family and that with
the rise of every penny in the loaf, he should receive an additional
3d. for himself and 1d. for each of his family. An unsuccessful attempt was made twice over in the House of Commons to
enforce what was called the Speenhamland Act of Parliament by
law, and Bills to this effect were introduced in 1795 and 1800 by
Mr. Whitbread.

There had been some rise in the rate of wages at the
conclusion of the century. The poor could not have subsisted
had not such a rise been effected; but it bore no proportion to
the rise in the necessaries of life. In 1801, Arthur Young
calculated that a Suffolk labourer could (at some date which he
does not give, but it must have been nearly sixty years before)
have bought with 5s. what, in 1801, would have cost him 26s. 5d.,
and that, therefore, as his wages and parish allowance would at
the best have given him only 15s., he was virtually put on little
more than half the scale of his earnings in the earlier period.
The workmen of the time put out statements as to their condi-

tion, in which they admitted a slight increase, but showed how inadequate it was when contrasted with their present outgoings. Thus, the journeyman tailors stated that their wages from 1777 to 1795 had been 21s. 9d. a week, with which they could purchase thirty-six loaves at the average prices, that they had risen to 25s. in 1795, and to 27s. in 1801, but that they were only able to purchase eighteen-and-a-half loaves with the larger nominal sum. Compositors had secured an advance from 24s. to 27s. in 1795, and to 30s. in 1801, but were really worse off than they had been. A similar rise had been effected, and with the same consequences, in the labour of carpenters, bricklayers, and masons. The rise was from 3s. a week to 1s. 6d. and 1s. But it was proved that the cost of maintaining a household at the beginning of the last quarter of the eighteenth century was, by a comparison of prices, more than trebled at the close of the period. It should be noted also that while prices were so high in England, they were remarkably depressed abroad, but that owing to the outrageous fiscal system in England, the famine in England was contemporaneous with a foreign glut. Now a free intercourse with other countries would have obviated much mischief and misery on both sides of the Channel. The report as to the state of the home trade is what might be expected. The trade of Birmingham was in a very distressed condition. A large number of workmen were out of employment, and those who got work had the utmost difficulty in subsisting, owing to the exorbitant price of food. The ribbon trade of Coventry was in a most deplorable state, the woollen trade of Yorkshire, if possible, still worse. The seasons had been unpropitious, and the law designedly intensified the scarcity.

Between 1800 and 1812 the nominal wages of agricultural labourers and artizans were considerably increased, either by actual payments or by parish allowances. Still the rise was not proportionate to the increased cost of living, for dearth had become an institution in the country. But the wages of persons employed in factories were not increased, or very partially, and many people were out of work altogether. In 1785, the poor rate was £2,004,238. In 1802, it was £4,267,965; in 1813, it amounted to £8,640.842. At the conclusion of the eighteenth century the rate of agricultural wages was 1s. 4d. a day. In the year 1810 it was 1s. 8d., and it is noteworthy that the carpenter's wages, generally about 50 per cent. above those of the agriculturist, did not go above the level of the latter at the time. For as Mr. Tooke ("History of Prices," ii. 71) said in 1837, "According to all experience, whether within modern observation or recorded in history, it may be laid down as an established maxim that labour is the last of the objects of exchange to rise in consequence of dearth or depreciation, and that commonly the price of labour is the last to fall in consequence of increased abundance of commodities or of increased value of money." The condition of labour was considerably bettered after the peace, was greatly benefited by the comparatively low prices which prevailed in the period intervening between the commencement of fiscal reforms and the repeal of the corn laws, and has, speaking generally, made further progress since that time.

The repeal of the ancient laws against the association of workmen for the purpose of raising their wages, led to the creation of trade unions. In course of time these associations took active steps, and especially in 1853 were successful in several directions. The lightermen on the river, the labourers in the docks, a number of artizans on the south of the river Thames, where there are great and important manufactures, the men employed in the building trades, masons, bricklayers, and carpenters, demanded and obtained an increase of 10 per cent. in their wages, and a considerable shortening in the hours of their labour. This movement has progressed, and at the present time the hours of labour are probably less in England than they are in any country, certainly considerably less than they are in the United States. Nor was this movement confined to artizans. The agricultural labourers, partly owing to their own action, partly to the greater mobilization of labour, brought about by the construction of the railways, which attracted numerous hands from the rural districts, partly to the easier means of communication, and the intercourse with other markets for labour which the railways opened up, made their demand also for a better remuneration, and generally achieved it. It is true that the wages of the farm hand are still low, and, as a consequence, country districts have suffered a great depletion of population, and it may be feared have lost their best hands, and, it is possible, the best stock. Emigration also became exceedingly active. Thousands went to the United States and the Colonies, although population, especially in the towns, continually increased, partly because, under better sanitary conditions, the number of births became greater and life was greatly prolonged, partly because there has been a steady inflow to the towns from rural districts, and even from foreign countries.

Working men have been far more effective in the combinations they have adopted than in the instrument which they have used for enforcing their demands. Strikes have so seldom been successful that a doubt has been expressed, as to whether the rise in wages, fortunately an accomplished fact, has not been due entirely to demand, and in no case to the combination. But it cannot, I think, be doubted that however little the battle between capital and labour has resulted in the victory of the latter, the contingency of a battle must have frequently averted its occurrence. The tendency towards the struggle, too, is always when trade is bad and a reduction threatened, *i.e.*, at a time when the minimum of loss is put on the employer and the maximum on the workmen. But the fullest proof of the real efficacy of trade unions as a means for improving the condition of the labourer and increasing his material benefit lies in the stimulus which they have given to the construction of boards, which should conciliate both parties and arbitrate between them. Many of us can well remember the time when the master repudiated the interference of arbitrators with great warmth, and men looked on the proposal with cold incredulity. But this to a great degree is changed, and though the mechanism of conciliation works still with not a little friction, all persons testify to the infinitely improved tone with which trade disputes are avowed, carried on, and settled. It was not to be expected that persons unused to argument, and inexperienced in the analysis of facts, much more of motives, should not at first be violent when they were angry. The tendency, however, has greatly changed, and, in the opinion of most fair judges, with great rapidity.

Working men in England have now their future very much in their own hands. They see, I suspect, much more clearly than their critics do, what are the limits of their power over capital and prices,—on the former because the profits of capital depend on the sufficiency of the latter; on the latter because they know that they may check or even destroy the market of what is voluntarily purchased, and may rise against themselves and their own order what must necessarily be used or consumed. But the joint action of working men is only in its infancy yet. As association becomes wider and more coalescent, many steps which have not yet been taken will become easy and natural; as, for instance, the maintenance of a standard of honour and efficiency in work, and the protection of the public against the roguery of producers, of which at present workmen are the silent witnesses, but should not be the willing accomplices. I know nothing which would exalt the reputation and justify the action of trade combinations more than the establishment of a rule, that members of such unions would denounce and expose dishonest and scambling work, and protect those of their order who may suffer ill-usage or wrong-doing for having reported and checked such nefarious practices. As yet the rules of trade unions are principally confined to the process of bettering the whole class. Hereafter they will, or should, extend towards purifying the class, and making it a potent instrument for the moral and material advancement of all. Other professions exclude, either formally or informally, misbehaving, disreputable, or incompetent persons from their ranks. It cannot be doubted that in time to come artizans and labourers will elaborate those necessary police regulations, by which they will increase the usefulness, elevate the reputation, and cultivate the moral tone of those who ply the craft whose interests they seek to serve, and whose character they ought scrupulously to maintain.

CHAPTER IV.

THE ENGLISH POOR LAW.

THERE has always been poverty in human societies when men are settled on the soil, though not, perhaps, more poverty than exists among peoples who are still wanderers, or hunters, or herdsmen. I make no doubt that the ordinary hardships of human life in England were greater, and I am sure they were more general, six centuries ago than they are now. Life was briefer, old age came earlier, disease was more deadly, the risks of existence were more numerous. The race was smaller, weaker, more stunted. But the extremes of wealth and poverty were, by the fact of these common conditions, less widely separated. Above all things, what is now characteristic of human life, that one-half of the world does not know how the other half lives, a very moderate statement of the fact, was not true of the early ages of English progress. Society was small, and not packed densely. Not only did each man know all about his neighbours'

affairs, but the whole machinery of government pre-supposed that
he did. The ancient jury was not a body of men brought together
to interpret the relevance of a set of facts which they hear for the
first time when they get into the jury-box, but a dozen men who
were supposed to know all the facts of the case beforehand, who
were held responsible for not knowing them, and still more
responsible for not giving a satisfactory verdict on the facts
which they knew.

As the English householder in the middle ages was supposed to
know the acts and the character of every man in the neighbourhood, he was equally well-informed as to each person's circumstances. No doubt people hoarded, the more because taxation
was on the visible means of the tax-payer ; but it is certain that
the periodical visits of the assessor must have brought out the
fact of narrow circumstances, poverty, and want very plainly,
perhaps over plainly, as destitution was, under certain circumstances, held to be a virtue, or, at least, the preparation for virtue.
I cannot say that people did not perish from want in very bad times.
I am tolerably sure that they did, and in considerable numbers,
during the great famines of 1315 and 1316, when all but the
very opulent must have been stinted. But fortunately for the
English people, as I have frequently stated, their habit, even
under the adverse circumstances of their existence and the un-
cleanly ways of their life, was always to subsist on abundant
provisions of naturally high quality. They ate wheaten bread,
drank barley beer, and had plenty of cheap, though perhaps coarse,
meat. Mutton and beef at a farthing a pound, take what
multiple you please, and twelve is a liberal one, were within the
reach of far more people than they now are. The grinding,
hopeless poverty under which existence may be just continued,
but when nothing is won beyond bare existence, did not, I am
convinced, characterise or even belong to mediæval life. That
men died from want I can believe, but I do not think that they
lived and died by inches, so to speak. There were many means
by which occasional distress was relieved. I am not sure that I
have been able to collect all the means.

In the first place, the relief of destitution was the fundamental
religious duty of mediæval Christianity, I might have said of

6

Christianity itself. In ancient polities it might be the duty of the state to relieve distress; it was always its prudence, if it cared for security. To get abundant supplies of food for the poorer citizens in one way or the other was the constant anxiety of democratic Athens and of imperial Rome. But from the very first Christianity transferred this duty from the state to the individual, and to the voluntary corporation. The early Church undoubtedly preached patience, but it much more emphatically inculcated the duty of almsgiving. The contribution of the tithe was enforced in order that a third part at least of the proceeds should go to the relief of the deserving poor. In the fifteenth century nothing moves the righteous wrath of Gascoigne more than the teaching of Pecok to the effect that ecclesiastical revenues enjoyed by churchmen can be disposed of according to the discretion of the recipient as freely as the proceeds of private property. After heresy, simony, and sorcery, the heaviest charge which could be levelled against a churchman was that of avarice, and a covetous priest who hoarded his revenues was lucky if the charge of avarice was not coupled with those graver vices to which I have referred. We may be certain, too, that the duty which was so generally imposed on them by public opinion—the force of which is not yet extinct—was inculcated by them on others. In times of plenty, too, food was often given with wages. A wealthy monastery or college would find a place at the servants' table for the artizans whom they employed without much grudging, and still more would the poor at the gate not be sent away empty-handed. Where mendicancy was no disgrace, almsgiving was like to be considered the most necessary and the most ordinary of the virtues.

It has been often said and often denied that the monasteries supplied the want which the poor law, two generations after the dissolution of these bodies, enforced. That the monasteries were renowned for their almsgiving is certain. The duty of aiding the needy was universal. Themselves the creatures of charity, they could not deny to others that on which they subsisted. But some orders were under special duties. The Hospitallers were bound to relieve casual destitution. Hence, when Waynflete procured the surrender of the house of the Oxford Hospitallers, he bound his college to the duties which the surrendered house had performed, duties which, it is almost superfluous to say, were speedily evaded. So again the preaching and begging friars were the nurses of the sick, especially of those who laboured under infectious diseases. There were houses where doles of bread and beer were given to all wayfarers, houses where the sick were tended, clothed, and fed, particularly the lepers. There were nunneries, where the nuns were nurses and midwives; and even now the ruins of these houses contain living record of the ancient practices of their inmates in the rare medicinal herbs which are still found within their precincts. In the universal destruction of these establishments, the hardest instruments of Henry's purposes interceded for the retention of some amongst the most meritorious, useful, and unblemished of them. It is possible that these institutions created the mendicancy which they relieved, but it cannot be doubted that they assisted much which needed their help.

The guilds which existed in the towns were also found in the country villages. They are traceable to the period before the Conquest, and Hickes long ago printed some of the rules under which they were constructed and governed, though these are in the towns of Cambridge and Exeter. Blomefield finds some in the Norfolk villages. Vestiges of their halls remained long in small villages, these halls being devoted to the business and occasional feasts of the society. They were convenient instruments for charity before the establishment of a poor law, and they employed no inconsiderable part of their revenues, collected from subscriptions and from lands and tenements, in relieving the indigent and treating poor strangers hospitably. Blomefield, speaking of their feasts, says: "But as the poor of the parish always were partakers with them, I much question whether their revenues were not better spent then than they have been since they were rapaciously seized from the parishes to which they of right belonged." (Norfolk, iii., 185). The guilds frequently survived the Reformation, though, of course, they had lost their property, and are probably represented in later times by the parish feast. Their property, as I have already said, was finally confiscated by 1 Edward VI., cap. 14, after having been comprised in the last of Henry's acts of rapine (37 Henry VIII., cap. 4).

Before the dissolution of the monasteries, but when this issue was fairly in view, in 1536, an attempt was made to secure some legal provision for destitution. The Act of this year provides that the authorities in the cities and boroughs should collect alms on Sundays and holy days, that the ministers should on all occasions, public and private, stir up the people to contribute to a common fund, that the custom of giving doles by private persons should be forbidden under penalty, and that the churchwardens should distribute the alms when collected. The Act, however, is strictly limited to free gifts, and the obligations of monasteries, almshouses, hospitals, and brotherhoods are expressly maintained.

The Supplication of Beggars puts the contributions given to the begging friars by the people at £45,333 6s. 8d. annually, supplied by 520,000 households. There was a considerable party in England which was willing enough to see the monasteries destroyed, root and branch, and one of the most obvious means by which this result could be attained would be to allege that all which could be needed for the relief of destitution would be derived from the voluntary offerings of those who contributed so handsomely to the maintenance of indolent and dissolute friars. The public was reconciled to the Dissolution by the promise made that the monastic estates should not be converted to the king's private use, but be devoted towards the maintenance of a military force, and that therefore no more demands should be made on the nation for subsidies and aids. Similarly when the guild lands and chantry lands were confiscated at the beginning of Edward's reign, a promise was made that the estates of these foundations should be devoted to good and proper uses, for erecting grammar schools, for the further augmentation of the universities, and the better provision for the poor and needy. They were swept into the hands of Seymour and Somerset, of the Dudleys and Cecils, and the rest of the crew who surrounded the throne of Edward. It cannot therefore, I think, be doubted that this violent change of ownership, apart from any considerations of previous practice in these several institutions, must have aggravated whatever evils already existed. It was idle to expect that they who saw ancient institutions, on which the duty of almsgiving was imposed, not only swept away, but devoted to en-

tirely different purposes, in which these obligations were utterly
neglected, would contribute of their free will to the relief of
destitution, even if their resources were as considerable as before.
But as I have already stated, there came upon this violent change
another and far more formidable calamity, the issue of base money
and the total derangement of currency and prices. Foolish people
talk of the influx of the new silver. It had not reached England,
and did not reach England till a generation after, and then
superficially. What England wanted was silver, and the Government put it out of her power to get it.

The guardians of Edward attempted, in a savage statute passed
in the first year of his reign, to restrain pauperism and vagabondage by reducing the landless and destitute poor to slavery, by
branding them, and making them work in chains. The Act,
however, only endured for two years. In the last year of Edward's
reign two collectors were to be appointed in every parish, who
were to wait on every person of substance and inquire what sums
he will give weekly to the relief of the poor. The promises are to
be entered in a book, and the collectors were authorized to employ
the poor in such work as they could perform, paying them from
the fund. Those who refused to aid were to be first exhorted by
the ministers and churchwardens, and if they continued obstinate
were to be denounced to the bishop, who is to remonstrate with
such uncharitable folk. In Mary's reign, when the Act is
renewed with a penalty on such collectors as decline the office,
the reference to the bishop is accompanied with the hint that
refusal to give might be construed as suggestive of heresy. This
Act put the canvass for weekly subscriptions at Christmas in
place of Whitsuntide. In the beginning of Elizabeth's reign
(5, cap. 3) the unwilling giver, after being exhorted by the bishop,
is to be bound to appear before the justices, in quarter sessions,
where, if he be still obdurate to exhortation, the justices are
empowered to tax him in a weekly sum, and commit him to prison
till he pays. This Act precedes that enforcing apprenticeship
and empowering the magistrates to fix wages, on which latter I
have often and fully commented, and should probably be taken
with it. The law has now proceeded from exhortation to
compulsion.

It seems highly probable that destitution and vagabondage were still further developed by the decline of that manorial jurisdiction which had been so effective in the thirteenth and fourteenth centuries, and the transference of the machinery of police from the parish to the justice's office or to the quarter sessions. The old system, concentrating as it did the functions of local discipline in the steward and inhabitants of a parish, exercised a control and enforced a responsibility which was indifferently compensated by the authority of an individual or a bench of magistrates. And this impression is confirmed by the almost insensible change from a jury who are witnesses to a fact to a jury who are merely judges of a fact,—a change so gradual that we get the first hint of it in the celebrated case of Throgmorton, who was acquitted in Mary's reign; though the legal irresponsibility of a jury which acquits in face of a judge's ruling, or what he conceives to be the law, was only affirmed by Chief Justice Vaughan as late as the reign of Charles II. in the Quakers' case.

There was only a step from the process under which a reluctant subscriber to the poor law was assessed by the justices and imprisoned on refusal, to the assessment of all property under the celebrated Act of 43 Elizabeth, cap. 3. The law had provided for the regular appointment of assessors for the levy of rates, for supplying work to the able-bodied, for giving relief to the infirm and old, and for binding apprentices. It now consolidates the experience of the whole reign, defines the kind of property on which the rate is to be levied, prescribes the manner in which the assessors shall be appointed, and inflicts penalties on parties who infringe its provisions. It is singular that the Act was only temporary. It was, by the last clause, only to continue to the end of the next session of parliament. It was, however, renewed, and finally made perpetual by 16 Car. I., cap. 4.

The economical history of labour in England is henceforward intimately associated with this remarkable Act. It was the result of a series of causes, each of which has been already commented on, the most dominant unquestionably being the rapid and serious rise in the money value of food and other necessaries, and the halting manner in which the rate of wages followed the rise. In the fourteenth and fifteenth centuries the labourer secured increased wages in the midst of decreasing prices. In the six-teenth, the reverse which he suffered was far more considerable than the advantage which his forefathers had gained. I do not, indeed, find that they who regulated his wages by Act of Parlia-ment were aware how seriously his condition had been deteriorated, or that even those who busied themselves with the phenomena of social life, as Latimer did in the worst times of the bad currency, and Stafford and Harrison did in the days of Elizabeth, took any thought whatever of the labourer's condition under these deplor-ably altered circumstances. Even Eden, whose careful investiga-tions into the condition of the poor, and whose comments on the various statutes which regulated their wages, their condition, and their movements, are fairly exhaustive, does not seem to have realized, though the facts were to a considerable extent before him, how great a change had come over the life of the labourer and the artizan. I cannot but think that a growing disaffection, which Elizabeth and her counsellors were not slow to discern, the remedy for which seemed to be the continuance of expedients adopted in the three previous reigns, was the cause which induced them and parliament to acquiesce in the Act of 1601. The Act was to be tentative, indeed, but in its general principles it lasted till 1835.

It is plain that had the Act of Elizabeth been carried out in all its details, the whole revenue of land would have ultimately been swallowed up in the relief of the poor. To some extent the framers of the Act saw that this was already locally possible, for the third clause of the Act contemplates the possibility of the resources of a parish being inadequate to the charge of maintain-ing the local poor, and directs that the deficiency, if any arises, shall be supplemented from the rest of the hundred. Now it was plain that if the magistrates in quarter sessions were to fix the rate at which labour should be paid, as they regularly did in the sixteenth and seventeenth centuries, they would have every motive to put the rate at the lowest sum which would sustain life, knowing well that if the labourer became destitute, all occupiers would have to assist in his maintenance, while the benefit of cheap labour would remain to those only who employed him, as, indeed, actually happened. In country places this would not at first be a very important matter, as there would have been few persons rated

to the poor who, being occupiers, were not immediate employers
of labour.   But in the towns, the incidence of the poor rate was
a very serious addition to the burdens of such occupiers as did not
employ labour, and at the latter end of the eighteenth century it
became a very heavy charge generally.

The effect of poor law relief on the wages of labour was to keep
them hopelessly low, to hinder a rise even under the most urgent
circumstances.   This will be seen most clearly in the history of
wages during the seventeenth century, when prices of corn were
very high, and the labourer's standard of subsistence undoubtedly
fell.   For even if he were still able to maintain himself on wheaten
bread, his power of purchasing other kinds of food was greatly
curtailed.   We must not be led into believing that because meat
was comparatively cheap—it rapidly rose to three times the old
rate, while wages did not increase more than fifty per cent. over
the rate in Elizabeth's reign after the first exaltation of prices was
established—it was therefore within the range of his expenditure.
On the contrary, the comparative cheapness of meat, beside that
of corn, is proof that the power of consuming it was narrowed by
the deteriorated condition of the mass of the people.   The fact is,
the relief of mere destitution was the removal of every prudential
restraint.   If the labourer got scanty wages, he was at least
guaranteed against famine in sickness, in infancy, and in old age,
and he was, therefore, discouraged from exercising any foresight
whatever.   I am persuaded that the singular indifference with
which, on the whole, the condition of the working classes was
viewed in relation to profits and rent was due to the impression,
that as the propertied classes had bound themselves by law to
ensure the labourer against the contingencies of life, the facts of
the case needed no further anxiety on the part of any person
whatever, except in so far as the maintenance of the destitute
seriously trenched on the value of land.

It has been said, and with great apparent justice, that the
legal relief of destitution, though perhaps incapable of an
economical defence, is justified on the highest political and social
grounds.   If the relief of misery is left to private charity, the
assistance given is capricious and imperfect.   Besides, the destitute
and unrelieved are always dangerous; and though the forces at

the command of modern society are powerful enough to check any outbreak, they cannot be, except at an enormous expense, so efficient as to protect property against desperate distress. Again, serious as the strife has been between labour and capital, when the former is at least guaranteed against the worst contingencies ; it would be infinitely sharper were the guarantee repudiated. Nor must one forget how harsh and bitter life becomes when it is familiarized with the signs of unrelieved distress. I cannot, indeed, doubt that in the magnitude of modern societies the relief of the poor is a necessity which cannot be, however much labour makes progress and betters itself, repudiated or neglected. Society may not be responsible for nine-tenths of the misery and poverty within it, but it will never restrain poverty and misery unless it takes them in hand, and to do so is to relieve them.

But the English poor law, after all, was the outcome of great crimes committed by government, and is aggravated even now by customs permitted by government. It could not be free from the vices of its origin, and it is still in many particulars made mischievous and harsh by those provisions and those contingencies which arise from the customs to which it is partly due. I have referred to the crimes of the Tudor government. The customs to which I take exception have an earlier origin, and are even more enduring, for they have given occasion to two of the greatest problems of our own day,—the housing of our poor in cities and the settlement of agricultural labour in the country.

How far beggary, wretchednesss, and crime, with their most fruitful concomitants, drunkenness and hopelessness, reciprocally act on each other we cannot and never shall be able to tell. We know that they are the miserable circle in which thousands of our people, especially in London, revolve. We know that they have destroyed all interest, except in the means of the present day, in thousands. There is a large population which would, if it could, make war on society, which measures its own misery by the opulence of others, and is profoundly convinced that every power which society has and uses is employed against it. These people live in squalid dens, where there can be no health and no hope, but dogged discontent at their own lot and futile discontent at the wealth which they see possessed by others.

But it cannot, I think, be doubted that when prudence and thrift are deliberately discouraged, and recklessness is inculcated by law or practice, the misery which must, it seems, accompany human life in society may become general and chronic. The legislature strove to tie the peasant to the soil, not, indeed, as a mere serf, for the Act of 1592 prescribed that every labourer's cottage in future should have four acres of land attached to it, —a law which roused the wrath of Arthur Young in 1770, and was no doubt habitually broken. But it also gave him, as a compensation for the policy which permitted entails and the accumulation of land in few hands, the right to be a pensioner on the soil, from all real and permanent share in which he was practically excluded. He had been robbed by the landowner, and he was to be hereafter quartered on the occupier. He had been impoverished by misgovernment, and was to be degraded by a charity which was to compensate him for the losses which he had sustained and for the hard measure which was being dealt out to him, but which would ultimately degrade him and make him helpless and hopeless. I can conceive nothing more cruel, I had almost said more insolent, than to condemn a labourer to the lowest possible wages on which life may be sustained, by an Act of Parliament, interpreted and enforced by an ubiquitous body of magistrates, whose interest it was to screw the pittance down to the lowest conceivable margin, and to inform the stinted recipient that when he had starved on that during the days of his strength, others must work to maintain him in sickness or old age. Now this was what the Statute of Apprenticeship, supplemented by the Poor Law, did in the days of Elizabeth. And if you go into the streets and alleys of our large towns, and, indeed, of many English villages, you may meet the fruit of the wickedness of Henry and the policy of Elizabeth's counsellors in the degradation and helplessness of your countrymen.

Still their evils have been aggravated by other agencies. The cost of living in large towns has been reduced by the excellent and regular services of supply. In the Middle Ages most articles of food and analogous necessaries were fully fifteen per cent. dearer in London than elswhere. It is probable that at present they are as much cheaper. But to these economies there is one notable exception. The cost of house rent is enormous. Some of this cost is doubtlessly due to the density with which the people are packed, and the advantage contained in proximity to one's calling. But the cost is greatly increased by the power which the law confers on corporations and private proprietors to withhold land from the market at a minimum of cost. It will be clear that if the law encourages an artificial scarcity, it creates an unnatural dearness. By permitting corporations to hold land in towns, and by allowing private owners to settle land in towns, it gives such persons a power of exacting the highest terms possible for the use of their property, by keeping it out of the market till they can enforce their price. To use an American phrase, taken from the slang of speculators, the Russells, and the Bentincks, the Cecils, the Portmans, the Grosvenors, and the rest, with the corporations, have had for a long period a ring or corner in the land market, and can force buyers to give famine prices. Now what is an injury to the moderately wealthy, is oppression on the poor. It is well known that vile and loathsome buildings, probably the property of some opulent landowner, yield from the misery of their inmates a far larger rent than the plots on which the most luxurious and convenient mansions are built. Dives is clothed in purple and fine linen, and fares sumptuously every day from the crumbs which he sweeps out of the wallet of Lazarus; and if Lazarus has to be fed occasionally, and at last taken care of permanently, the fund which helps him comes, not from the pockets of those who grow wealthy from his want, but from those of others who are made liable in their degree to the same extortion. The law which levies rates on occupancy instead of on property makes the evil worse, for it puts the minimum inconvenience on the person who holds the strongest position. But they say, rates are paid by property in the end. If so, there can be no hardship in making the possessor of property pay them in the beginning. The facts and their effects may be dwelt on at greater length below.

In the ten years ending with 1590, the average price of wheat was 20s. 6d.; in the next decade, 31s. 11¼d.; the average being heightened by two years of famine, 1596 and 1597; in the next, 29s. 5½d.; in the next, 34s. 9½d.; in the next, 37s. 5¼d.; in the next, 43s. 0$\frac{3}{4}$d. ; in the next, 46s. 1$\frac{1}{4}$d. ; in the next, from 1651 to 1660, 44s. 6d. ; the price being lowered in the last decade by the three abundant years 1653-5 inclusive. Now my readers will notice that the price of food is, on the whole, steadily rising, and he will readily discern that the two years of famine, 1596-97, when wheat was 46s. 3d. and 56s. 10$\frac{1}{2}$d., precipitated the passing of the Poor Law. At the commencement of the period, the artizan's wages were 1s. a day; the ordinary labourer's, 8d. At the conclusion of it, the former were 1s. 6d., the latter, 1s. ; and at these prices they remained under the Act of 5 Elizabeth and the quarter sessions' assessment for a century and a quarter, since this is the rate at which they ordinarily stood in Arthur Young's time. In the time preceding the issue of base money, when the average price of wheat was below 6s. a quarter, they were 6d. and 4d. In the earlier period, then, an artizan could buy $\frac{1}{12}$ of a quarter of wheat, the ordinary labourer $\frac{1}{18}$ of a quarter, by a day's work. But in the eight decades since 1581 they could get only $\frac{2}{41}$ and $\frac{2}{61}$ parts, $\frac{1}{32}$ and $\frac{1}{48}$ parts, $\frac{2}{59}$ and $\frac{2}{88}$ parts, $\frac{1}{130}$ and $\frac{4}{205}$ parts, $\frac{2}{75}$ and $\frac{2}{112}$ parts, $\frac{1}{43}$ and $\frac{1}{64}$ parts, $\frac{1}{46}$ and $\frac{1}{69}$ parts ; while, in the last decade, when 50 per cent. was added to wages, owing, perhaps, to the charges of war and the circulation of money, they rose to $\frac{2}{63}$ and $\frac{2}{88}$ parts, omitting minute fractions throughout. Such figures show plainly how lessened the wages of the workman had become since the prosperous age to which I have so often referred.

Estimated by his power of purchasing wheat, the artizan and labourer in the last twenty years of the sixteenth and the first fifty years of the seventeenth century got progressively less, so that in the ten years from 1641 to 1650, their wages were little more than the fourth of that which had been earned by their grandfathers and great grandfathers. In the *Percy Ballads*, one of the speakers, called Ignorance, sings :—

> " I'll tell thee what, good fellow
> Before the friars went hence,
> A bushel of the best wheat
> Was sold for fourteen pence ;
> And forty eggs a penny,
> That were both good and new "

The price of the wheat in the song is a good deal above the average, though it does happen to be the price which prevailed just about the time of the Dissolution. The peasants naturally connected the change with the great event which had occurred before their eyes, and from which, chronologically, the decline in their condition commenced. It may have had its effect in the general cataclysm. It is certain that the majority of persons, most of all those who are quite unused to analyse the causes which lead to a result, ascribe to one or two events, occurring concurrently with an effect which makes them anxious or distresses them, the whole effect of which they complain. The event may have no relation to the phenomenon on which they rely, it may have a slight relation to it, it may have a partial relation to it, but be only one in a considerable congeries of causes, of which the principal remain undetected. Now the principal factor in the progressive decline of the labourer's condition was, as I have more than once stated, the issue of base money by Henry and Edward.

When the prices of the necessaries of life rise, the wages of labour do not rise with them. Even under the best conditions of labour this will be found to be the case, or, what is the same thing to the economist, given a fixed order of things, under which the labourer is restrained from seeking employment in the best market, has his wages defined for him by a hostile authority, is made —as in the case of the agriculturist—the residuum of all labour, and is compensated by supplementary allowances raised by the taxation of occupiers, as, under the Poor Law, the exaltation in the price of food is never compensated by a corresponding increase in the rate of wages, or, indeed, of the supplementary allowances. By contrast with the facts which prevailed before 1640, the labourer's service sank to the worst scale of remuneration during the first half of the seventeenth century, for the price of food increased, while wages remained stationary. By contrast with what prevailed during the first three-quarters of the eighteenth century, the wages of the labourer were again depressed during the last quarter of the eighteenth and the first quarter of the nineteenth centuries, when the old rates coninued, and wheat kept trising ;

for the average price between 1801 and 1810 was 96*s.* 4*d.*, or more than double that which existed in the worst decade in the first half of the seventeenth century. At this time it is true that something slightly analogous to Henry's base money occurred—the issue of inconvertible paper; but the poverty of the poor was practically unalleviated, their wages only nominally improved, the assessment of their earnings unchanged, and no thought whatever was taken of their condition by the Legislature, unless it be that the attempt to repress the violence with their unparalleled sufferings drove them occasionally to commit by atrocious penal laws may be called thought.

As, therefore, wages do not rise with prices, no crime against labour is more injurious than any expedients adopted on the part of government which tend to raise prices. Unluckily for them, many working people have been misled by interested sophistry into believing that high prices for employers mean good wages for workmen. I do not deny that if an artificial stimulus is given to some particular industry, the demand for the produce of which is limited but continual, and the craftsmen in which are also limited, such a calling may get enhanced wages for a short time. But others soon crowd into the calling, and very speedily the thing is made dearer, and the producer remains no better off, having lost in the interval the knowledge which competition gives as to the best conditions under which industry can be exercised. But it is idle to argue that such an artificial stimulus can be given to every kind of industry. Were it universal, the country would be debarred from all intercourse with foreign commerce, and the legislature would raise a blockade round the ports far more effective than anything which the most successful belligerent could enforce. If it be partial, it will either affect all consumers or some. If all, it induces a universal scarcity without benefiting any one, for internal competition is sure to do its work on profits and wages; if some, it simply narrows the area of consumption, and with even more rapid results on profits and wages. These elementary principles, which one is almost ashamed to allege, could be illustrated by a thousand facts.

The case is rather more difficult when, in a country where

labour is free and mobile, a marked addition is made to the currency, in the only form in which the addition can be made, a debased coinage, or a large increase of circulating credit. Here we find temporarily all the appearances of great industrial activity,—wages rise, profits are large, at least when the labourer is free to choose his locality and his employer, though wages never rise to the level of profits. But the benefit is only for a time, and generally for a very short time. The labourer is the first to lose his advantage. Then profits shrink, and ultimately the collapse ensues, with its disappointments, its bitterness, and its degradation. The English labourer, indeed, has had little experience of such advantages as come from inflation, though something analogous to it occurred in 1873, when the capitalists made much money, and circulated a great many calumnies about the hands. But in the sixteenth century, whatever advantage ensued was entirely on the side of the employers, on those who could interpret a base currency, could make the labourer pay for their commission on the exchange, and could succeed in permanently degrading him.

The first half of the seventeenth century is a magnificent political drama, in which the stage of public life in England is crowded with those historical characters on whom the better off and more educated of the English people dwell with a peculiar and lasting interest. We seem to see before us the Scottish king who had dropped into the English throne, who looked and spoke like a fool, but was not such a fool as he looked and spoke, with his strange brogue, his strange manners, his named and unnamed vices ; and his son, who seemed grave and wise, but was hotbrained and foolish, proud and false, the type of those unlucky liars who are always found out. Then there is the first leader of the constitutional opposition, Phelips, and the wily but dangerous counsellor of the court, Cecil. There is Carr, with his wife, one of the harlots of the House of Howard, who had so bad an eminence in the century ; and the grim Coke, loyal to the law and himself ; and Bacon, whose splendid reputation has obscured the baseness of his life; the shrewd Cranfield, who almost made James absolute ; and Buckingham, who ruined the Treasurer, and bringing his schemes to nought, assisted in pulling down that which Cranfield had laboriously striven to build up; and behind, below, but infinitely above these, are those men of genius whose writings are the choicest treasures of the human race and the special pride of the English tongue, for the same generation witnessed the maturity of Shakespeare and the precocious intellectual wealth of Milton. As time passes on, the whole energy of the nation is concentrated on the struggle between absolutism and free institutions, free, alas! only for the few, but these, as yet, the best types of our race. The rare learning of Selden, the grave, inflexible patriotism of Eliot, the dexterous tact of Pym, the resolute gentleness of Hampden, the stern prescience of St. John, the wise moderation of Bedford, and, ultimately, the military genius and clear foresight of Cromwell, were to be arrayed against the perfidy of Charles, the passionate bigotry of Laud, the fierce energies of Strafford, against the herd of Finches and Noys, against bullies from the Thirty Years' War and pettifoggers on the Bench. The age was so dramatic, the men were so typical, that Hyde was able in his first exile to sketch their portraits as no one has sketched individuals since, because men were so individual; for the imaginative drama had died out, since living men were more characteristic than the subtlest pictures of the poet. There has been and there will be no period in English history which commands and deserves such attention as the first fifty years of the seventeenth century, for memory sees gods ascending out of the earth.

By the middle of the century there were probably four millions of people in England and Wales, for hardships and poverty do not always check the growth of population. The half at least of these lived by weekly wages. There are no annals of these people, of their work and their sufferings, except in the record of their wages and the cost of their living. We see the characters on the stage, and a little more, but nothing of those who enabled these great actors to play their parts, or of the work which was being done behind the scenes. History, which crowds its canvas with these great names, tells us nothing of the people. But they who take note of the pittance which the peasant or artizan earned, and of the cost at which he spent his wages on his needful food, can interpret the hardships of his lot, the poverty of his life, the barrenness of his labour, the growing hopelessness of his condition. The eager spirits who crowded into the House of Commons, the mounted yeomen who rode with Hampden, the men who fought and won at Marston Moor and Naseby, thought no more of the peasant and the workman, had no more care for bettering him, than the Irish patriots of 1782 cared for the kernes and cottiers on whose labours they lived. For in the midst of this battle of giants, when the king was made subject first, and his foe, the parliament, followed him in submission to the great army which Cromwell wielded as dexterously as a swordsman does his weapon, the English people who lived by wages were sinking lower and lower, and fast taking their place in the contrast with the opulence which trade and commerce began, and manufacturing activity multiplied, as the beggarly hewers and drawers of prosperous and progressive England. In 1651, the magistrates of Essex in quarter sessions at Chelmsford fixed the wages of artizans and labourers at 1*s.* 6*d.* and 1*s.* a day respectively; and this was the price which they generally secured. The price of wheat in this year was nearly 50*s.* a quarter.

I have little doubt that during the civil wars and the Protectorate there was some little stirring among the labourers. Their wages were raised, as I have said, fifty per cent. above what they stood at in the times which preceded these civil convulsions. It is probable, too, that trade and manufactures made progress; it is certain that agriculture did. It was natural that labour should seek after a better market, and should acquire some mobility. The government of the Protector was not likely to stop this movement, and it is plain that labour began to stir. But the Restoration came, the landed interest became dominant; the principle that the crown and the parliament should be employed in the interest of the landlord and the trader was stereotyped, and the law of parochial settlement was forthwith enacted. This law consummated the degradation of the labourer. It made him, as it has left him, a serf without land, the most portentous phenomenon in agriculture. It applied equally to the artizan, but he was able to extricate himself at an earlier period from the toils of this hateful law.

The Act 13, 14 Car. II., cap. 12 (1662), begins with a hypocritical preamble, that it was enacted for the good of the poor, for the correction of rogues and vagabonds, and for the proper employment of such as were legally chargeable to the parish of their settlement, and so empowers the churchwardens and overseers of any parish into which a person comes and occupies a tenement of less than ten pounds annual value, within forty days of such a person's coming, to apply to a justice of the peace for the removal of such a person to his place of legal settlement, under the hands of two justices. The person in question may, however, give security that he will not become chargeable, and may in any case appeal from the justice's decision to quarter sessions, *i.e.,* from Herod to Pilate. The Act, however, permits, with tender care for the farmer's interest, that strangers may, under proper precautions, be employed in harvest work.

The great Revolution, which established the authority of Parliament, put an end to arbitrary power, and relieved the consciences of those who could not accord themselves to the worship of the English Church, brought no liberty to the peasant and artizan. It stereotyped their servitude by constraining (3 William and Mary, cap. 11) that notice of new comers should be published after service in Church. Labourers had ceased to be factors in political action, and are simply ignored for a century or more. But an Act of William III., 8 and 9 cap. 30 (1697), recognises the effect of the law of settlement passed thirty-five years before. It allows that persons are imprisoned in their place of settlement, where they cannot get work, though work may be wanted elsewhere, where the increase of manufactures would employ more hands, and that the provision of the Act of 1662, requiring the new comer to give security that he would not be chargeable to the parish of his new residence, confines them to live in their own parishes. It therefore permits churchwardens or overseers, who acknowledge their contingent liability, to give licenses to those who might wish to migrate, the effect of the license being that, if the incomer became chargeable, he could be forthwith removed with his children, even though they had been born in the new settlement. It is superfluous to say that such licenses would be looked on with suspicion, as expedients to relieve a parish of its quota of poor. Hence it became customary for those who employed foreign labour to give certificates of indemnity to the parish (often to a considerable amount, £100 or more) that they would bear the risk of the new comer's chargeability, the recognisance being stored in the parish chest. The effect of the law of parochial settlement was not only to annex the labourer to the parish of his residence, but to make him a serf. Those persons who possessed the whole of a parish took care, whenever they could, to pull down cottages on their estate, and rely on labour from a distance. By this system they hired labour at quarter sessions' rates, *i.e.*, at factitiously low wages, while the parish of the man's residence had to supplement his wages and to bear all those contingencies which were enhanced by the labourer being constrained to travel a consider-able distance to his work in all weathers. The law of settlement, therefore, not only fixed the tenant to the soil, but enabled the opulent landowner to rob his neighbour, and to prematurely wear out the labourer's health and strength. All this, too, was done when the patriots and placemen chattered about liberty and arbitrary administration, and fine ladies and gentlemen talked about the rights of man, and Rousseau, and the French Revolution, and Burke and Sheridan were denouncing the despotism of Hastings. Why at his own doors at Beaconsfield, Burke must have daily seen serfs who had less liberty than those Rohillas, whose wrongs he described so pathetically and dramatically.

Most writers of the eighteenth century take the law of parochial settlement as a matter of course. There were persons who, such as Alcock and Burn, took a different view from the complacent landowners and farmers, but above all Adam Smith. The former dwell upon the effects which the law of parochial settle-ment and chargeability had on the condition of the poor; but the great philosopher of social science detects the inherent injustice of the system. "To remove a man," says Smith, "who has committed no misdemeanour from the parish where he chooses to reside, is an evident violation of natural liberty and justice, and an oppression, to which the people of England, though jealous of their liberty, but like the people of most other countries, never rightly considering in what it consists, have for more than a century together suffered themselves to be exposed without a remedy." The people of England have a very just view of what constitutes their own liberties when they are in a position to vindicate them, and can bring sufficient force to bear upon the machinery by which those liberties have been outraged and may be restored, but which has had no very great consideration for unrepresented and powerless interests. It is generally vain to expect political justice on behalf of those who can by their own action bring no pressure to bear on Parliament. And this is as much matter of modern as it has been of past experience.

It is one of the commonplaces of an ignorant optimism to allege that the remedy is supplied by taking away the cause of the disease; but the maxim that the effect ceases when the cause ceases, is true in inorganic nature only, and not always true there. The present condition of English society, its violent contrasts of opulence and penury, of profligacy protected by law and misery neglected by law, is the outcome of causes which have a longer pedigree than the recorded generations of any family. The people of this country have become what they are by reason of events and acts which it is the duty of the genuine economist to discover, as contrasted with the economist who constructs a system out of a few axioms and a multitude of postulates. The reproach of political economy is that it is a hard and dry system, which has no sympathies, and only proposes to suffering humanity a bundle of unwelcome truths which it affirms to be natural laws. In many cases these are neither truths nor laws, but parodoxes, which have not even the merit of experimental inductions, but at the best are doubtful tendencies elevated to the rank of principles. I cannot take up any ordinary work on political economy without finding in every page a dogma which is controverted by facts, and, with the great exception of Adam Smith, I know no writer in England who has been at the pains to verify what he confidently affirms by the evidence of what has actually taken place. Mr. Mill is an ardent advocate of human liberty, and deserves all honour for his labours on behalf of it, but I do not remember that throughout his work on political economy he has been at the pains to point out how powerful a factor the law of parochial settlement has been in bringing about the unthrift and recklessness of the working classes, or how it has stereotyped improvidence and justified incontinence.

No trifling percentage of the funds collected for the maintenance of the poor was expended in litigation on the cases which sprang out of the Act of Charles II. It was an evil inheritance to the English people, perhaps the worst Act of the worst Parliament which ever sat, but it was a Potosi, an Eldorado to the lawyers. Many a barrister owes his place in Parliament and on the Bench to his skill in arguing settlement cases, to the ingenuity with which he was able to tighten the bonds on the peasant. The wealthy landowners clung to it with desperate tenacity, for it increased their rents at the expense of the occupiers and the poor. What mattered it to them that the English peasant's life was aged soon after his prime, if they could get cheap labour and increasing rents? The whole force of law was for nearly two centuries directed towards the solution of this problem, How much oppression can the English people endure, how much privation, misery, starvation, without absolutely destroying the labour on which growing rents depended? We, in our generation, though a portion of this evil has been prevented for the future, inherit the outcome of these two centuries, and with it problems of the gravest kind daily pressing for solution, and to which it is idle to offer the nostrums of over-population, emigration, competition, and the other formularies of an ideal society.

Towards the conclusion of the eighteenth century, the Berkshire magistrates, struck with the appalling discrepancy between wages and the price of food—for the labour of the peasant could only procure him for several years one-eighth of the amount of wheat which the same person could have earned before 1540,—met and proposed, not that the mischievous law of Elizabeth which established quarter sessions' wages should be repealed, or that the infamous law of parochial settlement should be done away, but that able-bodied labourers should have their wages supplemented by allowances from the overseer, proportionate to the number of their children or the general charges of their family. By this means they would be able to prevent a general increase of wages, to fix the wages of the single and the childless at a low amount, and compel all occupiers to contribute towards the cost of agricultural operations. This expedient, sanctioned by the courts, and, indeed, implied by 9 Geo. I., cap. 7, and 22 Geo. III., cap. 83, was known as the allowance system, and has been criticised adversely, not for its manifest harshness and injustice in giving that as charity which was due for work, but because it removed a check on population, at that time not much more than one-third of the number which now subsists in infinitely greater comfort in England than the lesser number did at the beginning of the century.

The English Poor Law would have ultimately devoured the rent of all open parishes, that is, those in which there were many owners, and consequently the possibility of housing the poor, and have enormously exalted the rent of all close parishes, *i.e.*, those in which there was one owner only, who cleared off every cottage on his domain, had it not been for the almost simultaneous discovery of steam power and the substitution of machine for hand-loom weaving. The capitalist inventors of these processes found that they wanted labour (though at first it appeared that the discoveries would dispense with labour), and were therefore indifferent to the contingencies of an unlicensed settlement. But it may be doubted whether their discoveries were an immediate boon to labour. The parochial system of relief must have been condemned long before it was imperfectly abandoned, when the system of close and open parishes had been thoroughly developed and the outrageous injustice of the practice had been exhibited in its fulness. The wages of the mill-hand were settled by the justices, like those of the artizan and peasant. Children and women were worked for long hours in the mill, and the Arkwrights and Peels and a multitude more built up colossal fortunes on the misery of labour. Any attempt on the part of workmen to combine for the purpose of selling their labour at better rates was met with stern repression, any overt act with sharp punishment. The English workmen earned all the wealth and bore nearly all the cost during that long war on which the fortunes of manufacturers and landowners, the glory of statesmen and generals, were founded. High profits were extracted from the labour of little children, and the race was starved and stunted while mill-owners, landowners, and stock-jobbers collected their millions from the toils of those whose wages they regulated and whose strength they exhausted. The student of economical forces can tell whence that wealth came by which England stood almost singlehanded against Europe, and subsidized the wretched governments whom Napoleon humiliated,—governments which were saved by their subjects, but who repaid these subjects with the Holy Alliance, a name, after that of the League of the Public Good, which was the most hypocritical lie ever forged in the devil's chancery. The story of the workmen's sufferings is told by Mr. Porter in his "Progress of the Nation."

At last, and not at its deepest midnight, a change began. The laws directed against the right of workmen to combine together in order to sell their wages in the best market, which had lasted for nearly five centuries, were repealed in 1824. So was the Quarter Sessions' assessment of wages. The workman was not indeed free to find his market, for the law of parochial settlement remained, as the shadow of it remains to this day. But a trade union ceased to be a crime. It was no longer forbidden by law. It was not, indeed, under the protection of law ; and I conceive that much of the savagery which for a long time characterized the conduct of trade unions was due to the outlawry under which those wholesome institutions were placed.

For nearly five centuries the legislature had declared that labour partnerships, that is, associations of working men formed for the purpose of selling their labour collectively to the best advantage, were under the ban of the law. The motive for this repression was never concealed. It was designed in order to increase and secure rents and profits at the cost of wages. For two centuries it failed, for nearly three it succeeded. The experience of the English workman had been of its success. It was therefore in human nature that he should believe in the efficacy of that which the legislature had so long striven to repress. It is commonly noted that those men who have been persecuted are more apt to be intolerant, when the persecution has passed away, than those who have never been oppressed. It is much more reasonable, then, that those who have been denied a right should conceive that the right is of inestimable value and should overrate its efficacy. Stolen waters are sweet, says the Hebrew apothegm, and bread eaten in secret is pleasant. But such joys are as nothing to the early delight of obtaining a liberty which has hitherto been forbidden. One has a right also to ask a reason for any restraint put on us. A workman might have laid out his money better at his master's tally shop than at the village store. But he objected to being forced to buy there, and rightly. The public-house may be a convenient place even for a total abstainer to receive his wages in, but a master should not be allowed, and latterly has not been allowed, to elect such a place, and constrain his workmen to take their money there, for all the Liberty and Property Defence League may say.

Eleven years after the repeal of the Acts against combination the new Poor Law was enacted. The change was needed, but it should have followed, not preceded, the repeal of the Corn Laws. The Corn Laws were defended on the ground that if they raised the price of food the Poor Law assured the peasant his subsistence from the land. The Act of 1835 took away this right, except under hard conditions, but it left the artificial scarcity. The result was that for once in English history a genuine communistic movement took root in the minds of the English workmen, for Chartism had only a political mask, the principal object of the organization being the repeal of the new Poor Law. When the Corn Laws were repealed, the movement collapsed. If it be ever revived, the motive force will be the laws and customs which direct the devolution and permit the settlement of land; laws and customs which are barbarisms, and would be infinitely grotesque, if they were not infinitely mischievous and infinitely dangerous. Already there is an ominous sympathy with the theory for making that a national estate which Englishmen have been studiously excluded from sharing by ordinary purchase as private owners. A political interest, like a political party, may seem to be strong when it is, after all, on the edge of a precipice. If it topples over, strength and weakness are all one.

Three processes have been adopted by the working classes, each of which has had a vast, and should have an increasing influence in bettering the condition of labour and making the problem of dealing with individual distress, however caused, easier and readier. They should be viewed by statesmen with unqualified favour, and be treated by working men as the instruments by which they can regain and consolidate the best interests of labour. They are trade unionism, or, as I prefer to call it, labour partnership ; co-operation, or the combination in the same individuals of the function of labour and capital ; and benefit associations, or the machinery of a mutual insurance society. So important do I conceive these aids to the material, intellectual, and moral elevation of the working classes to be, that I would, even at the risk of being thought reactionary, limit the privileges of citizenship, the franchise, parliamentary and local, to those, and those only, who entered into these three guilds—the guild of labour, the guild of production and trade, and the guild of mutual help. Nor do I think it extravagant to believe that were those associations rendered general, and finally universal, the social problems which distress all and alarm many would ultimately arrive at a happy solution. The first and third are only revivals of ancestral practice, the second is not very unlike the habit which prevailed in ages which I hope I have made in some degree familiar. I must, however, advert to them in another chapter, for this is already unduly long. Only let me assure my readers, that though it is a foolish dream to think that everything was better in the past, it is arrogant presumption to conclude that all progress is a modern acquisition, and that we can complacently despise the wisdom of our ancestors. Would that we could unite the opulence of the fifteenth century to the civilization of the nineteenth, and diffuse or distribute both.

CHAPTER V.

The Slow though Real Progress of Agricultural Improvements—The Passion
for Agricultural Pursuits at the Beginning of the Century, and its
Continuance for some Time in the Next—Failures due to too much
Land with too little Capital, and Slovenly Book-keeping—Motives for
this Fashion of Agricultural Pursuits—The Gains of Commerce in the
Eighteenth Century—The Pride of the English Nobility—The Immedi-
ate Benefit of Improved Agriculture—Arthur Young's Testimony—
Increased Stocks of Animals—Manures, Marling—The Increase of
Production estimated—Rental of England—Farmers' Profits—Leases
Necessary and Universal—The Estimated Value of Stock in 1770, and
of Wages in Agriculture—Rise in Rents—The Earnings of Labour—
Young's Estimate of Earnings—Comparison of Wages in the Eighteenth
and the Fifteenth Centuries—The Particulars of Agricultural Progress
in 1770—Abundance and Scarcity, their Effects on the Landed Interest
—Corn Laws—The Seven Barren Years of the Seventeenth Century—
Enclosures in the Eighteenth and Nineteenth Centuries—The Period of
Scarcity in the Eighteenth Century—The Corn Law of 1773 and 1791
—The Rise in Rent at the Close of the Century—Eden's Information in
1795—Weekly Earnings and Annual Deficits—Porter on the Cost of
Poor Relief in Wheat—Summary of the Action of Government on
Labourers, and their Consequent Condition—Its Effects on their Minds
now—The English Workman no Socialist—The Function of Employers
and Labourers—The Attitude of Farmers—The Result.

I HAVE stated already that while the agricultural progress of the
seventeenth century was chiefly in the direction of utilizing the
fallow for roots, that of the eighteenth was especially characterized
by the extension of artificial pasture, and the increased use of
clover, saintfoin, and rye grass. By this I mean that the development of each was the principal feature of agriculture in three
successive centuries. The winter roots were known in gardens in
the sixteenth century, at least towards its close, for Tusser speaks

of them as garden plants. Saintfoin was known to be useful to the agriculturist as early as 1637, for in this year a small work was published in which its cultivation is strongly recommended. Clover seed is to be found in prices current some time before the end of the seventeenth century, and that not in the London market only. But these seeds are regularly bought from the beginning of the eighteenth century by any farmer who had any idea of improved agriculture. On the other hand, the extension of the cultivation and the improvement of the article were of very slow development. The roots were small, and the crop at first was scanty. In course of time the farmer procured good seed, and increased his produce by judicious treatment; and similarly he studied the best means by which to supply himself with clover and saintfoin hay, and to utilize the aftermath. No record, however, of the progress is left us. It is the characteristic of agriculture that its improvements are so gradual as to be almost imperceptible, and it is only by contrasting rents and produce at different times, and perhaps prices, that we are able to arrive at any exact conceptions as to the progress which was effected. Writing in 1772, Arthur Young says that "saintfoin, cabbages, potatoes, carrots, are not common crops in England. I do not imagine above half, or at most two-thirds of the nation cultivate clover. It is a surprising number of years that are necessary firmly to introduce the culture of a new plant." " If gentlemen of the present age," says Young, " had not assumed a spirit in agriculture vastly superior to former times, I much question whether that excellent vegetable would make its way fairly through the island in a thousand years."

The Englishman of the eighteenth century was greatly addicted to agriculture as a business or a pleasure, or both. It was the " reigning taste " of the age. There was scarcely a nobleman or country gentleman who did not betake himself to the cultivation of land, not merely in the sense of keeping a home farm in his hands, which he managed by his steward, but as an overseer of his land, and as an experimenter in husbandry. Writers of the time note that country gentlemen talked about land and its properties, the benefit of certain courses, the advantage of turnip fallows, and the economies of agricultural machinery, about breeds of cattle, sheep, and pigs, with the same interest which their fathers and grandfathers used to exhibit on the subjects of the stable and the kennel only. The fashion had been set in Norfolk by Lord Townshend, after his quarrel with Walpole and his retirement, when he devoted himself to agricultural pursuits, especially to turnip growing. "There have been," says Young, "more experiments, more discoveries, and more general good sense displayed within these ten years in agricultural pursuits than in a hundred preceding ones." And the same writer adds, that "if this noble spirit continues, we shall soon see husbandry in perfection, and built upon as just and philosophic principles as the art of medicine."

The pursuit was universal. Citizens who were engaged in London business five days in the week were farmers for the other two ; men who had been brought up to other pursuits deserted them for a trade which appeared easy and independent. It was a bye industry with those who had other callings. Physicians, lawyers, clergymen, soldiers, sailors, and merchants were farmers as well. "The farming tribe," says Young, "is now made up of all ranks, from a duke to an apprentice." This habit continued till the beginning of the second quarter of the present century, especially in places remote from towns, out of the way of main roads, and before the first railways were constructed. Parson Trulliber, though perhaps an exaggeration, was not an imaginary character. Fielding must have seen such clergymen by hundreds. I am old enough to remember the type, very little changed, in my own youth; as I can also remember the doctor and country lawyer to have been as keen after the cultivation of their fields as they were after patients and clients, and a number of country gentlemen, with pedigrees of undoubted antiquity, as proud as the haughtiest noble and as coarse-mannered as the most illiterate rustic.

Of course, experimental farming such as this often was frequently ended in failure. The principal cause of ruin a hundred years ago was precisely the same as it has been and is to-day,—too much land in occupation, and too little capital to cultivate it with. Young considers an average of £6 an acre the minimum necessary for successful agriculture ; and it is certain that stock, live and dead, and labour, some few items excepted, cost the husbandman less than half the sum which they do now, the produce, as a whole, being sold for much less than half the price it reaches in our days. If he were criticising English agriculture at present, he would certainly set down £12 an acre as the average minimum. Every one knows that much less than half this was, unluckily, the capital of the agriculturist when the course of bad seasons came five years or so ago (1878). English agriculture has, as I have good reason to know, been in the course of the six centuries of its recorded history subject to severe strains. But there was no period in which the ordinary farmer was less able to stand the shock than he was when the present crisis came. Five years ago I was told by a land agent who managed a large amount of property in two of the most fertile among the arable counties in England, that the average capital of the farmer on land let at about 30s. an acre was considerably under £6 an acre.

Another frequent cause of discomfiture in the agriculture of this highly progressive period was the neglect of keeping proper accounts. Exact and careful book-keeping, Young urges, is the only way in which one can not only demonstrate the success of an experiment, but the prudence of imitating the experiments of others. In the case of a gentleman who farms with the aid of a bailiff, accurate book-keeping is the only satisfactory check which the landowner can employ in order to test his servant's integrity. The ordinary farmer, he tells us, guesses, and often with remarkable accuracy, at the items and the totals, though he is unable to reduce his profits to figures. But such a rule of thumb process is always unsafe, and is fatal to the inexperienced. I can imagine the delight with which Young would have studied the particulars and the accurate balancings of a bailiff's roll in the thirteenth and fourteenth centuries, and how his preconceptions as to the rudeness of the age four or five hundred years before his time would have been modified by an examination of the facts. Though the farmer of the eighteenth century was far better provided with agricultural appliances and far more competent for the work of agriculture than his ancestor of the thirteenth,—the rent he paid would be a sufficient proof if other proof were wanting,—he was, I suspect, more illiterate.

this struggle. I am persuaded (on the rule that it is wise to assign action to the rational and intelligible motive of self-interest in matters innocent and in their effects laudable, instead of postulating mere whim) that the English landowners set the fashion of making the best of agriculture, because they desired to make one wealth-producing agency become a rival in personal interest and in popular sympathy with another. The inference is obvious, that a person who makes wealth is more useful than one who gets wealth. It is not clear that the man who gets wealth does not destroy at least as much as he gets, and sometimes more,—a thief does so plainly, as society concludes. A speculator often does, as those who have to purchase the materials of industry discover. A hundred men live in opulence on time bargains. Somebody pays for their enjoyments, There is a superstition among old-fashioned economists that all parties are the better for the middle man. Experience is gradually proving that the abstract theory is incorrect. Hence under competition producers are getting rid of the middle man, and the modern economist, who studies facts instead of spinning theories and dilating on tendencies, is beginning to prove that he is generally a nuisance. Now that a man who wins more food from the earth is more useful than one who wins more food from somebody else's labour without offering anything solidly desirable in return for his function, needs no proof. If you can entirely get rid of the middle man, all the better; if you cannot, it is an economy which even he can hardly dispute, to narrow his functions and to curtail his profits.

It is curious to see how alive Arthur Young is to this sentiment. He is no economist at all in the most shadowy sense of the word, for he has no real conception of the harmony of interests, the exposition of which is the true function of the economist. His entire sympathy is with agricultural production. Everything must lend itself to this result. The labour must be cheap, whatever it cost in penury to the workman. The produce must be increased by every effort of ingenuity and skill. The energies of the farmer must be stimulated, and his ignorance and sloth cured by a rack-rent ease. The continuity of these beneficent processes must be secured by prodigal bounties on the exportation of agricultural produce and judicious restraints on its importation. The great landowners have been the pioneers of agricultural progress. Young is not at all a lackey. He speaks plainly about the shortcomings of those landowners who do not come up to his ideal. But he is so grateful to those who do that he describes their houses, measures the largeness of their reception rooms, and comments on their pictures as learnedly as Goldsmith's critic does in the story of his charming vicar.

The principal result which agricultural improvement exhibited on such estates as were cultivated with assiduity and skill was the increased stock of animals. The general adoption of root crops in place of bare fallows, and the extended cultivation of clover and other such plants by the use of the plough, supplied the farmer with a great increase of winter feed, besides materially improving its quality and sustaining powers. In consequence, on abundance of fodder, abundance of stock followed. But abundance of stock implied the great increase of barn-yard manure, the principal fertilizer of the time, indeed of all times, on the spot. So great is the increase that the farmer is in difficulty as to the means by which he can adequately compost or dilute it before he distributes it over his fields, and it is expedient to convey the whole of the straw or stubble produced on the farm to the yards. The grazing of meadows in winter time he considers injurious to cattle and destructive to the pasture. But the littering of cattle with straw will increase the litter in its conversion into manure five-fold in quantity, and the littering of pigs will increase it ten-fold. Better, he concludes, purchase straw, fern, or stubble than sell a single truss. The manure was mixed with earth, better still with chalk, best of all with marl. A dressing of twenty loads an acre of barn-yard manure thus composted will give a four years' fertility to the land which is so treated. The greatly increased produce of the eighteenth century was entirely due to the increased use of natural manures. The lessened price of agricultural implements had the effect of diminishing generally the cost of production.

Marling had now been revived, and was, relatively speaking, far less costly than when it was practised in early English agriculture, as compared with the value of land; for in earlier

times, the expense attending it was from half the value to
nearly the whole value of the fee simple. In Young's time it
cost from 50s. to £4 the acre. This is about twelve times
the average price at which the improvement was made five
centuries before. In Young's day the operation cost, at the
value which he assigns to arable land, from one-fourth to one-
eighth of the fee simple. The benefit of the operation, we are
informed, lasts for twenty years; but, he adds, it yields no
advantage for the first year, and but little in the second. In the
third it is distinctly useful ; but most of all from the fourth to
the fifteenth, when its effect is nearly worn out. Soils were also
treated with clay, with chalk, and with lime. But the principal
agent in successful husbandry is stable and shed manure ; and
my author estimates that land properly dressed with this fertilizer,
and continually dressed, will yield, if the land be capable of such
treatment, from 40 to 48 bushels of the different kinds of corn.
The average produce of the fourteenth century in prosperous
years, and when low prices prevailed, was under 11 bushels of all
kinds of grain. Manure was carted from towns, but the price
was high and the carriage costly. The dressing of land with
soot, ashes, bones, malt-dust, woollen rags, and even oil-cake was
known ; but the price was so high, and the evidence of the
advantage so scanty, that the use of these articles had not yet
transcended the stage of experiment.

The productiveness of agriculture in the eighteenth century
was, it is plain, when land was properly cultivated, four times
that of the thirteenth, both as regards corn and stock. The
weight of the fatted ox was raised at least three-fold; for the
maximum weight in the earlier period, and even up to the
beginning of the eighteenth century, was 400 lbs., while in
Arthur Young's time he constantly reached 1,200 lbs. A similar
but not so extensive an increase had taken place in sheep, while
the weight of the fleece had become fully four times above the
average of the earlier period. Now if the produce of England in
the middle of the fourteenth century was sufficient to feed two
millions and a half, that of the middle of the eighteenth was
sufficient for ten millions. But it is almost certain that when
Young wrote, the population was only seven and a half millions,

or possibly eight. England was, therefore, a considerable corn-exporting country, and would have been, even without the bounty, which was, of course, a virtual addition to rent. The bounty being, as was believed, a settled maxim in English policy, accounts in part for the fact that land, the value of which was constantly rising, sold in the beginning of the latter half of the century at $33\frac{1}{2}$ years' purchase.

Young tells us that in his northern tour he traversed and inspected more than 70,000 acres of land under cultivation, and that he registered the rent of the whole. He concludes, and with very good reason, that the parts which he visited are a fair sample of the whole of England. He sets the acreage of the whole country at thirty-two millions, a skilful calculation arrived at seventy years before by Halley the astronomer, by means of a most ingenious process, and only in error by about half-a-million acres. The rent of the land which he visited is, good and poor included, 10s. an acre ; and he therefore concludes that the total agricultural rental of the country is £16,000,000. He continually urges that this rental, especially for good land, is too low, and that good husbandry and an enlightened self-interest suggest and even demand a considerable exaltation of rents. There is, he says, a proverb current among farmers that a man cannot pay too much for good land and too little for bad ; and he illustrates his proverb by showing what is the rate of production and the cost of land rented at 5s. an acre and that which is rented at 20s. He makes out the profit of the former to be 8s. 8d. an acre, under the best known husbandry, and that of the latter 29s. It may be observed that, according to Young's calculations, the profit of the farmer, all charges deducted, is considerably in excess of the rent he pays. But it is considerably less than that procured under the ancient system of capitalist agriculture, or that which succeeded, the land and stock lease, and even than that of the short lease which followed.

Young considers it impossible that agriculture should thrive except under the security of a lease. Leases in his day were well-nigh universal, often with the obligation of repairs being imposed on the tenant. There was no motive as yet for keeping the tenant in a state of political independence. No tenant on term of years had a vote, not even a copyholder had one. . The only county voter was the freeholder; and even the freeholder for life would not guarantee subservience. I suspect that the Chandos clause in the first Reform Bill is to a great extent answerable for precarious tenancies, though the constantly rising rent of land in the fifty years preceding that famous clause is more responsible for the result. When the country gentlemen became passionately protectionist, it was an aid to their policy that the tenant farmers should be not only enlisted in the same interest with themselves, but should be plainly informed that their livelihood depended on the interpretation which the country party chose to give of that interest.

In the estimate which Young makes of the capital value of agricultural wealth in England, land is put at $33\frac{1}{2}$ years' purchase of the rent and valued at 536 millions, farmers' stock at nearly 110 millions, while house property is estimated at 100 millions. He reckons the wheat and rye crop at over 9 millions of quarters annually, that of barley at $11\frac{1}{2}$ millions, that of oats at $10\frac{1}{4}$ millions. It will be seen that this estimate, which he bases on the amount of those kinds of grain which he found to be actually produced in the district over which he travelled, corresponds closely with the inference which I have arrived at as to the possible population which could be maintained on English produce at two periods which are separated from each other by an interval of five centuries. The tithe payable from the produce he estimates at $5\frac{1}{2}$ millions; and he is clearly alive to the injury which a tithe in kind inflicts on progressive agriculture. The whole earnings of agricultural labour are set at $14\frac{1}{2}$ millions, shared among 836,235 persons ; or, in other words, the cost of agriculture, as far as labour is concerned, is supplied at nearly £17 9s. per head of persons. The estimate includes harvest labour, but not that of the tenant himself, which Young says was general, and, for farmer's profits, necessary.

The average rent of land is, he tells us, actually 9s. 11d. an acre, but for the sake of convenience he puts it at 10s. In the middle ages, and down to the rise in prices, it was let at not more than 6d. an acre. The payment, therefore, made for the occupation of land has risen twenty times. The average rise in the price of wheat is about six-and-a-half times, and the average rise in the price of labour is almost exactly three-and-a-half times, for the price of wheat is set at about 40*s.* a quarter, while that of the labourer is 7*s.* 1*d.* per week, the corresponding prices in the earlier period being 6*s.* and 2*s.*; and it should be remembered that while the labourer in Young's time had his earnings of hay and harvest time included in the aggregate average, the labourer of the earlier period had his harvest earnings over and above. The agriculturist of the eighteenth century called the forty-one weeks which remained before and after the harvest period winter, when the regular wages were about two-thirds of the better paid eleven weeks. As, however, I have often said, the agricultural labourer in the first half of the eighteenth century was better off than he had been at any period since the fifteenth and the first half of the sixteenth.

The rise in rent is the result of diffused agricultural skill. The cost of production had so far diminished, that the farmer could afford to pay out of the enhanced general profits twenty times as much for the use of land as his ancestors did some two centuries before. If the peasant's wages had risen with the general progress of that skill, in which he shared to the full with the farmer, the rise in rent would have been checked. The labour bill on a 500 acre farm in Young's days, on his estimate, was £335 8*s.* 4*d.*; the rent, £250; the profit, about £400. But assuming the profit to remain the same, and the labourer to have received a rise of wages at all proportionate to the rise in the price of wheat, rent would have again sunk to zero. The farmer's profit is estimated at from 14 to 18 or even 20 per cent. on his capital, a return, on the smallest of the figures, which is sufficient to account for the popularity of agriculture and for the generally prosperous condition of the farming class.

Two facts exceedingly puzzle this careful statistician. He finds that the local price of labour does not correspond with the local dearness and cheapness of provisions, and that relatively high and low wages are not connected with relatively low and high poor rates. It never seems to have struck him that the

Law of Parochial Settlement, and the consequent temptation put
before the owner of a whole parish to check the local growth of
population, would, directly there arose a demand for labour in
particular localities, tend to decrease the liabilities of one district
and increase those of another, but that the demand for labour
and the consequent rise in local wages might very well go on
with pauperism and overcrowding.   Similarly he does not in the
least discern the effect of the quarter sessions assessment in
stereotyping apathy and helplessness.   What he complains of is
the occasional prodigality of the justices in their valuations of
labour and the rate at which they fix the price of the peasant's
contribution to the general growth of opulence.

In estimating the earnings of labour, Young gives many and
elaborate tables based upon a preposterous postulate, the unreality
of which he admits.   The labourer is supposed to be in constant
work, and to earn the average of the three seasons, hay-time,
harvest-time, and winter, the latter being forty-one out of the
fifty-two weeks.   His wife is to work in hay and harvest-time,
and to get six weeks' work in winter.   His eldest son is to be a
first hand, his second an ordinary hind, his third a farmer's boy,
each at the average wages which such a calling supplied.   One
of his daughters is to be a dairy-maid, and the other a common
maid.   This family of seven are all capable of work, all at work,
and are all collecting their wages into a common fund.   He finds
the average of such a family's wages to be close to £51 8s. a year.
Now it is plain that not one family in a thousand corresponded
at that time or afterwards to Young's hypothesis, and that,
therefore, the calculations based on the statement are, as regards
the remuneration of labour, entirely fictitious.   What they do
represent, and as I believe accurately, is the average cost at
which a farmer in the Eastern Counties could procure the
services of seven persons in the distribution of occupations in
husbandry.   Each of these services was necessary, and was,
indeed, traditional in English husbandry on the large scale from
the very earliest times, and they would be and could be proved
to be equally necessary in the economy of modern English
agriculture.   How far the figures which Young has collected fell
short of the facts in the case of an agricultural labourer's

aggregate earnings will be shown in the evidence supplied by Sir Frederic Eden, on which I shall hereafter comment.

Now if any of my readers will take the pains to calculate what a family of seven, engaged as Young contemplates, would have received in the aggregate under the Act of 11 Hen. VII., cap. 22, in the year 1495, he will find that it amounts to £24 10s., or nearly one-half of that which the same persons employed in identical industry received in the tenth year of George III. In 1495, the four-pound loaf of bread cost ½d.; in 1770, 5d.; and to take and contrast Young's other prices with those of the earlier year, butter, 1d. and 7d.; cheese, ½d. and 4d.; meat, ¼d. and 4d. Of these prices the first is very low, for the year 1495 is a very cheap year. The others are the average price for the whole period of 283 years. Now if we apply the same rule to bread, we should raise the price of the four-pound loaf to ¾d.

If, therefore, it were the case, as it certainly was not, that the same amount of labour was required to secure the produce which was obtained in the eighteenth century as was needed in the fifteenth, it is clear that had wages in the later period been made to possess the same purchasing power which they had in the earlier, the family of seven would have received, in nominal or money wages, seven and a half times more than they received in 1495, in order that they might obtain the same amount of the necessaries of life, *i.e.*, £183 15s. instead of £51 8s. It will be plain that such a rate of wages would have reduced rent first, and profits afterwards, and have left no opportunity for the growth of the former, except in so far as labour might be economised by the increased productiveness of land at less cost, by substituting mechanical for manual labour, by cheapening the carriage of goods, by increasing the fertility of the soil, and by improving seed and stock. All these were, except perhaps the second, affected. But I do not think that any one who examines the facts will doubt that much of the increase of rent which was effected in the first half of the eighteenth century, and nearly all which was obtained in the seventeenth, was obtained at the expense of the agricultural labourer, whose real wages were, as I have shown here and elsewhere, reduced by all the difference between their earlier and their later purchasing power.

The advance which agriculture had made by the year 1770 was great and remarkable. Tools and implements were far cheaper and far better. The breeds of cattle and sheep were greatly improved, threefold in many cases within living memory, and the comparative cheapness of agricultural produce, a cheapness which is general and fairly uniform, is proof that, apart from the continuous abundance of the seasons and the success of agricultural operations, for a time at least production had gone ahead of population. Of the character of the seasons, Young asserts that a proper distribution of cultivation over the area of the farm, and especially the adoption of that husbandry which recognises the place of root and hay or grass crops in connection with crops of corn, will practically make the farmer independent of the weather, since he will get his compensation, in the vast majority of cases, for what he loses in one kind of produce by what he gains in another. Now I am ready to admit that much of this improvement was due to the public spirit and enterprise of some who had turned their attention to the good of their own estates, and (as the farmer must work in the open, and has neither the inclination nor the power to make a secret of a profitable process) who had benefited their neighbours by the proof of their success. It is possible, if wages had advanced on the same lines as rents and profits did, that the margin of advantage would have been so narrowed that there would have been little impulse given towards either experiment or improvement. An industry may be discouraged by the excessive cost of labour, especially when the product is of optional use. But the production of food is not so much affected by these considerations, at any rate in the same degree, as long as rent exists and profits are large.

When there were seasons of great abundance and, consequently, of low prices, there was general complaint on the part of the landed interest, who considered, because nature was propitious and prices were low, that the country had become poor. We are told that in the few cheap years in the first half of the seventeenth century the tenants could not pay their rents, and that land was reduced in value from twenty to sixteen or seventeen years' purchase. The abundance of the seasons between 1666 and 1671 led to the prohibitive Act of 22 Chas. II., cap. 13, under which a duty of 16*s.* 4*d.* was imposed on wheat as long as it was below 53*s.* 4*d.* a quarter, and one of 8*s.* when it was below 80*s.* The Act which was intended to keep up prices, failed of its effects, for the prices again became low. In order further to secure high prices and full rents, a bounty of 5*s.* a quarter, when the price did not exceed 48*s.*, was granted immediately after the Revolution. To the operation of these two enactments the scientific agriculturists, who affected to discuss the economic bearings of husbandry on the growth of opulence, ascribed the development of agriculture in the eighteenth century and the plenty of its produce. It is probable that the belief in the efficacy of these legislative remedies led to the very numerous enclosures which begin under the authority of Parliament in the reign of Anne, under which, in the eighteenth century, nearly 3,000,000 acres were enclosed, and in the nineteenth, up to 1854, nearly 6,000,000 more. The amount so enclosed is more than one-third of the whole cultivable surface of England and Wales.

The seven barren years at the conclusion of the seventeenth century were long noted for the distress of the people and for the exalted profits of the farmer, as they probably gave occasion to the celebrated law of Gregory King, that when there ensues a scarcity in an absolute necessary of life, and the quantity falls off in an arithmetical ratio, the price is exalted in a geometrical one. But when prices fell, as they did in the period between 1715 and 1765, there was a general outcry of agricultural distress, which, when it comes to be analysed, is always resolved into the shrinkage of the landlord's rent. Noblemen and country gentlemen demanded the aid of the legislature in order to enable the farmers to pay their rents. In eleven years nearly £2,000,000 were paid in bounties. But much new land was brought under tillage, and the price of labour, as I have said, rose twenty per cent. Mr. Malthus accounted for the rise characteristically, by alleging that there was no proportionate increase of the population, for that the English people, having now achieved a notable increase in the real wages which they received, decidedly elevated the standard of their comforts and conveniences. It is doubtful whether moral or prudential reasons had much to do with the matter. Wages are always, both in nominal amount and in real power, greater when food and the other conveniences of life are cheap; and the demand for labour was receiving an additional stimulus from improvements in agriculture and the increasing area of land which was taken into cultivation. But whatever may have been the cause, a reverse was near at hand.

Up to 1765, England has been an exporting country in divers agricultural products. Subsequently it became an importing country. It was supposed to have suffered this change from the fact that the population increased rapidly. The view is untenable on two grounds. In the first place, an increase of population cannot take place at a bound; in the next, it has always been found that a time of distress, when food is dear, checks population. Undoubtedly after the Peace of Paris an extraordinary development of English trade occurred. The colonial empire of England was doubled, and the monopoly of the trade, according to the accredited policy of the age, was conferred on English shippers and merchants. Undoubtedly, too, the manufacture of textile fabrics took a great start, the production of them being cheapened and the market for them widened by the successful application of machinery to the process. But the displacement of industries must have produced much local suffering, and the check to population which this loss of revenue induced must have more than counterbalanced the miserable stimulus given to it by the increased demand for the labour of the young. In the long run, labour has gained by the inventions of Arkwright, of Watt, and of Cartwright, but the process which preceded the gain was accompanied by profound suffering, part of which, to the benefit of all parties, was remedied by the prohibitive regulations of a later time.

The seasons from 1765 were as generally unpropitious as those up to that period were abundant; and in 1773, the opponents of the existing corn law secured the alteration of the Act of 1671. By this law importation was permitted at 6d. a quarter, when wheat was at or above 48s., and the bounty was to cease when it was at or above 44s. But whenever the seasons happened to be abundant, the old cry was raised that landlords were distressed and farmers ruined. As a consequence, in 1791, a new corn law was enacted, under which a very heavy duty was imposed while wheat was below 50s., though it was slight when the price rose above this amount. But the general scarcity of these later years produced its effect on rent. Arthur Young, writing more than forty years after the date of his celebrated tours, comments on the singular and rapid rise in rent which took place after 1782, and the development of competition for occupancy. The landlords were alarmed at their own good fortune, and for a time hesitated to take advantage of it; but tenants rushed into the occupation of husbandry, which was thenceforward highly profitable when scarcity ruled, as was the case generally till 1820, and was correspondingly depressed when occasional abundance intervened.

After the deficient harvest of 1795, wheat rose to 104s. a quarter, and remained at that amount, or near it, for a whole year. It was during this time that Sir Frederick Eden collected his evidence as to the wages of labour and the cost of maintenance. The facts are in remarkable contrast to the hypothetical earnings which are drawn up with such fulness by Arthur Young. It must be admitted that the Government of the day adopted very active measures against the dearth. They seized all neutral ships laden with corn and bound for France, and compelled them to discharge their cargoes at English ports, and at a handsome profit to their owners. They offered a bounty of from 16s. to £1 on imported corn. But the scarcity was universal, extending even to the United States, though the barren lands of the eastern and central states could never have been relied on for any great amount. The two Houses of Parliament signed an engagement to reduce their domestic consumption by at least one-third, and the distillation of corn spirits was prohibited. Many of the poor perished by want, and nearly all persons were stinted. But it was a time of great prosperity to the landed interest,—to the landlords, whose rents were rapidly rising, and to the farmers, who were realising enormous gains during the currency of their leases. The deficiency was variously calculated at from one-fifth to one-third short of an average crop.

During the first two months of the year 1796, Eden collected the amount of wages actually earned by families engaged in agricultural labour in different parts of England, many of them being records of 1795 wages. Five are taken from Clopshill, in Beds; four from a village near Carlisle; four from Buckden, in Hunts; six from Hinksworth, in Herts; four from Kegworth,

in Leicester ; four from Lincolnshire parishes; four from Diss, in
Norfolk; five from Northampton ; six from near Oxford ; six
from Suffolk; four from Stogursey, in Somerset ; and one from
Yorkshire,—fifty-three in all.   The collective earnings of these
families average 11s. 9d. a week in Beds, ranging from 9s. to
14s. 6d. ; and these wages fall short of their expenditure, poor
enough, by an average of £3 15s. 9d., though a part of this
deficiency is made up by harvest earnings.

At Carlisle the average earnings are 10s. for the whole family
and the average deficiency in the whole is £3 2s. 4d.   In Hunts
the average wages are 9s. 3d., and the average deficiency £2 15s. 4d.
The six families in Herts earn an average of 12s. 6½d., but their
necessary expenditure exceeds their receipts by an average of
£22 3s. 6½d.   The average earnings of two families in Leicester
are 13s. 9d., and the average deficiency is £18 0s. 3¾d.   In one
family in Lindsey the earnings are 11s. 6d., the expenditure in
excess of wages being £21 18s. 4d. ; another family is only 7s. 4d.
short, but the wages of man, wife, and child are only 11s. 3d., and
the family live on bread alone.   In the case of three Norfolk
families, the total earnings are 11s. 3d., and the average deficiency
£13 11s. 4d.   In Northants, four families earn an average of
10s. 7½d., but are on an average £3 15s. short in the year.   The
six Oxfordshire families earn an average of 12s. 10d., the total
being heightened by one household, in which three boys earn
nearly as much as their father does.   Here the average deficiency
is £3 5s. 9d.   In Suffolk, four families, in each of which the
children contribute largely to the earnings, the average wages are
15s. 1d., and the average deficiency £12 13s. 6d., which in these
cases is slightly lessened by harvest wages.   In Somerset, four
families earn an average of 8s. 9¾d., and their annual expenses
exceed their annual income by an average of £11 3s. 10d.   The
Yorkshire labourer is worst off.   His own earnings are under 6s.
a week, his wife's a little over 1s., and his child's an infinitesimal
sum.   His expenses exceed his income by £12 13s. a year, though
his fare is the humblest conceivable.   I have taken those rates of
wages only which were paid in 1795 and 1796.   Between 1792
and 1795 such provisions as these labourers could procure had risen
by about 125 per cent.   The poor rate rose to £4,000,000, and yet

the people were starving. Mr. Porter has acutely observed, that in years of dearth, in which the largest sums have been expended on the poor, the amount estimated in wheat is the lightest borne by the community. He has inferred, indeed, that this is right, that the poor in seasons of dearth should suffer with those by whom they are supported, and feel the inconvenience which the niggardliness of nature has put upon the whole community. The inference is just, if it be also true that the position which they occupy is one which they have chosen for themselves, and for which they are therefore responsible.

The examination of the facts shows that this was not the case. We have been able to trace the process by which the condition of English labour had been continuously deteriorated by the acts of government. It was first impoverished by the issue of base money. Next it was robbed of its guild capital by the land thieves of Edward's regency. It was next brought in contact with a new and more needy set of employers—the sheep-masters who succeeded the monks. It was then, with a pretence, and perhaps with the intention, of kindness, subjected to the quarter sessions assessment, mercilessly used in the first half of the seventeenth century, the agricultural labourer being still further impoverished by being made the residuum of all labour. The agricultural labourer was then further mulcted by enclosures, and the extinction of those immemorial rights of pasture and fuel which he had enjoyed so long. The poor law professed to find him work, but was so administered that the reduction of his wages to a bare subsistence became an easy process and an economical expedient. When the monarchy was restored, his employers, who fixed his wages by their own authority, relieved their own estates from their ancient dues at the expense of his poor luxuries by the excise, tied him to the soil by the Law of Settlement, and starved him by a prohibitive corn law. The freedom of the few was bought by the servitude of the many. Fletcher of Saltoun, an ardent republican for a narrow class, suggested hopeless slavery as the proper doom of the labourers, argued that the people existed only to work, and that philosophical politicians should have the power to limit their existence by labour. Throughout the eighteenth century the most enlightened men gave the poor their pity, occasionally their patronage, sometimes would assist them at the cost of other workers; but beyond a bare existence, never imagined that they had rights or remembered that they had suffered wrongs. The weight of taxation fell on them in every direction, and with searching severity. It was necessary to find funds at all risks and from every source, and it is obvious that the most fruitful source of taxation is that of necessary consumption and cheap luxuries. It was, of course, impossible to tax the absolute necessaries of the individual workman, else he would starve and perish. But the process left him nothing but a bare subsistence. The interpretation of his wages is always incomplete unless one takes into account the virtual reduction which taxation made of them; and to know this would require an exact and searching analysis of the customs and excise, and of their incidence. Even this would be insufficient, because to adequately interpret the situation we should have to estimate the privation of enforced abstinence, as well as the contribution of universal taxation, and measure the labourer's losses not only by what he consumed but by what he was forced to abstain from consuming. And withal the existing condition of things bred and strengthened that mean and malignant passion for profiting by the miseries of others which became the policy of the landed interest, and to some extent even now remains a dominant hope in the minds of landlords and farmers. To crown the whole, the penalties of felony and conspiracy were denounced against all labourers who associated together to better their lot by endeavouring to sell their labour in concert, while the desperation which poverty and misery induce, and the crime they suggest, were met by a code more sanguinary and brutal than any which a civilized nation had ever heretofore devised or a high-spirited one submitted to.

Such was the education which the English workman received from those evil days, when the government employed and developed the means for oppressing and degrading him. It is no marvel that he identifies the policy of the landowner, the farmer, and the capitalist employer with the machinery by which his lot has been shaped, and his fortunes, in the distribution of national wealth, have been controlled. He may have no knowledge, or a very vague knowledge, as to the process by which so strange, so woeful an alteration has been made in his condition. But there exists, and always has existed, a tradition, obscure and uncertain, but deeply seated, that there was a time when his lot was happier, his means more ample, his prospects more cheerful, than they have been in more modern experience. From one point of view, the analyst of "the good old times" may be able to show that life was shorter, disease more rife, the market of food more unsteady, the conveniences and comforts of life fewer and more precarious than they now are. From another point of view, and that by far the most accurate and exact, the relative position of the workman was one of far more hope and far more plenty in the days of the Plantagenets than it has been in those of the House of Hanover; that wages were, relative to their purchasing power, far higher, and the margin of enjoyable income over necessary expenditure was in consequence far wider.

The remarkable fact in the history and sentiments of the English workman is that he is neither socialist nor anarchist. He believes, and rightly believes, that in the distribution of the reward of labour his share is less than it might be, than it ought to be, and that some means should be discovered by which the unequal balance should be rectified. He does not indeed detect the process by which this advantage can be secured to him, and relies, though doubtfully, upon certain expedients by which he thinks he can extort better terms. He has good reason for believing that he can gain his ends, in some degree at least, by association with his fellows; for he cannot have forgotten how angrily any action of his in this direction has for centuries been resented and punished, and how even now it is assailed by sophistical and interested criticism. But he has never dreamed of making war on capital or capitalist. In his most combative temper he has simply desired to come to terms with capital, and to gain a benefit by the harmonious working of a binding treaty between himself and his employer. He is wise in his contention, though not always wise in his strategy.

Food and the materials of industry constitute the capital of a community, of which money is the symbol. Labour is engaged, whether of head or hand, in replacing the former as it is consumed, and of imparting utility to the latter. The produce of the former is that upon which all subsist, those by whom it is procured and those who, by one plea or another, are able to make good their claim to a portion in the common stock. All who are engaged in industry strive to complete their work in the briefest and easiest manner. The employer of labour works as truly as the peasant and artizan, with head and hand, though in a different manner. His principal function, as far as the common interest is concerned, is to interpret the means by which labour may be continuously employed. When the product is secured and exchanged, always ultimately for food and other necessaries and conveniences, this question is always arising. What is the share, all expenses being deducted, which the employers shall have on the one hand, and labourers on the other, of the residue? The quarrel between capital and labour, as it is called, but, as it would be more accurately styled, between employer and employés, is, What is the amount of the share each should have in profits and wages? For centuries the law and the government interposed on the side of the employer in order to lessen the labourer's share. For a very long period, two centuries, the efforts of law and government were unsuccessful. At last they gained their object, and gradually reduced the labourers' share to a bare subsistence, so bare that in order to get their necessary work from him they supplemented his wages by a tax on the general public, as they do in a less degree to this day. The worst time, however, in the whole history of English labour was beginning when Eden collected the facts which he gives us as to the labourer's earnings. This condition of things was continued for twenty-five years.

The farmers competed against each other for occupancies, and constantly offered higher rents, which the enforced cheapness of their labourers' wages enabled them to pay, and the necessities of the public artificially created by the corn laws enabled them to increase. They made common cause with the landlord, and worked against the interests of the labourer and the general public, the body of consumers. They saw that if they pledged themselves to higher rents, they must needs procure the means by lowering the cost of what they produced and by heightening its price. They achieved the former by driving wages down to a bare subsistence, and the latter by maintaining an artificial dearth

Now it is plain that contracts founded on such unnatural conditions were certain, sooner or later, to bring mischief on those who agreed to them. It was certain that at an early period the nation would resent the existence of laws which were designed to stint them. It was certain that manufacturers and traders, now secure of a foreign market, if trade were open to them, would demand that they should be able to sell their goods for that which the people would always readily consume, and would, therefore, be the best and safest object of exchange. It was probable that workmen would not be for ever content to accept nothing but a bare subsistence, and that they would seek to extricate themselves from so ungrateful a position. But the vitality of the old system was singular. It took the active agitation of a quarter of a century before free trade in food was granted. The labourer, unused to the action which springs from the consciousness of a common purpose, even when the liberty of union was given him, was too ignorant and too apathetic to use t iat force of combination which his ancestors five centuries before had employed with such effect. He fled from his calling. Other and better paid industries hired him from the farmyard and the harvest field, sometimes, indeed, to his ultimate injury. The most enterprising sought in the United States and the colonies a future which was denied them here.

But though there was a shrinkage on both sides in the quality and quantity of labour, in the price of certain farm products, and in the profits of agriculture, rents went on steadily increasing. It was an open secret that even when these enhanced rents were being paid, the farming class had so narrow a margin of profits that even slight reverses would become serious. It was known that agricultural capital had greatly diminished, and that the cultivation of the soil was gradually becoming slovenly and imperfect. At last the crisis came, and the foolish payment of excessive rent, and the equally foolish receipt of excessive rent, have led to disasters in English agriculture to which there is no parallel in the annals of that industry. The case is made worse by the fact that there appears to be no prospect of an early and vigorous recovery, even though much rent is sacrificed.

CHAPTER VI.

WAGES IN THE NINETEENTH CENTURY.

The Rate of Wages and the Price of Food—Pressure on the Operatives in Factories and the Weavers—Machine Breaking—The Manufacturing Districts worst off—Causes raising Wages—These not Operative till Late—Difficulties in the formation of Labour Partnerships and their Management—The Competition of Capitalists, and its Effects on Labour—Recent Events—Effects of a Relaxation of Foreign Tariffs— The Depreciated Currency of the War—Abrogation of the Quarter Sessions Assessment—The Allowance System—Illustrations of its Working—The Abolition of Compulsory Apprenticeship—The Defence of Apprenticeship—The Objection to it—The Cost of the War—Hostility of Capitalists to the Workmen's Advance—Their Sinister Predictions— Animosity felt by the Workman towards the Combination Laws— Hume's Committee—The Union—The Agricultural Labourer—History of his Wages and the Poor Law—The Factory Acts not extended to the Children of Peasants—Agricultural Gangs—Mr. Girdlestone— Joseph Arch—The Difficulties of an Agricultural Labourers' Union— The Work of the Primitive Methodists—The Attitude of the Farmers Erroneous—The Moral Education of Labour Partnerships—The Present Position of Agriculture.

DURING the first twenty years of the nineteenth century, the price of wheat was on an average 98s. 6d. a quarter, i.e., 16·4 times the rate which prevailed on an average for the 280 years in which there was practically no variation in money values, beyond those which arose from exceptional scarcity. In the year 1800, when the working man was within the range of this extraordinary exaltation in the price of his food, the average wages of artizans were 18s. a week in London. They gradually rose by about 75 per cent. during the years of dearth, being generally highest in the years which were characteristically dear. When greater plenty prevailed, they fell. In the country they were about one-third less than they were in London. It does not appear that artizans had their wages supplemented by the allowance system, for when, in 1824, Lord John Russell moved for a committee to inquire into the consequences of a practice which had now become general, and drew his motion in such general terms as to include all kinds of labour, Mr. Peel objected that the reference to the committee would include superfluous subjects, and, in consequence, the inquiry was limited to agricultural wages.

These wages, which I shall refer to more particularly, in so far as evidence is forthcoming, further on in this chapter, were largely supplemented by parish allowances. The maximum sum expended in the relief of the poor under the old law was in 1818, when it was nearly eight millions, or 13s. 9d. per head of the population. The factory hand was even worse off than the labourer, and, as machinery was gradually being introduced into the manufacture of textile fabrics, the hand-loom weaver was worst off of all. Great as was the demand for labour under the new system, it was, unfortunately, not countervailed by an increase of real wages, hardly of nominal wages, for the demand was for both sexes and nearly all ages. But the severest penury fell on those who had been, in the older days of manufacture, the specially skilled artizans in textile fabrics, for the effect of machinery is to reduce labour as much as possible to the functions of attention and guidance. The weavers, therefore, who either could not or would not accommodate themselves to the new order of things, suffered the direst reverses. It was no wonder that they looked on machinery with the profoundest hostility, that riots and machine-breaking were frequent, and that the bitterest animosities were engendered. Thus in 1811-12, stocking and lace frames had been applied to the staple manufactures of Nottingham, and the discontented labourers, foreseeing or fancying that their livelihood would be imperilled, broke into houses and destroyed frames. The legislature thereupon passed an Act inflicting, as usual, the punishment of death on the frame-breakers. The Act only lasted two years; but on the occasion of its second reading, Lord Byron warmly attacked it, and recommended that if the Act were carried, it should be so amended as to provide that the jury should always consist of twelve butchers, and that a judge of the temper of Jefferys should be always engaged to preside in the court. Such a judge would not have been hard to find at that time.

It is easy to prove that the great movement of modern days, the employment of mechanical in the place of human forces, operates ultimately in cheapening produce and in bettering the wages of labour. But until that is brought about, the producers on the old lines may be subjected to severe privations. Nay, unless precautions are taken against the abuse of labour on the part of employers, it is very possible that the mass of those who work under the new system may sink into a lower position than that which they previously occupied when they were engaged with the old. The efficiency of labour may, by the use of mechanical expedients, be greatly enhanced, but unless the demand for labour is simultaneously enlarged, the profits of the employer may be increased enormously, while the wages of the workmen may even be lessened. Such a result may be further assisted by the temporary monopoly of patents. That the patents of Arkwright and Peel secured enormous fortunes for these inventors or purchasers of inventions we all know, that they ultimately cheapened production is equally clear ; that they gave England well-nigh a monopoly in the supply of textile fabrics, is as manifest ; but it does not strictly follow that the English workman was better paid. The handloom weaver was undoubtedly impoverished, but I do not find that the machine weaver bettered his position. His wages remained low, his means were even more straitened, and the misery of the manu-facturing districts was even greater than that of the agricultural.

There are three processes by which the wages of artizans may be increased concurrently with the adoption and development of mechanical appliances. Any of these has its effect on the fortunes of labour, and as they have worked together, though at a comparatively recent period, they have had a marked influence on their wages, in results which can be clearly traced. They are restraints imposed by law on the employment of labour ; restraints imposed by the joint action of labourers ; and the competition of capitalists as producers. Further, since the existence of such restraints and such a competition sharpen those inventive faculties which are ever on the look out for the means by which the process of production is cheapened, and when, in addition to these causes, there is the further stimulant of a market restricted by the policy of other countries, and therefore only open under the conditions of such a further cheapening as will enable the product to get over the barrier of foreign protection, the most powerful stimulants are applied to mechanical intelligence and productive invention.

Now for the early part of the nineteenth century, for nearly the first half of it, these conditions did not exist concurrently with the development of mechanical appliances. There was no control put on the employment of the young in any calling, and the manufacturer who had cheapened his production by the introduction of machinery could add to his profits by the employment of children in that kind of work which, under an earlier system, was carried on by adults. He could further, the poverty of workmen assisting the silence of law, make a saving by paying his wages, in part at least, by tallies on a shop which belonged to himself, and could add the profits of retail trade to the profits of cheap labour. The Factory Acts, which prohibited the employment of some persons altogether, and regulated the hours during which some other persons could be employed, increased the wages of labour absolutely and relatively, and, as has been shown, without diminishing, as also did the prohibition of the truck or tally system, the legitimate profits of the employer. The restraints which could be imposed by the joint action of labourers, though legally possible at an earlier date, were very slow in their operation. The illegal combination, branded as a conspiracy and sometimes treated as a felony, was certain to resort to violent action when its aims were thwarted, and in the earlier days of its imperfect legality constantly out-raged the liberty which it purposed to secure. The trade unions of the earlier period had very much to unlearn, in that they were to substitute confidence for distrust, prudence and judgment for haste and rash action, conciliation for force, foresight for passion, and a careful interpretation of their powers in place of headlong vengeance for the wrongs which they conceived that they were still suffering. They who try to combine individual forces and purposes, and to substitute joint-stock action, with its methodical subservience to a central authority, for independent action, find that they may make serious errors before they discover the proper use of the new powers which they are wielding. The founders of the Bank of England collected subscriptions from their shareholders, and applied them with all the judgment they possessed in a novel way to trade and finance. During the first twenty years of its existence the managers of the Bank committed errors which, had it not been for the great commercial and political value of the institution, would have been fatal to its existence. The errors and failures of joint-stock enterprise have been incessant and disastrous. The railway passenger in England would be providing ample dividends to the shareholders in those companies if he paid a halfpenny a mile on the most convenient conveyance, had not these undertakings been permanently burdened, and their nominal capital increased threefold by the blunders of those who projected them, by the rapine of those who gave them a legal status, and by the follies and recklessness of those who have managed them.

But no undertaking requires more care, more prudence, more tact, more patience, more watchfulness, than the application of the joint-stock principle to labour. In the first place, persons whose means are exceedingly slender have to make a sacrifice for an object highly advantageous if it can be secured, but the success of which is always problematical and generally doubtful. In the next, they have to surrender their judgment to the determination of those who have to interpret the most difficult of problems,—the question whether the market for labour will bear the cessation of labour. My readers are aware that the leaders and managers of labour partnerships have very rarely formed a correct estimate of the powers at their disposal, and the powers which they strive to resist and overcome, for the immediate object of a strike has only occasionally been obtained. In the next, they who combine for these ends have the mortification of knowing and seeing that their sacrifices and labours in the machinery of their organization are made by a small portion of the order to which they belong, while the benefit of their action, if it be successful, is shared by those who decline to participate in the movement, and even take advantage of the occasion to baffle those who assert, and with perfect sincerity, that they are labouring for the common good of all their fellows. I do not wonder that passion and violence have in past times accompanied the action of trade unions, when the promoters and members of them have felt that they were thwarted, not by the resistance of employers, but by the selfishness, as they hold it, of those who profit by their policy and take advantage of them in the crisis of their struggles.

The third cause which has affected favourably the position of labour and wages is the competition of capitalists, aggravated, though not perhaps adversely affected, by the restrictions put on foreign markets. This competition is rendered intense by the occurrence from time to time of exceptional demand and of real or imaginary scarcities. Thus the waste of wealth and the demand for foreign products consequent upon the civil war in America added largely to the permanent industries of this country, and induced the investment of great masses of capital in undertakings from which the capital could not be extricated or the capitalist disengage himself. Within ten years of this event, a war, brief in its duration but exceedingly destructive and dislocating, occurred in Europe. By a financial blunder of the gravest kind, the vanquished nation was called upon to pay a vast ransom to the victor. This, a new capital, was at once thrown on the market, and beyond doubt Germany paid, in enhanced prices and inflated but unsafe activity, far more than she exacted. Now the waste of wealth, which had to be restored by foreign imports in the one country, and the vast exaltation of prices, which for a time levelled the dam of protection in the other, called other masses of English capital into active and permanent investments for such industries as were stimulated at the time. Hence, with increasing production, we hear of declining profits and unremunerative trade. But, on the whole, wages have not declined. The phenomenon, often adverted to in these pages, that a time of low prices is a time of good wages, has been exhibited during the last ten years. I make no doubt that there are compensations. It is admitted that the efficiency of labour in attention, rapidity, and exactness keeps pace with the growing perfection of the machinery which it manipulates ; that the special skill of the mill-hand is getting more marked and complete; and that, perhaps, were it not for the increasing number of those who share in the employers' profit, the cheapening of the process would more than compensate for the cheapness of the product.

Undoubtedly, if a relaxation of foreign tariffs were to take place, this concurrent efficiency of machinery and labour in England, which, as far as I can observe, is far greater than in any country which I have visited, would be followed by a large increase of profits, and, relatively speaking, a far larger increase of wages. At present I believe that the workmen of this country, speaking of them in the mass, are better paid than those of any other settled and fully peopled community, if one takes into account not merely the money wages which they earn, but the power which these wages have over commodities. But the rise is entirely of the last thirty years, and, unfortunately, it has not been shared by all in equal proportion, while the case of some has been rendered worse.

The distress of the English workman during the earlier years of the nineteenth century was heightened by the issue of a depreciated paper currency. The history of that depreciation, the causes which brought it about, and the consequences which followed from it, have been told so exactly and so exhaustively by Mr. Tooke, that, in my opinion, that branch of monetary science which is concerned with the functions of paper currency has had no substantial addition to it since he wrote, though one frequently meets with the heresies and the fallacies which this acute writer detected or refuted by anticipation. The effects of the depreciated currency fell, as usual, with more severity on labour, and on those generally who had small incomes, than it did on those who could interpret the discount on the currency, and make a profit by their interpretation. In 1813, the premium on gold—*i.e.*, the depreciation of the paper—was nearly thirty per cent., and nominal wages were therefore in reality little more than two-thirds of their reputed value. The injury which was done to all was made a pretext for continuing the mischief beyond the time in which it could have been removed; but it has often been found to be the case in the economical history of England that a demonstrated wrong has been defended and its continuance supported on the plea that to do justice to the many would inflict a loss on the few.

In 1814, the quarter sessions assessment and the compulsory apprenticeship enacted by the Act of Elizabeth were abrogated. They had done their work thoroughly, and the regulation of the labourers' wages had been so completely successful that they were made mechanically to follow the price of food—a sure proof that wages are down to the level of subsistence. Thenceforward they were regulated by the farmers and the employers. There had been symptoms already that the justices were a little too considerate of the labourers' necessities. Besides, the Speenhamland Act, as it was called, of 1795, had authorized the allowance system, under which the employer of labour paid half the wages, and the ratepayers, employers or not, contributed the other half. The farmers, therefore, had only to meet together, when wheat was 100s. a quarter, and meat by the carcase was 7½d. a pound (having been less than half the price twenty years before), and agree that they would pay their workmen a shilling a day, with the rider that the rest of the public should pay him another shilling, which they took care to assess, collect, and distribute at their discretion. It is no wonder that, except in the fact that the breadth of arable land was greatly increased, and that locally certain improvements were made in the breed of sheep, very little real progress was made in agriculture during the sixty years between 1780 and 1840. The Board of Agriculture, over which Young presided with such efficiency and diligence, was dissolved, and agriculture has never since, unfortunately, been made the object of a department of State. For some unexplained reason, the political party which has had the principal management of public affairs since the first Reform Bill has always been averse to the revival of this department, and their rivals, who are perpetually talking about the necessity for it when out of office, have as strangely neglected to renew it when they have been in.

Vicious, demoralizing, and unjust as the allowance system was in principle, it occasionally gave an opportunity to individuals who had sufficient prudence and thrift to make use of it. In my native village in Hampshire, I well remember two instances of agricultural labourers who raised themselves through the machinery of the allowance system to the rank and fortunes of small yeomen. Both had large families, and both practised a bye industry. The village was peculiar in its social character, for there was not a tenant-farmer in it, all being freeholders or copy-holders. The rector was opulent and generous, and there were a few persons of some private means in the parish. But, on the whole, the rates and the allowances came from the resources of occupying owners, and were, therefore, the contribution of the vestry from its own resources, the only non-employers being one or two humble tradesmen, the rector, and a country gentleman, whose house and grounds were not a hundred acres in extent. There was no poverty in the whole place. Most of the labourers baked their own bread, brewed their own beer, kept pigs and poultry, and had half-an-acre or an acre to till for themselves as part of their hire. But they had regulated wages, and, when their families were large, allowances. There were not infrequent sales of land in the village, as families came to an end, but rarely in large quantities. The rector built extensively, parsonage, schools, and finally church, from his own means, and, therefore, employment was pretty general. The village mason became a considerable yeoman. But the two labourers of whom I am speaking had their allowances, lived on their fixed wages with the profits of their bye labour, one being pig-killer to the village, and, therefore, always busy from Michaelmas to Lady-day, at a shilling a pig, and the offal, on which his family subsisted, with the produce of their small curtilage, for half the year. In the end, the allowance, saved scrupulously, and, I presume, made a profound secret, was invested in land by each. The one bought some forty acres of poor soil, on which he got a comfortable and independent living ; the other some twenty, on which he did still better, for the land was some of the best in the village.

The abolition of compulsory apprenticeships in such callings as were specified in the Act of Elizabeth, or had been interpreted to come under its conditions, and the settlement of wages by the quarter sessions assessment or other magisterial authority, was not considered a boon by the artizans in 1814. In the first place, the repeal of Elizabeth's Act was demanded by the employers of labour, and it was, therefore, suspicious. In the next, the legislature from time to time had referred trade disputes between employers and employed to certain permanent authorities. Besides, the capitalists were exceedingly averse to any restraints on the employment of apprentices under the old system ; and it was concluded, not without reason, that the repeal of the legal necessity would be followed by a rush into the calling. It should be remembered also that the change was effected at a time when the distress of the working classes was the deepest, that the avowed object of the repeal was to cheapen labour, and that every effort was made then and thereafter to sharpen the edge and expedite the use of the hateful laws which had been constantly enacted up to 1800 against combinations of workmen, and were still strictly enforced.

The defence of apprenticeship is two-fold. It secures, if the apprentice is adequately taught, a supply of good workmen, thoroughly instructed in the craft. It lessens the number of persons employed in the calling, by putting an impediment in the way of earning full wages. In the former of these ends the public is interested, though it may be doubted whether, in the absence of a trade regulation under which the workman should refuse to work for a dishonest manufacturer, and should be assisted by his union, and probably protected by the law, in case the denunciation is made a means of oppressing him, the skill of the workman is not sometimes enlisted in concealing the dishonesty of the employer. In the second aim of those who insist on or advise aprenticeship, the trade alone is concerned. The further precaution taken in some callings of limiting the proportion of apprentices to journeymen, though defensible on certain grounds, is much more open to challenge. It is a restraint on the choice of callings, and is, therefore, apparently at least, an injury to those who are kept outside a calling which they would desire to enter. Mr. Howell has stated the case in his work on capital and labour with great fairness. But it would appear from his own admissions that while up to 1814 the practice of unlimited apprenticeship was general, and the results disastrous, the abolition of the law and the consequent discontinuance of the practice has been followed by an epoch of better and continually increasing wages

necessity has restraint has

wages were said to have been less in the twen

1820 and 1840 than they were in the previous twenty years, it is admitted that the intrinsic value of these wages, as measured by their purchasing power, was greatly increased. But if we can rely on Mr. Leoni Levi's figures, taken from the record of prices paid at Greenwich from 1800 to 1820, and between 1821 and 1840, we shall find that, in the former period, the rate of wages as compared with the cost of food was at 55·25 to 232·5, the first figure being the daily wages in pence, and the second the aggregate cost in shillings of seven chief necessaries; while in the latter period, the wages stand at 62·75, and the same articles cost only 146·35. Wages, then, had actually risen, and the price of the necessaries of life had greatly fallen.

The chief economical objection to apprenticeship, which has not been anticipated by Mr. Howell, is that it tends to create an ever-increasing residuum of unprotected labour. That all human societies as they grow more populous will have a proportionately larger element of helplessness, misery, and crime within them, is apparently inevitable. It is most visible in countries where emigration goes on largely from the best and most vigorous stocks, and immigration into towns from poorer districts and foreign countries is active; for when immigration is from near localities, the least desirable addition to the growing population is likely to take place. Now during the existence of the famous Statute of Apprenticeship, the residuum was driven to agricultural labour, or to the new industries where apprenticeship did not prevail. That the whole body of working men suffered greatly is only too manifest; that those callings suffered most which consisted of the non-apprenticed classes is proved, if by nothing else, by the resistance which the workmen made to the abolition of the custom. The common defence for the limitation of apprentices is that if bad times come, it is better for few to suffer than that many should, and that the limitation of hands is analogous to and identical with a limit of output in production. But the answer is, that the restraint puts a permanent suffering on those who would otherwise enter a better paid calling, and reduces an increasing number to permanently low wages.

fact, the sufferings of the working-classes during
d on which I have dwelt might have been

aggravated by the practices of employers, and were certainly intensified by the harsh partiality of the law ; but they were due in the main to deeper causes. Thousands of homes were starved in order to find the means for the great war, the cost of which was really supported by the labour of those who toiled on and earned the wealth which was lavished freely, and at good interest for the lenders, by the government. The enormous taxation and the gigantic loans came from the store of accumulated capital, which the employers wrung from the poor wages of labour, or the landlords extracted from the growing gains of their tenants. To outward appearance, the strife was waged by armies and generals ; in reality the resources on which the struggle was based, and without which it would have speedily collapsed, were the stint and starvation of labour, the overtaxed and underfed toils of childhood, the underpaid and uncertain employment of men. Wages were mulcted in order to provide the waste of war, and the profits of commerce and manufacture. It is no wonder that working-men have no great trust in government by party, for the two great historical parties have fleeced and ground them down with impartial persistence.

Employers have constantly predicted that ruin would come on the great industries of the country if workmen were better paid and better treated. They resisted, and have resisted up to the present day, every demand which workmen have made for the right of association, for the limitation of children's and women's labour, for the shortening of hours, for the abolition of truck, for the protection of their workmen's lives and limbs from preventible accidents, and are now appealing to the doctrine of liberty of contract, after having for centuries denied the liberty. This misconception as to the consequences which would ensue from just and, as events have proved, wise concessions, has not been due to a cunning selfishness, but to the natural disinclination which all men have to make those efforts which have always compensated the loss which they thought that they foresaw, and have frequently turned it into a gain. For it is a remarkable and an indisputable result of those interferences with what is apparently free action, that when their justice or necessity has been demonstrated, and the change or reform or restraint has been adopted, benefit instead of injury to the imperilled interest, strength instead of weakness, have been the consequence. The concession of the right of combination was thought to be an infinite peril, and the workmen have gradually learnt their proper strength, and what is far more important, the strength and solidity of the calling in which they are engaged, and the profits which are required in order to secure its continuity and their employment. They are getting to know what is the point at which cost will cripple production, and may be safely trusted not to destroy by excessive exactions that by which they live. The Factory Acts were believed to be the death-blow to English manufacture, and they have made labour more efficient, more intelligent, more decent, and more continuous, without trenching on profits. Only three years ago, the legislature determined on abolishing some of the fictions which lawyers had induced over the theory of common employment, and the same predictions of ruin were uttered. The law was passed, however, and a concession being made to the employers, under which, as is so often mischievously done, they were allowed to contract themselves out of the law, they eagerly clutched at the opportunity, as though the whole life of their industry depended on their being able to save a few shillings a year in remedying the losses of their own heedlessness, or a few pounds which might, properly spent, obviate the risk and ensure that justice should be done. The Parliament and the Law, which never do better work than when they arbitrate between timid interests, have over and over again by their action demonstrated the futility of these apprehensions and the folly of these fears. The only pity is, that Parliament has not had the courage to extend its action.

The old laws against combination and the doctrine of trade conspiracies were so dangerously wide, so capricious and uncertain, that at last the exasperation and anger of the workmen became excessive. The country was honeycombed with secret societies, and political disaffection was coupled with social discontent. The complaints of hungry workmen were met by the Peterloo massacre, and the demands for political reform, which the workmen had been instructed to consider remedial, by the Six Acts. In the early history of the English people, the bias of judges and law courts was directed towards the emancipation of the peasant and the maintenance of personal rights. The process by which the serf became the copyholder was greatly assisted by the interpreters of the common law. But from the days of the Stuarts, the judges were servile, timid, and the enemies of personal liberty. Over and over again Parliament has interposed to sweep away precedents which have coerced natural liberty, and interpretations which have violated justice. For generations it seemed that the worst enemies of public and private liberty were those courts whose duty it was to adjudicate equitably and to state the law with fairness. The English people owes much to the persevering acuteness of Bentham and the high-minded courage of Romilly that it was delivered at last from the Kenyons and the Eldons.

The credit of abolishing the combination laws is due to Joseph Hume. He procured a committee in 1824, took evidence, reported to the House, and obtained an instruction from it to the Chairman of Committees that a Bill should be drafted on the lines of eleven clauses dealing with the combination laws, and four which examined the effect of certain prohibitions put on artizans going abroad. The Committee declared itself unable to express any opinion on the propriety of removing the prohibition then put on the exportation of machinery. The Bill appears to have passed without debate or opposition, for I find no record of any such debate in Hansard. The Act inflicted penalties on such combinations as attempted to further their ends by violence.

It was inevitable that the working classes should immediately take advantage of the powers which the law had at last awarded to them. For nearly five centuries law after law had been passed under which the workmen's wages had been regulated, for the reputed advantage of their employers. The English law has never affected to fix the price of food, though sometimes proclamations have pretended to do so, and local authority has occasionally been empowered to publish fair prices. But when a scarcity of labour occurred, due to natural causes, it attempted to control the claims of the workmen. For more than two centuries the law was a complete failure. For nearly three, as I have shown at length, it was a complete success. Now it was entirely natural for the workmen to believe that what they had

gained at last was a boon, since their employers had so long and
so successfully deprived them of its use. The employers and
Parliament became alarmed, and revised the Act of 1824, though
they did not venture on materially modifying it.

The ingenuity of the judges, always interested in the defence of
property and very little friendly to that of liberty, discovered
that the common law against combinations was still alive, and a
series of prosecutions on false or frivolous grounds was undertaken, convictions recorded, and punishments inflicted. Mr.
Howell has collected several instances of these trials, and comments on the general dissatisfaction felt among working men at
the administration of the law. The ultimate emancipation of
trade unions or labour partnerships from the difficulties and
hindrances to which they were still exposed, and from the disabilities which precedents had put on them, is of very recent date.

The condition of the agricultural labourer has been different
from that of the artizan. Scattered, and incapable of combined
action with his fellows, bowed down by centuries of oppression,
hard usage, and hard words, with, as he believes, every social
force against him, the landlord in league with the farmer, and
the clergyman in league with both, the latter constantly preaching
resignation, and the two former constantly enforcing it, he has
lived through evil times. Under the allowance system, he seems
to have been guaranteed against starvation, and under the law of
parochial settlement he avenged himself on some of his oppressors,
though not on the worst, those who, on one pretext or another,
quartered him on another parish, employed him on quarter
sessions or farmers' vestry assessment wages, and left others to
supplement his wages by the allowance, and to support him when
they had worn out his body, as they had worn out his spirit long
before. There is nothing in the history of civilisation more
odious than the meanness of some English landlords, except it be
their insolence. They have been abetted by the foolish farmers,
who ground down their labourers in order to enrich the landlords,
and have finally sacrificed themselves to the rent-rolls of profligates and gamblers.

The sharpest trial they had to bear was the wholesome surgery
of the new poor law. This famous measure, which was so

necessary, so harsh, so inopportune, so unjust, was modelled on the practice which had been adopted in two Nottinghamshire parishes, Southwell and Bingham, in the former of which the workhouse test was organised by Sir George Nicholls, in the latter by Mr. Lowe, the father of an eminent statesman and very rigid economist of the *laissez-faire* school. The experiment of these two parishes was made the type of the new system. It is only just to say, that what might have been fairly equitable to all, though still severe in the last degree to the agricultural labourer, was mutilated by the owners of the close parishes, who succeeded in making others pay for the maintenance of their labourers, as all the landed interests had made the occupiers pay.

The average wages of the agricultural labourer, according to Arthur Young's calculations, had been 7s. 6d. a week from 1767 to 1789 ; 10s. from 1799 to 1803 ; and 12s. from 1804 to 1810. In 1811, they were 12s. 9d. They continued at this rate for three years ; sunk about 17 per cent. from 1814 to 1818 ; about 20 per cent. more in 1819-20 ; about 12 per cent. more in 1821 ; and 5 per cent. more in 1822. Then they began to rise, and, according to Mr. Villiers' returns in 1861, were 9s. 4d. in 1824 ; 10s. 4d. in 1837 ; and 11s. 7d. in 1860. In 1866, Mr. Levi sets them at 13s. It may be doubted, however, whether these several increases of money wages were not, so far as the labourers were concerned, more than counterbalanced by the increase of house rent, the curtailment of allotments and similar indirect aids to labour, to say nothing of the excision of the allowances under the old poor law. In 1837, the cost of maintaining the poor was less than in any year since 1800, and was three millions below what it had been in 1832, though the average price of wheat in the former year was 58s. 8d. ; in the latter, 52s. 6d.,—a difference in the ordinary consumption of a labourer's family, as estimated in bread, of about 4d. a week. The rise thus effected in 1837 probably represents the compensation for the loss of the allowances, for some expenses under the new poor law were considerably increased. I may add, that Young argued in 1813 that the wages of the agricultural labourer were below his necessary food, omitting all estimates as to house rent, fuel, clothing, and extras.

The beneficent restraints of the Factory Acts were not extended to the children of agricultural labourers engaged as helps to the paternal employment. Much of the activity which assisted the agitation for those excellent acts and insured their success, was the hostility felt by benevolent landowners to over-prosperous manufacturers. Even if the language employed by them did not warrant this inference, and the tactics they adopted did not confirm such a conclusion, the fact that agricultural children were not protected against premature labour would prove my contention. One does not see why they should not have been protected. The exposure of young children to weather, the custom of putting them under brutal carters and ploughmen, the common practice of sending them to drive birds from newly-sown fields in the most inclement seasons of the year, with scanty food and clothing, was, I imagine, as likely to be injurious to their health and growth as employment in mills. But the desire to secure an increasing rent, to be procured by the stint of the labourer, is, I imagine, as keen a passion in the bosom of the landlord as that of getting an increased profit from the unsuitable labour of women and children or from the misery of the factory hand has ever been in the constitution of the manufacturer.

I do not remember, in the very extended study which I have given to the history of agricultural labour and wages during the six centuries for which there is recorded and continuous evidence, that, in the worst experiences of the labourer, he was till very recently open to the risk of having his young children of either sex taken from him, and put under the care of a gang-master, with a view to their labouring in the fields, being housed for the night in barns, without the pretence of decency, not to say comfort, and apart from the obvious degradation of their condition, exposed to the coarse brutalities of the manager of children's labour. But in the Eastern Counties it appears to have been till recently the practice, perhaps still is, for farmers to contract for the services of agricultural gangs, *i.e.*, of crowds of children set to work under an overseer who had hunted them up. The practice, I remember, was defended on the ordinary gound of cheap labour being a necessity for profitable agriculture, which, when it is interpreted means that tenant farmers are too cowardly to resist rents which they cannot pay, except by the degradation of those whom they employ. That a peasantry, underpaid and underfed, should be constrained to submit their children to such an odious and demoralising slavery, is unhappily intelligible ; that the middle-man can be found to undertake the office of such an agency, is a fact to be regretted but expected ; that farmers should allow themselves to employ such an expedient, is scandalous : but that they who pretend to consider the condition of the poor, and to be active in the interests of humanity, should be complacent and silent, is a negligence which ought to bring its punishment, or is an acquiescence in ill-doing which I do not care to characterize.

Some twenty or more years ago, Mr. Girdlestone, a clergyman in a country parish in the west of England, and then or subsequently a canon of Bristol, called attention to the miserable condition of agricultural labour in that part of England with which he was familiar. The agricultural labourers of Devon are more than ordinarily numerous, for within the memory of man, a lucrative local industry, cloth weaving, has decayed, and the ordinary population has been swollen by the accession of unemployed weavers. Mr. Girdlestone had the ordinary fate of those who attack the doings of the landed interest. His better behaved opponents denied the accuracy of his statements, and published their own account of the facts. His rougher critics, the farmers, threatened him with violence and the horse-pond. It is not quite clear that his poor clients thought him their kindest friend in letting the world know what was their condition, for employers in country places have many opportunities of letting their workmen feel that discontent or complaint, even if expressed by an advocate, is dangerous. Quarter sessions' justice is very often, apparently, partial, but the tender mercies of farmers to their labourers are the reverse of gentle. Nor, indeed, is there much good done in calling attention to such facts as Mr. Girdlestone disclosed, unless the remedy is clear and can be applied immediately. Even the activity of the press, now far more searching than it was twenty years ago, and the tenderness of the public conscience, are apt to be transitory. Besides, though modern England is curious and sensitive, we may be certain that much unrecorded

wrong is done. The public prints do not know everything, and
might find it inconvenient to know everything.

Some years later, Joseph Arch, a Warwickshire peasant, undertook the heroic task of rousing the agricultural labourer from his
apathy, of bearding the farmers and the landowners, and of striving to create an agricultural labourers' union. I believe that I
was the first person in some position who recognised his labours,
by taking the chair at one of his meetings, and I have been able
to see how good his judgment has been, how consistent his conduct,
and how prodigious are his difficulties. I believe he has done no
little service to his own order, but I conclude he has done more
for the general interests of labour, if only by showing how universal is the instinct that workmen can better their condition only
by joint and united action. And it should be said, that other
workmen, trained for a longer period in the experience of labour
partnerships, have aided, and that not obscurely, the undertaking
in which Arch is engaged.

The difficulties in creating and maintaining a labour partnership
of agricultural hands are very great. In the darkest period of
their history, artizans, even when their action was proscribed by
the law, still clung together, had common purposes, took counsel,
though secretly and in peril, and struck against oppressively low
wages. But for three centuries at least, agricultural labourers
have had no organization whatever on behalf of their class interests.
I shall have written in vain if I have not pointed out how effectively the employers of rural labour contrived to enslave and
subdue them. It is hard to see how any one could have hoped to
move them. But even when they were moved, it was still more
difficult to make the units cohere. I remember that an eminent
clergyman of my acquaintance, now deceased, told me that when
he first took a country living,—some of Arch's kindred were among
his domestic servants, and he was entirely friendly to Arch's
policy,—nothing struck him more painfully than the evident
suspicion with which the labourers in his parish met kindness.
He said that he very early despaired of their confidence, for he
noticed that invariably any trust he showed in them was distrusted,
was supposed to be tendered with the object of overreaching them.
I do not comment on the experiences which must have induced

this habit of mind on them, but simply say that this was the material with which Arch had to deal.

I am willing enough to admit that my clerical friend's position was more awkward than that of other persons. The landlord, generally non-resident, is, ordinarily speaking, as unknown to the English peasant as if he were a foreign potentate, and I suspect that the Arcadian pictures we now and then get of the peasant-labourer, his wages and his allowances from the great house, are, with rare exceptions, rustic ornaments in the immediate neighbourhood of the country seat, cottages with trim gardens, with honeysuckles trained on the walls, and neat borders of old-fashioned flowers in the little garden by the road, the creations of a benevolent despot, who from some good nature and more ostentation keeps his poorer neighbours in apparent content. But the peasant who has to do with the tenant-farmer enjoys none of these amenities, and the parson who took the peasant's part would be thwarted in a hundred ways, and perhaps threatened with the horse-pond. I do not doubt that most country clergymen are kind and conscientious, but they are poor hands at arbitrating between employers and labourers; and when the former are farmers and the latter are hinds, I have generally found that the clergy put a personal interpretation on the apostle's advice, and seek to live peaceably with all men.

But though, being one of their order, the advocate of an agricultural union occupies a more independent and more confidential position than the intelligent parish clergyman, the temper of the peasants must be, even to an enthusiast, no easy instrument to play on. He has to combat with the persistent apathy of despair. He has to contend with the sluggishness of ignorance. He has to interpret the habitual mendacity of distrust. He has to rebuke the low cunning with which the oppressed shirk duty, for only those who are worthy can take a good part in the emancipation of the English serf. I well remember that a friend of mine, earnestly anxious to better his labourers on his model farm, gave them high wages, regular work, and showed them infinite consideration. At last he despaired and sold his property, because they thought him, in their poor puzzled way, a fool; and he found that he had made them worse knaves than he found them.

Again, such a man, constrained to be a leader of men, is obliged to assert an authority and exercise a decision, which others, inevitably less informed, cannot understand and are loath to submit to. This difficulty is universal. The most awkward persons to deal with when debate is needed are two mobs, one of uneducated, and the other of fairly educated persons; for the former are generally suspicious, the latter generally conceited. Neither will concede to the expert unless there is danger, or till patience wearies conceit. The greatest difficulty, we are told, even with the comparatively well-trained artizan, is willing obedience to necessary discipline. It is said that the ill-success which has attended various schemes of co-operation has been due to the disinclination of operatives to obey the necessary orders of one who is of their own order, whom they have invested with authority. They will obey an overlooker whom their employer selects, even though his rule be harsh and severe; but it is not so easy to induce them to acquiesce in the directions of those whom they could depose at their pleasure. But the difficulty is greater the less instructed persons are, and the less familiar they are with the process by which the reality of liberty is achieved, —by the sacrifice of a portion of liberty itself. I have heard that in Mr. Arch's efforts he has been constantly baffled for a time by revolts from the necessary authority with which the manager of a labour organization must be invested.

Again, the scattered character of the agricultural population must needs be a great difficulty in the way of adequately organizing them. The heads of a trade union in towns can summon their men speedily; and take action, if action seems desirable, promptly. But it is far more difficult to manipulate the scattered elements of an agricultural union, especially when the hostility to it is so marked, as has been generally shown, and the opportunities of giving effect to that hostility are so numerous. I do not believe that the mass of peasants could have been moved at all, had it not been for the organization of the Primitive Methodists, a religious system which, as far as I have seen its working, has done more good with scanty means, and perhaps, in some persons' eyes, with grotesque appliances for devotion, than any other religious agency. I have often found that the whole character of a country parish has been changed for the better by the efforts of those rustic missionaries, who possess many of the qualities, and have reproduced not a little of the discipline which the preaching friars of the thirteenth, and the Lollard Bible-men of the fourteenth and fifteenth centuries displayed or enforced. I believe it is true that all successful religious movements have aimed at heightening the morality and improving the material condition of those whom they have striven to influence.

The poverty of the agricultural labourer is a serious bar to the organization of the order. If trade unions have done, as I feel persuaded they have, much to raise the moral and better the material condition of artizans and operatives, they still cost money. I see from the excellent and, on the whole, complete apology for trade unions written by Mr. George Howell, that the charges put on the members by the machinery of the union of engineers amounts to an annual average of £1 17s. 2d. for the last six-and-twenty years; and, if I remember, my friend Mr. Broadhurst told the foreign workmen at the Paris conference, that the funds necessary for the mechanism which he recommended would be a shilling a week from every member. But though the work of an agricultural union is greater than that of an urban association, there is no hope that peasants will be able to contribute at this rate. The economies of the agricultural labourers' union are rigid, the expenditure is cut down to the narrowest limits.

I am persuaded that the jealousy which the farmers feel and the resentment which they express against Arch and his union are mistaken. The first condition under which a workman can be expected to be honest and intelligent, efficient and effective, is that he should have a sense of self-respect. Half a man's worth, says the Greek poet, is taken away on the day that he becomes a slave. The increase in the labourer's pay, if it be obtained, will be much more than compensated by the moral education which he has got by submitting to discipline and by understanding the principles of a labour partnership. When working men make a free contract, and they can never make such a contract as individuals, I am persuaded that they will make more intelligent and more beneficial bargains for the use of their labour than they ever will if they are hindered from corporate and collective action, remain under the impression that their wages are fixed without any discretion on their part, or are constantly called upon to defend or apologize for what they believe is their undoubted right,—a right which no consistent economist would dispute. The public is profoundly interested in the efficiency and the independence of the working man. By the former the industrial success of the country is guaranteed and secured. In the latter, there lies the only hope that we shall ever be able to realize in our day what the trade guilds of the middle ages aimed at, and in some directions unquestionably secured,—the character of the workman, as contained in his moral and professional reputation, and the excellence of the work which he turned out, to say nothing of the practical refutation of social fallacies. Among the members of the Agricultural Labourers' Union, sobriety, independence of public charity, and education, are conditions. The trade unions of London and other large towns do not perhaps exercise the moral discipline over their members which they might do if their fellows more generally enlisted in the system, and they will do, as they get stronger and better informed. But I am abundantly convinced that the English trade unionists include in their numbers the most intelligent, conscientious, and valuable of the working men.

I have referred to the difficulties which beset those who strive by the machinery of trade partnership to better the condition of the agricultural labourer. At all times they would be many, but they are sensibly enhanced at the present time. It is patent to every one, that a vast amount of English land is going out of tillage. It is known that the value of land during the last five years has sunk to panic prices, for much of the price of land was due to the expectation, realized during three centuries, that agricultural land would continually rise in value. Now the mischief cannot have come from lowered prices, for they are incontestably higher than they were ten years ago. It cannot have come from the fact that effective agriculture is a lost art; for if one takes every particular in the schedule of the conditions under which agriculture is successful, the progress of the art in the United Kingdom is as remarkable and as continuous as it is possible to conceive it. Agricultural machines are better, breeds of animals are better, seeds are vastly better, manures have been multiplied by chemical skill and tested by elaborate experiments, and in every direction progress of a solid and substantial kind has been made. But in spite of all this, there is serious agricultural depression and serious national loss. For once, at least, the complaints of the farmers are substantial, for they have in numbers abandoned their calling.

There is only one explanation possible for the decline of agricultural profit. It must be that the income is not proportioned to the outlay, that the cost of agriculture with a number of individuals who have hitherto followed the calling has been excessive. Now there may be four causes for this result, any one of which would be serious, but altogether may be now, as in past times, fatal. They are, first, insufficient capital; second, excessive rent; third, insecure tenure; fourth, inefficient labour. No writer on agriculture has ever hesitated to ascribe disastrous consequences to the occurrence of any one of these incidents. What may we expect if all four are coincident? That there are many agriculturists who during the last few years have escaped these evils I can readily believe. But that many have failed through the pressure of the whole is manifest. And it should be remembered that excessive rent is a relative term; that rent is excessive to one farmer which is easy to another; and to discover what was the rent that not only the land but the cultivator could bear should have been, as it assuredly has not been, the business of the landowner, and his too often most dangerous adviser, the agent or surveyor. Of this I am convinced, that the effect of unpropitious seasons has been trivial when compared with the other causes. Foreign competition has had no effect except in the muddled and selfish heads of protectionists, as may be proved by obvious and measurable facts. Whether the partial and halting security which the late Act gives to the tenant will have any solid effect is too problematical for any one to anticipate.

The inefficiency of agricultural labour, its alternate scarcity and abundance, is, I believe, to be admitted. Low wages, harsh usage, and the temptation of advantage in other localities, explain much of the evil. Perhaps changes in the mode of cultivation, the extension of pasture, and the use of machinery may have contributed in some slight degree. But the most hopeful prospect in this direction appears to me to lie in the extension of union principles among agricultural labourers. It is quite possible to pay too little for labour. Low wages, as economists have frequently demonstrated, do not always mean cheap labour. What Young says about land, that you cannot give too little for poor soil or too much for good soil, is true of your workmen. Some few years ago, an eminent agriculturist of my acquaintance told me that he preferred to have union men on his land, and bore testimony to their sobriety, steadiness, and integrity. Discontent with one's lot is not always a vice; it may be the prelude to many virtues, the parent in the end of that which its timid or jealous critic would be the first to welcome. It seems that the foolish and frantic calumnies which have been told about labour partnerships have this foundation. They who utter these statements are uneasy at the supreme utility of labour, and are afraid that it will destroy public prosperity. Labour knows the conditions of its existence and continuity better. Meanwhile the retention of foolish and suicidal privileges has created a dangerous interest, as yet wild and undefined, about the relation in which the people of England stand to the land of England. The lack of wisdom and foresight is, I am convinced, more prevalent among those who have governed the nation than in the nation whom they have governed.

CHAPTER VII.

THE PRESENT SITUATION.

Summary of the Preceding Statements—Mr. Newmarch's Inferences—Labour Partnerships—Views of Senior, Thornton, and Mill—Trade Unionists and Political Economists—Certain Writers and their Views—Utility of Rigid Theories—The Statesman's and the Social Philosopher's Use of these Theories—Effect of Interference with the Natural Development of Society—This Universal in all Civilised History—The Services of Political Economy to Free Trade—The Distribution of Wealth, its Importance in the Theory—Restraints on Some Labour Necessary—The Remaining Facts of the Past which need Reform—The Land System and Local Taxation, Exceptional Advantages Given in Each to Certain Classes, and the Results—Rent of Land in Towns—Mr. George—Effects of Putting Local Taxation on Occupiers, on Public Opinion, on the Value of Land—Incidence of Local Taxation—The Common Statement—The Fact—Effects on Agriculture, Trade, Labour—The Practice in America—The Effect on Workmen of State Paid Dwellings—Comparison of Fifteenth Century Wages in Building Trades and Present Rates—Women's Wages at the Two Epochs—Allowances other than Wages now and then—Effects of Machinery on Agriculture—The Old Day of Eight Hours—The Character of the Work done under it—Effects of Great Business in which Labour is Employed—Spontaneous Increases of Wages—Power and Weakness of Labour—The Course of History.

I HAVE now, I trust, stated with sufficient distinctness the facts which bear on the history of wages and labour for six centuries in England. The evidence is taken from unimpeachable sources, from the record of what was actually paid, and the power which the wages earned had over the necessaries and conveniences of life. For nearly half the period, I have myself supplied all the evidence from which the inferences have been derived, or could be as yet. For another century I have relied on the notes which I have already collected for the history of prices during the period extending from the middle of Elizabeth's reign to the accession of Anne. For the rest I have trusted to Arthur Young and Eden to the end of the eighteenth; to Tooke, Porter, and others for the nineteenth. I have been able, I hope, to discover and explain the special causes which affected the labourer from the middle of the sixteenth century to the end of the first quarter in the nineteenth. I have shown that from the earliest recorded annals, through nearly three centuries, the condition of the English labourer was that of plenty and hope, that from perfectly intelligible causes it sank within a century to so low a level as to make the workmen practically helpless, and that the lowest point was reached just about the outbreak of the great war between King and Parliament. From this time it gradually improved, till in the first half of the eighteenth century, though still far below the level of the fifteenth, it achieved comparative plenty. Then it began to sink again, and the workmen experienced the direst misery during the great continental war. Latterly, almost within our own memory and knowledge, it has experienced a slow and partial improvement, the causes of which are to be found in the liberation of industry from protective laws, in the adoption of certain principles which restrained employment in some directions, and most of all in the concession to labourers of the right so long denied, of forming labour partnerships.

Though the materials before him were exceedingly inadequate, and in many particulars quite untrustworthy, my late friend Mr. Newmarch, one of the very few persons who have been competent to interpret related statistics, discovered and announced, in the last volume of the " History of Prices," that the best condition of the English workmen was during the fifteenth century, and subsequently, but in a less degree, in the first half of the eighteenth; the worst in the first half of the seventeenth and in the first quarter of the nineteenth. The periods, however, for which his information was defective were the fifteenth and seventeenth centuries, for one of which, till I published my third and fourth volumes, no evidence of value had been adduced; for the other, none has been printed. I am glad to have the opportunity of referring here to the great synthetical abilities of my late friend, the more so because one is so constantly vexed by the rashness of many who attempt the work of one who did it so well and thoughtfully, and even put their names to it.

My reader will observe that I set great store by the reparative energy of labour partnerships or trade unions in improving the material prospects of the working classes. These institutions were repressed with passionate violence and malignant watchfulness as long as it was possible to do so. When it was necessary to relax the severities of the older laws, they were still persecuted by legal chicanery whenever oppression could on any pretence be justified. As they were slowly emancipated, they have constantly been the object of alarmist calumnies and sinister predictions. I do not speak of the language used by newspapers and reviews which merely take the capitalist side of the question and give anonymous utterance to the passion of the hour. Far graver were the allegations of such persons as Senior and Thornton, economists whom I knew and respected for their clearness of sight and the excellence of their intentions. Even my friend Mr. Mill treated these forces of industrial life with a strange indifference. I confess to having at one time viewed them suspiciously; but a long study of the history of labour has convinced me that they are not only the best friends of the workman, but the best agency for the employer and the public, and that to the extension of these as o-_ciations_ political economists and statesmen must look for the solution of some among the most pressing and the most difficult problems of our own time. I shall hope to show this after I have dealt with the facts of the present situation.

The trade unionists speak with considerable bitterness of political economists, and with some reason. The ordinary teaching of political economy admits as its first definition that wealth is the product of labour; but it seldom tries to point out how the producer should obtain the benefit of his own product. It treats of the manner in which wealth is produced, and postpones or neglects the consideration of the process by which it is distributed, being, it seems, attracted mainly by the agencies under which it is accumulated. Writers have been habituated to estimate wealth as a general does military force, and are more concerned with its concentration than they are with the details of its partition. It is not surprising that this should be the case. Most writers on political economy have been persons in opulent or at least in easy circumstances. They have witnessed, with profound or interested satisfaction, the growth of wealth in the classes to which they belong, or with which they have been familiar or intimate. In their eyes the poverty of industry has been a puzzle, a nuisance, a problem, a social crime. They have every sympathy with the man who wins and saves, no matter how; but they are not very considerate for the man who works. Ricardo, an acute stock-broker, went so far as to say that there should be no taxation of savings, so profound was his interest in the process of accumulation by individuals. It was strange that he did not see that the only fund which can be taxed is what the individual may save. To tax what he must spend is to destroy industry.

In point of fact, ordinary political economy does not go further than to describe the process and some of the consequences of a state of war. The war is industrial, in which each man is striving to get the better of his neighbour, to beat him in the struggle for existence. Malthus and the elder Mill laid down the Darwinian hypothesis before the modern prophet of the physical life of the future and the past began to speculate on natural forces. Malthus, a most excellent and benevolent person, was so convinced that the limitation of what produces wealth should be effected in the interests of wealth, that he proposed to do away with all relief to destitution. The elder Mill endorsed the dismal and absurd theorem of Ricardo that the production of food was obtained only in diminishing quantities by increased labour, and his son insisted on it with pious zeal. John Mill was so impressed with the risk of over-population that he hints, not obscurely, at unqualified restraint, at even more than the coercion of prudential foresight. It is needless to add that these writers magnify the function of the capitalist employer, are under the impression that capital can be transferred from object to object with almost the facility of a balance from one banker to another banker, and are alarmed at the risk that national wealth may be sacrificed by a change in the relation which exists at any given time between profits and wages. Nothing illustrates this alarm better than Mr. John Mill's famous paradox that the fund available for paying wages was a fixed quantity. The countenance which he gave to this doctrine has been made the basis of a perennial attack on trade unions. It insists on the inference that when the representatives of one industry strive to better themselves, they can do so only at the expense of other labourers. This doctrine, which Mill at last saw was an error, has been the greatest difficulty in the way of the trade unions. It is as baseless in industrial life as the quadrature of the circle is in mathematics. But this postulate would not, I think, have been gravely alleged had not Mr. Mill been affected by the supreme significance of the production of accumulated wealth, the ideal of the speculative economists.

It is exceedingly useful for men to know what will be the consequences of an industrial war, of a struggle for existence in society, of the results of that kind of competition, in which the strongest is entitled to use all his strength, and the weakest is to be judged, not by his utility, but by his success in the scramble. In these days we are told that the inferences of the economist are only tendencies. Had they been veritable, living realities, society would have long since collapsed, for they would have left only the alternative of two conditions—the relentless despotism of the few, or the anarchy of the many. I do not believe that, however great are the forces at the control of government, the logical consequences of rigid political economy would have been suffered to ensue. Force could extinguish discontent for a time, but the extinguisher would have had to be hired, and would in the end itself take fire.

The political economist of the strict school tells you what will happen (though he seldom tells you all that will happen) under certain conditions. Fortified with this information and warned by it, the statesman in the true sense sees what must not happen, and takes his precautions, applies his remedies, and neutralises the disastrous consequences. The struggle for existence, interpreted strictly, is not progress but retrogression, and civilization is constantly engaged in moderating the struggle, even at the risk of sometimes burdening itself with indefinite liabilities. The information as to what will come to pass under the unrestrained action of certain social laws, is a boon which we cannot overestimate, provided, of course, that the antecedent causes are fully stated and properly estimated. The student of social science thus discovers, or tries to discover, which of these causes are preventible, and the statesman, if he be worthy, deals with the problem. In

the sense that the researches of the economist tell us the truth,
his laws are beneficent, just as the physical laws, which connect
disease with its causes, and show us thereby the means of preven-
tion, are also beneficent. It is only when the economist becomes
arrogant, and avows that he is a guide to all social action, instead
of being the interpreter of certain definite results, that he is
informed by the workman that his conclusions cannot be accepted
as final in the practice of life, and by the statesman that they
may consist with the constitution of another planet, but not with
this.

The case is rendered infinitely more complicated, and abstract
political economy becomes still more unpractical, when the social
condition of any community has not grown naturally, but has
been distorted by selfish laws and mischievous practices, the effects
of which still survive, though the causes have passed away; and
more difficult, when some of the most potent among these causes
still survive. There has never yet been a civilised society in
which nature was allowed to have her way, and where, in consequence, the economical condition of the people is one of spontaneous
growth. One class has oppressed another; and even when the
oppression has been remedied for the future, the present still
bears, and for a long time will bear, the inherited tendencies of
the past. Even in a country which, like that of the United
States, has had an apparently spontaneous development, and has
been freed from tyrannous customs, the immigrants bring with
them the traditions, the weaknesses, the resentments of the
country which they have quitted—feelings and habits which have
been engendered by past experience,—and have been cunningly
introduced to political and social heresies, promulgated for the
benefit of the few, in their new home.

Political economy has indeed taught one lesson of enormous
value, though the truth has only been accepted in its fulness
among ourselves. It is that any hindrance put by law or
custom on the purchaser's market is a wrong to every one—
to the community first, to the labourer next, to the capitalist
employer last. It is due to the facts that the injury comes
last to the capitalist, and that before the mischief is worked
out such a person is able to gain abnormal profits by the losses

of others; and that they who get these profits are an organization, the consumers and the labourers, as a rule, are only a mob ; that protectionist laws, as they are called, exist for a day. When labour is thoroughly organised, and workmen find out the significance of the truth, which I have insisted on and illustrated in this work, that wages have always increased absolutely, — *i.e.*, in their money amount, and relatively, *i.e.*, in their purchasing power, when prices were low,—they will be still less disposed to listen to the insidious advice of those who counsel them to help the movement for raising prices, through restraints on trade, under the plea of fairness. But it will be found that all the best inferences of the political economist have had the advantage of being inductions from experience, and have been supported by practice after they had been demonstrated in theory.

Had economists worked out the most important part of their science, that which deals with the distribution of wealth, instead of merely busying themselves with hypothetical theories about rent, profits, and population, they would have inculcated every one of those legislative acts which have seemed to control the production and distribution of wealth, but in reality have assisted the former, and have made the latter more natural, and therefore more equitable. I think that my contention, which I see quoted by Mr. Goschen, could be exhaustively proved, that every act of the legislature which seems to interfere with the doctrine of *laissez-faire*, and has stood the test of experience, has been endorsed because it has added to the general efficiency of labour and, therefore, to the general well-being of society. A civilised people desires that they who produce its wealth should be intelligent, honest, thrifty, far-seeing, prudent, and, to the fullest extent possible, cultivated and well-mannered. It is impossible that these advantages should be secured, and the economies which they invariably effect secured with them, unless the workman is adequately remunerated for his labour, and is encouraged to hope. "The liberal reward of labour," says Adam Smith, "as it is the necessary effect, so it is the natural symptom of increasing national wealth. The scanty maintenance of the labouring poor, on the other hand, is the natural symptom that things are at a stand, and their starving condition that they are going fast

11

backward." The first sentence is indisputably true; but the phenomena referred to in the second may be artificially induced and were induced for a generation or two after Smith wrote. Employers will get labour cheap if they can; it is the business of the State to prevent them getting it so cheaply, that they imperil the future of the race by the process; and it is the business of particular crafts of workmen to sell their labour at as good a price as they can. They never have ruined, and they never will ruin, the capitalist employer by the process, for they may be trusted not to ruin themselves, since they are quite as acute as their employers in discerning what price the market will bear.

There still exist in all their mischievous force two factors in the evil legacy of the past, which exercise a mischievous influence on the fortunes of English industry. One of these is the permission still given to accumulate land under settlements, and to suggest its devolution by primogeniture. The other is the unfairness which puts local taxation on the occupier in place of putting it, in part at least, on the owner. The first of these is partly an inheritance of the Norman Conquest, partly a result of the great War of Succession in the fifteenth century, partly the acquiescence of corrupt courts of justice in conveyancing practices, which were contrary to public policy and to the declared purposes of the common law. The second begins with the poor law of Elizabeth. At that time the occupier was generally the owner, and the rule was commended for its simplicity. But the slow operation of the former practice changed the conditions of the latter, and the occupier is rarely the owner, and can rarely become the owner. The convenient rule of Elizabeth's law became the interested practice of every other kind of assessment imposed by Parliament. The cost incurred in the maintenance of roads, the police of town and country, the health of towns, the education of the young, are imposed on the occupier; and the owner, except when he happens to be the occupier, is freed from all direct payments. As the revision of assessments is put into the hands of the quarter sessions, and the magistrates are not only generally landowners, but have a necessary property qualification, these authorities have invented a special system of valuing their own property, and on the plea that they assess their houses and grounds at what they would let for, have put nominal rates on themselves.

Now that the owner of land should be allowed to get the best price he can for that which he has to sell or let is, I conceive, as fundamental a right as that of the manufacturer to secure the fullest price which the market will allow him for his produce, and the labourer the best price for his labour. Nothing is, I think, more foolish than the theory that the State should regulate the prices of land, produce, or labour, should fix a maximum or minimum of either. Nothing, I think, could the theory become a practice, would be more disastrous to all. The English law attempted to carry out the theory with regard to labour, as I have shown, for centuries, and with the most mischievous results to land, produce, and labour. But, on the other hand, nothing is more natural and proper than that a person who owns land, produce, or labour should get the best price he can for it ; should not, in short, be constrained to sell it to the first applicant, either at that person's price or at a fixed price determined by law.

But it is another thing for the legislature to give any vendor exceptional powers under which he can enhance the price of what he has to sell by constraining him to keep out of the market a large portion of that which is strictly limited in quantity. The custom was originally permitted, in order to protect the successors of an existing generation of landowners against the consequences of their own vices, and the result has been to make them more vicious. This might be of no consequence, except in so far as it is not in the public interest that profligates in high position should be deliberately engendered by law ; but the protection accorded to them is injurious to others, however good the personal character of the protected individual may be. It stands to reason that if the market of a necessary of life is deliberately straitened, its cost will be enhanced. I have not the slightest doubt that the miserable condition of the poorer classes in our large towns is greatly due to the accumulation of land in few hands in such towns, and to the possession of land by corporations. I cannot doubt that if settlements of land were forbidden by law, and corporations were constrained to grant leases in perpetuity to purchasers, the market for convenient sites would be adequately stocked, and the price of land in towns would fall. It is, of course, impossible to find a parallel object to the existing area of a country, its land. But if we could conceive that the supply of the precious metals in any given country became a rigid quantity, and the law permitted individuals to take portions of this quantity out of currency, and hinder its natural distribution, it is certain that all prices but those of the precious metals would constantly fall. Something analogous to the case is to be found in the fact that the paper currency in the United States is limited by the necessity of purchasing government stock by the issuing banks. The debt in the States is rapidly being decreased, and the price of the residue is gradually advancing. It has been found necessary to permit an issue based on silver certificates, that is, on deposits of silver estimated at the factitious value of the silver coin. This expedient will, however, soon be ineffectual, and it will become necessary, unless the paper currency is to bear a premium, to find a further basis for the security of the issues, or to discover some new means for supplementing the paper circulation.

No parallel, however, can be found to exactly illustrate the effect of an artificial stint of marketable land. It is a perpetual corner, to use an Americanism, created or permitted by the law to the injury of the multitude and for the advantage of the few. It gives the owner the power, not only of constraining the public to purchase in an artificially narrowed market, but of compelling him to part with capital which he has laid out on a terminable lease at the expiry of the term. Now this may be no injury to the middle man, for he will recoup himself from the necessities of the public, his customers. It may be no injury to the trader, though there are signs, not very obscure, in the growth of so-called co-operative shops, that the public are beginning to see that enormous rents for shops enter into the price of commodities purchased in them ; and it may be no injury whatever to persons whose transactions are very large, because the addition of a percentage to cover office expenses is infinitesimal under such circumstances. But where rent is the most important and the most increasing part of the cost of subsistence, as it is with the urban labourer, especially in large towns, the mischief is prodigious. The self-complacency with which some persons—

owners of land to a great extent in London, for the temporary use of which the severest terms which the law allows and the market gives are extorted, to say nothing of taxes on renewal, equivalent to the appropriation of the tenant's good-will—advocate the housing of the London poor at the cost of the London occupiers, and, of course, to the enormous benefit of those who hold this induced monopoly, and will be vendors under forced sales, would be absolutely amazing in any other country besides England. But this kind of complacency is dangerous.

While in the United States in 1881, I found that the reading public was interested and amused by Mr. George's work on "Progress and Poverty." A clever man had caught up a few real facts and a few doubtful theories, and had constructed from them a sketch of social life, which was characterized by growing evil and waning hope. The sketch was not lacking in dramatic force, and in that probability which is frequently unreal, because it is based on, or appeals to, narrow or exceptional experiences. For this misery of the present and the future, Mr. George prescribes a single and, in his opinion, a complete remedy, just as the owner of a patent medicine is ready to assert and advertise that his nostrum will prevent or cure every disease to which either sex and every age is subject. The book was written with great clearness. The Americans, always pleased with clever paradoxes, and not devoid of that interest in speculative pessimism which well-to-do people like to indulge in, especially when it is illustrated from foreign practices, read the book, not seriously, I conclude, and have, I presume, forgotten it. In England it has run through numerous editions, and is said to be eagerly accepted as a new gospel of labour by multitudes of intelligent workmen, who recognize in the English land system the aggravation of their discomforts, the spoliation of their wages, and the present beggary of agriculture. The situation, it seems to me, is sufficiently ominous, and the attitude which landowners take, have taken, and appear likely to take in the future, discourages the defence of what is their proper right in the minds of competent and disinterested advocates. It is clear that class is set against class; but who is to blame, in the past and in the present? for this distrust is not always made manifest. It is certain, however, that if discontent retaliates injustice by injustice, they are most in fault who gave the original provocation, and affect to be ignorant that they gave it, and continue to give it.

The other serious cause of dissatisfaction is the practice of putting all local taxation on the occupier. This is especially felt in towns, where local taxation is increasingly severe. The industries which aggregate in towns have, by their natural competition for building sites, aggravated by artificial scarcity induced on a limited area, continually enhanced the ground value of house property in densely peopled localities. I could show, if the nature of my work required the proof, that land for two miles round St. Paul's has increased during the last hundred and fifty years a thousand fold in value. In so far as such an exaltation in value is not the arbitrary creation of a partial law, it is a natural result. If it could be shown to be the entire creation of labour and capital, as the Thames Embankment was, it is as much the property of the producers as a bale of cloth or a cask of sugar. Now it is the opinion of many, and these very respectable persons, that a very large portion of this enhanced value should become the property of the tax-payer, and that the revenue of it should be employed to diminish his burdens. Others go further. As a matter of fact, the owner contributes nothing to local taxation. Everything is heaped on the occupier. The land would be worthless without roads, and the occupier has to construct, widen, and repair them. It could not be inhabited without proper drainage, and the occupier is constrained to construct and pay for the works which give an initial value to the ground rent, and, after the outlay, enhance it. It could not be occupied without a proper supply of water, and the cost of this supply is levied on the occupier also. In return for the enormous expenditure paid by the tenant for these permanent improvements, he has his rent raised on his improvements, and his taxes increased by them. The occupier in towns is worse used by far than the Irish tenant was before the changes of the Land Act, for if the landlord made him pay interest on his own outlay, the cost of local taxation was shared between the parties.

It is commonly and confidently said that these taxes are only paid through the occupier, and not by him; that if they were

shifted to the landlord or the owner of the ground-rent, the price
would be enhanced by all the tax. To this it is a sufficiently
practical answer to say, that in such a case no wrong can possibly
be done by transferring local taxation to the ground owner and
building owner in towns, where the tenancy is precarious ; and
where the tenancy is a term, by dividing the charge between
house landlord and ground landlord, according to the respective
capital values of their interest, with the object of imposing the
whole of the taxation on the ground landlord at the termination
of the lease. When this period arrives, the ground landlord may,
if he pleases, not now being supplied by the law with a protected
market, and under another condition to be stated hereafter, make
his subsequent bargain with the tenant. Such an arrangement
would test the truth of the allegation, and would clearly not
mulct the owner of the unearned increment, since it would come
back to him in an increased rent. I have never found that
ground landlords welcome or even relish this proposal, which,
on their own showing, would only involve a re-arrangement.

The fact is, the statement is not true. It is, of course, the
case, that when a tenant-farmer takes a farm he inquires about
and calculates the outgoings before he offers a rent. A tithe
rent charge, he knows, is only part of the rent, and if the and
be tithe free, or if the landlord pays this rent charge, he gives
all the more for the land. If the two other charges were
remitted, it entirely depends on the way in which they are
remitted whether he will include them in his rent or not. I
am referring to poor rates and highway rates. If the legal
relief of the poor were extinguished, he would pay less rent,
for he would assuredly have to pay more for labour, plus what
those pay in poor rates who do not employ labour. If the
highway rates were extinguished, and the state of things recurred which was general before the Act of 1773, under which
every occupier or owner was bound to find at least six days'
labour on the roads, he would probably pay less rent, because
the cost of carriage would be enhanced, and the charge of
taking goods to market would be increased. The fact is, the
two principal rates levied on rural occupancy are in reality
beneficial outlay, since without labour and roads no land has

value. They are antecedent conditions of agriculture in the first place, and rent in the second, in satisfying which the landowner and the farmer get subventions from other occupiers, who do not employ labour and yet contribute to the double fund.

These taxes are transferred from the farmer to the landowner in the shape of a reduced rent, because they are associated with what is essential to agricultural operations. A tax levied on an individual remains with him, unless he has some relation of exchange with another person, when he always strives to transfer that tax to such a person. If an income tax is levied on a farmer, he cannot transfer it to his landlord, or to the purchaser of agricultural produce : not to the former, because there is no transaction to which it can be annexed ; not to the latter, because it is excluded by the competition of the market. A landlord who pays an income tax cannot make his tenant or any one else reimburse him. A tradesman who pays an income tax can possibly add it to the price of his goods, and would certainly attempt to do so, and it seems, from what tradesmen have said, may succeed in doing so. But in the case of beneficial outlay, such as that on poor rates and roads, the poor really pay the former in stinted wages, and the landowners do, and should do, most of the latter.

These operations do not apply, or do not in anything like the same degree apply, to dwellings in towns. That the tenant takes the outgoings into account is certain. But what determines his rent in the vast majority of cases is not the profit which he makes on the occupancy, but the proportion which rent bears to his income. It has been long since seen that the ground-rent of shops, and also the rates, in popular and business thoroughfares, are compensated for by enhanced prices to purchasers, or, at least, by a much more rapid turnover, the latter being frequently a matter of personal reputation. If the local taxation were transferred from him to the ground-landlord, he might lower his prices, but there is no reason to believe he could be made to pay more rent. A man does not pay an increased rent because he makes more profits, but because the owner of his place of business can reduce his profits by offering, when opportunity occurs, this site to a rival tradesman. The local tax, therefore, tends to remain with him, but is transferred along with the greater portion of his rent to the customer, under the head of trade charges, in so far as his energy and ingenuity can effect the transfer.

With the mass of those who live in town tenements, these circumstances do not apply. A London labourer, I conclude, does not get better wages because he lives in London and pays a higher rent, but because, as a rule, the best labourers gravitate to the best market. I have pointed out before, that during the period in which the best wages were paid to the labourer, London wages were about 25 per cent. more than country wages of the same kind, and that when labour was depressed universally, the London labourer lost his advantage. During the first twenty years of the present century, London wages were higher than country wages, but then both were on the margin of existence. At present, the more important orders of artizans in London are in receipt of higher wages than those who ply the same craft in the country; but I have always been told that this was because they were worth all the difference. I have been constantly informed that it pays the employer to take London workmen into the country, at London wages, because their superiority is so marked.

The practical immunity of ground rents from all taxation except income tax raises, naturally, the cost of sites. Local taxation in London is in the aggregate about one-third the annual value of ground and building rent together, the proportion of the two varying from many times more in the ground rent, to equality, and to the reverse. I am persuaded from my experience as a director in an industrial dwellings company, whose buildings are erected in the borough which I represent (1883), that if the charge of local taxation were distributed equitably over the ground landlord and the building landlord, the effect on the cost of sites would be such as to render the housing of the industrious poor, in a two-roomed flat, with all conveniences of decency and cleanliness in each habitation, a matter of comparative ease and of moderate commercial success. The solution of the problem would be easier still, if the law permitted a cheap registration of title and an inexpensive mortgage on advances made by Government, with a wide margin for security. The unnatural cost of sites and the unnatural cost of legal instruments are the great hindrances

to the economical housing of the poor in large towns. In the
worst parts of London the ground rent is almost the whole of that
for which rent is paid; and it is well known that when the
Metropolitan Board of Works purchased the rookeries, they often
paid for a filthy and dilapidated tenement the price of a mansion
in a fashionable square.

In the eastern and middle states of the American Union, local
taxes are levied on owners, and not on occupiers; upon property,
and not on the use of property; no kind of property being exempt
from contribution, as is, I think, absolutely just and necessary.
Hence the owner of a magnificent house, with well-appointed and
ample grounds, does not, as in England, escape with a nominal
assessment, on the ground that the letting value of the property
is problematical and, therefore, low. Again, the owner of void
tenements is not excused from contributing on their assessed
value. It is not the duty, American statesmen argue, of the
public to remit an obligation on the ground that an owner does
not dwell in his own house or discover a tenant for it. This
system of taxation values stock-in-trade, furniture, even the
balances of customers at bankers, and taxes all. There is no
reason why an empty house or shop should escape, because the
owner does not employ it for the purpose which led to its erection.
Hence, while in England landowners, being relieved from a tax
on void tenements, escape everything but loss of interest on their
property, and, therefore, if rich, are able to withhold their
property from the market, under terms of special advantage, the
American owner gets the sharp reminder of local taxation that it
is his business to inhabit or sell or let his tenements.

I have no doubt that strenuous efforts will be made to impose
the expenditure necessary for the adequate housing of the
industrial classes in London and other large towns on the local
ratepayers or on the general public; and that, if possible, the
purchase of sites for the erection of such habitations as are needed
will be made a means for procuring exaggerated prices for those
owners of town property who have been able hitherto to evade all
contributions to local purposes from their property, and to employ
the machinery which the law allows them or confers on them in
order to enhance the price of that which is needed to satisfy what

either social danger, or a sense of moral duty, or an awakened humanity declares to be urgent. What the other cities may do, I do not pretend to predict, nor how far they will realise that they will be called on to perform a duty at a great cost to themselves and at a great profit to the landowners. But London is helpless. Nothing can be conceived more ludicrously incompetent than the Board which manipulates its expenditure and at present transacts its municipal business. It is to be hoped that London may have an audible voice given it before the Legislature attempts to aggravate its burdens. But as yet London is administered, and not self-governed.

It is noteworthy that the demand for some action on the part of the Legislature for the better housing of the poor has not proceeded from labour itself. The working classes have made no claim on the State for the supply of one of the necessaries of life at an arbitrated rate. It is probable that they can foresee that this process is not friendly to the object which they have before themselves,—to sell their labour at the best possible price ; and to effect that object by selling it collectively, and on the joint-stock principle. On the other hand, they have not resented, except when the action proceeded from the masters, the competition of foreign workmen. Nor have they been, in the only capacity in which they deliberate, deluded by the sing-song of the fair trade syrens. To commend them for this is to patronise their good sense ; for it is certain, and they are, I conclude, as convinced as any one can be, that state gifts, like charitable donations for purely business transactions, are always more than compensated by the reduction of what is, without them, the natural market rate of wages. If they are wise, they should be resolute in determining that the conditions under which they will engage in the social warfare and the social harmony are that those with whom they are concerned shall have or shall retain no privilege, and that they will be beguiled with no gifts, the most insidious manner in which the workman may be led to sacrifice the advantages of his position.

Some of the working classes in London, and those who have been long educated in the machinery of labour partnerships, have at last regained the relative rate of wages which they earned in the fifteenth century, though, perhaps, in some particulars, the recovery is not complete. I can illustrate what I mean by giving the details which I promised above. From 1449 to 1450 divers workmen were engaged in building at Oxford. The head mason got 4s. a week for nine months in the year; the others, 3s. 4d. for ten. For two months the under masons got 2s. 10d. Now a multiple of twelve will fairly represent, except in house-rent, the general difference in the cost of living at the present period and that to which I have referred. In modern values, then, these sums represent 48s., 40s., and 34s. Mr. Howell informs us that the building trades in London in 1877 had reached 7s. 1½d. a day, or 42s. 9d. a week. I am not informed whether this rate is for the whole six days, and for how many days in the year it may be reckoned on. The workman of the fifteenth century only missed eighteen days of the year, of which a fortnight was at Christmas, three days at Easter, three at Whitsuntide, and six on other days scattered over the year. My reader may care to see the average prices for the two years 1449-50. Wheat was 5s. 10d. a quarter; malt, 3s. 10½d.; oatmeal, 5s.; beef, 4s. 1d. the cwt.; mutton, 4s. 6d.; pork, 5s.; geese, 4d.; fowls, 1½d.; pigeons, 4d. a dozen; candles, 1s. 1d. the dozen pounds; cheese, ⅓d. a pound; butter, ½d.; eggs, 5¾d. the hundred of 120; firewood, 1s. 10¼d. the load; shirting, 6d. a yard; and cloth 1s. 5¼d. If my reader cares to construct a table for himself from these facts, he will find, I think, that, leaving out house-rent, the most formidable item in modern, the most trivial in ancient times, my multiple of twelve is moderately low.

I have taken the best prices of artizan labour in the best English market for such labour in order to contrast them, improved as they are by the mechanism of a trade union, with the prices paid spontaneously in a country town in England 434 years ago. I will now contrast the lowest prices of the most poorly paid labour (not, indeed, that in London, where the extremes of poverty are to be expected and are witnessed, but) in places where, if kindness can discover and aid struggling and ill-paid industry, the search will be made and the assistance accorded, with the remuneration of the same kind of labour more than four centuries ago.

Women's labour in agriculture is rare in the fifteenth century. When it is found, it varies from 2s. a week paid in hay and harvest time to 1s. 6d.; for ordinary field work, such as hoeing corn, I have found it as low as 1s., the rate paid old women for weeding pitched pavements. In the calculations made as to the rate of women's wages in the agricultural districts supplied by Mr. Villiers in 1860, the average given is 4s. 2d. But if the price of this kind of labour had risen as highly as that of other commodities has, the wages of a woman labourer in husbandry would be from 24s. the best paid, and 18s. the ordinary rate, to 12s. the most poorly paid. I do not know whether any material increase has occurred in such wages since 1860, very little information being given as to the amount generally paid, and I think that such an outgoing would have been put prominently forward as a further cause of agricultural distress; but even if it be the case that it has increased some twenty-five per cent. and is now at 6s., the wages of ordinary agricultural labour earned by women are not more than a third of the amount which they were four centuries ago.

In almost all comments on the wages paid the agricultural labourer, they who invite our attention to the facts in the public prints, and are invariably the landowners, dwell with satisfaction on the indirect allowances made to the peasant, his low-rented house and garden, his bit of potato ground, his occasional payment in kind by a periodical bushel of unsaleable wheat, and the concession of collecting wood or getting an allowance of loppings and roots as fuel, and insist that these are substantial additions to his weekly earnings. Undoubtedly he would be worse off without them, and generally when they are given they are an addition to such wages as the labourer could not live upon alone. But it should be remembered that these are to be compared with the facts of far better days, of a time in which the peasant's hut and curtilage was occupied at a fixed rent of 2s. a year, which, treated by the multiplier given above, would be less than sixpence a week at present; that the curtilage of his cottage was far larger than the villager's garden is in our time; that he had his share in the common of pasture; that he was able to keep poultry, probably a cow,

certainly pigs; that his employers constantly gave him portions
of food, under the name of nonschenes, daily; and that in
harvest-time his wages were not only increased, but he was
frequently boarded as well. I do not imagine that the present
privileges and allowances of labourers in husbandry are to be
reckoned as spontaneous acts of generosity on the part of
employers, in whom I have never seen any such tendency, but
simply as the curtailed and by no means equivalent survivals
of much larger and more solid advantages, which could not,
perhaps, with safety be suddenly and entirely extinguished.

It is probable, too, that the wages of labour were far more
continuous in agricultural operations than they are at present.
The farmer, before the use of machinery in substitution for
human forces was adopted, and for a considerable time after
it was familar, employed his hinds in many kinds of service
for which mechanical means are now found. We learn from
Young that many improvements had been made in the implements employed in agriculture, and his English tours are full
of engravings of such machines as he found in use. But
sowing, reaping, mowing, and threshing were all done by
hand; ploughing, of course, and the building of ricks. It was
Young's great desire to see improved ploughs adopted, and
with them much more rapid and clean work, with less wear for
man and cattle. Now, many of these necessary processes are
effected by machinery, sowing universally, mowing generally,
reaping and binding frequently. Ricks are often built by
means of elevators, and the threshing of corn is invariably
done by machines. But the six or eight weeks of the labourers'
hay and corn harvest were what he relied on for supplementing
the scanty earnings of the rest of the year, and were constantly
the source from which he supplied himself with the extras,
over and above the bare food, of fuel, house-rent, clothing, and
casualties. He expected to have much work in the barn during
winter at threshing, and now the use of the flail is a lost art.
It is more than likely that the shortening of his exceptional
advantages, and the change which has come over the previous
regularity of his occupation, would be very indifferently compensated by a rise of 25 per cent. in his wages when he is employed.

I stated in a previous chapter that the day was one of eight hours' work, and grounded my opinion on the fact that winter wages were reckoned to be payable only in the months of December and January, and from the fact that extra hours, sometimes as many as forty-eight in the week, are frequently paid for by the king's agents when hurried work was needed. These hours, of course, were not continuous, being broken for nonschenes, dinner, and supper in the summer, and for nonschenes and dinner in the shorter days. During the winter solstice it seems that only the dinner-time was allowed. Even when the Act of Elizabeth and the regulations of the quarter sessions prescribed a day of twelve hours all the year round, for this is in effect the meaning of the clause, two hours and a half were allowed for rest, and the day was brought down, on an average, to nine hours and a half. But this was precisely one of those prescriptions which labourers would be sure to resist and employers would find it expedient not to insist on. That it was evaded is, I think, clear from the fact that the quarter sessions' ordinances constantly call attention to the law, and remind artizans of the penalties they incurred,—a penny for every hour of absence. Employers were very likely to discover that the labourer's resistance to an excessively long day was not entirely personal, and that the work might suffer from the workman's weariness or exhaustion. Now the quality of the work in the old times of which I have written is unquestionable. It stands to this day a proof of how excellent ancient masonry was. The building from the construction of which I have inferred so much as to work and wages, is still standing as it was left four centuries ago. I am persuaded that such perfect masonry would have been incompatible with a long hours' day. You may still see brickwork of the next century, which I venture on asserting no modern work would parallel; and within five minutes' walk of it Roman brickwork, probably sixteen centuries old, which is as solid and substantial as when it was first erected. The artizan who is demanding at this time an eight hours' day in the building trades is simply striving to recover what his ancestor worked by four or five centuries ago. It is uly to be hoped that he will emulate the integrity and thorough-

ness of the work which his ancestor performed. According to
Mr. Leone Levi, the average amount of hours in the building
trades at the date of his work on the wages of the working
classes (1867) was fifty-five hours.

The magnitude of commercial undertakings, due to the cheapening which ensues when business is concentrated in few hands, is a
characteristic of modern times. In some particulars it is better
for the working classes; in some it induces inconveniences; in all
it makes the organization of labour a necessity, and, as I hope to
show hereafter, a solid advantage to the public. I have already
stated that in the past, which I have been contrasting with the
present, the relation of employer and employed was exceedingly
direct; nor do I doubt that it was to this directness that the high
remuneration of the artizan was due. A church or a mansion
was to be built, a new wing or new offices to be added to a con-
ventual house or college. Perhaps the owner supplied the plans.
If not, the master mason knew how " to draw his plot," and the
master carpenter his. The employer bought all the raw materials
direct from the manufacturers, and put them ready for use on the
spot. He could calculate within a very moderate margin what
the whole would cost, and what would be the charge of labour.
In the building to which I have referred, the cost of materials, on
much of which labour is expended, was £54 10s. 3½d.; of labour,
£73 0s. 0½d.; and the extras connected with the structure, but not
immediately associated with the materials and labour, £14 9s. 0½d.
Thus in the aggregate charge, the cost of materials is 38·3 per
cent.; that of labour, 51·4 per cent.; and of extras, 10·3 per
cent

The multiple of twelve would put this structure at a cost of
£1,703 12s. 6d., from which should be deducted the sale of certain
cranes, worth, on the same estimate, £73 12s., and therefore
leaving £1,630. Now I make no doubt that at the present day
the tower would cost from £4,000 to £5,000, and I infer that the
additional cost would be entirely due to the charge of contractor's
profit, architect's commission, and middle-men's advantage. It is
upon the saving of this enormous waste that the energies of the
intelligent employer are directed, and the advocates of increased
wages for workmen should be. When the economy is effected, it

will be found, concurrently with another reduction of charge alluded to already, that workmen may get better wages and may be more cheaply housed. It is assuredly from the stint of wages that the profits of middle-men have been derived.

The employer in our day is unknown probably to nine-tenths of his workmen. Their relations are generally with his agents and overlookers only, and probably must remain so. But it will be evident that the more able and shrewd the employer is, the greater will be his profits, because such mental qualities are rare ; and the more difficult his workmen make his position, either by slackness or slovenliness of work, or by the necessity of supervision, the greater do they themselves make his profits to be. He has a large margin from which he can save in the competition with those who are engaged in the same calling, by the reduction of the middle-man's charges. He has another large margin from which he can save, in the character of his workmen and the goodness of their work, for the better this is than the average, and the greater its efficiency is, the cheaper it is to him. If, however, this quality of excellence becomes general in workmen, they ultimately have it in their power to attach a portion of his profits, by a demand for higher wages, and by a conviction that he will not forego a cessation of his advantage by refusing to part with a portion of it. It will be found, I believe, that those heads of firms who best know their business are most amenable to the reasonable demands of their workmen, and the analysis given above shows that the reason of this is that they make greater profits than their rivals. For though it is true that, in the first place, an increase of wages can only be derived from profits, and where rent is a principal result from profits, as it is notably in agriculture, from rent, the efficiency of labour may be so increased in the end that profits and rent may rapidly recover themselves. This is the way in which the judicious employment of machinery tends to raise wages. That it lessens the demand for labour immediately is possible, just as a successful demand for more wages lessens profits, but in the end it increases them, for it cheapens production, and thereupon sets up a fresh demand for labour, and lessens cost, and thereby leaves a larger margin of gross profits to be divided. The increase in the wages of agricultural labour between 1730 and 1760 was not merely due to the fact that agricultural produce was cheap, but to the fact that profits in agriculture were large, that a rapidly increasing area of cultivation was taken in hand, and that a rapidly increasing capital was put into the land.

Now it cannot be denied that capital may seek labour, and that labour may, without an effort, be able to gain the advantage of this demand. Such an event has occurred when there has been a sudden deficiency of labour, as after the great pestilence of 1348. It has occurred when the distribution of employment has become so exactly proportionate to the current demand for labour that demand has been always in excess of supply, as was the case in the fifteenth century, and is normally the case in countries where labour is scarce and the opportunities of wealth are great, as in the western, and especially the mineral districts of the American Union. Such an event has occurred when there has been a sudden and increasing demand for special products, as happened to the coal and iron trades in 1865 and 1873. It does to some extent when the supply of labour is in equilibrio, and the competition of capitalists is great,—a rarer phenomenon. But in the great majority of cases, the whole advantage of a new discovery, a new process, and a new machine rests with the capitalist employer. The great inventions of steam and the machinery employed in textile fabrics remained with those who invented and applied these capital forces and processes. The artizan, by whose labour the development of this wealth was alone possible, became more impoverished and stinted. If population was stimulated, it was made more miserable, and population will grow rapidly when the condition of the people is deteriorated. Now it is impossible to doubt that had labour partnerships been general and legal in the latter part of the eighteenth century, the Englishman of that epoch would have been as assuredly able to make better terms with his employer as we are told he did in the fourteenth, when the Legislature vainly strove to put down the combinations of those ancient trade unions.

It would be possible to go through the various kinds of labour which were carried on in those remote times, and are still special industries. But enough has, I trust, been said to sustain the main conclusions at which I have arrived. From what is supposed to be the natural, and, on the whole, justifiable, tendency of the parties to a contract, the employer strives to enlist the services of the common factor with himself of profit and wealth on the most favourable terms for his part of the bargain. The labourer or workman, on the other side, seeks as naturally to achieve his advantage, though he is seriously hindered by his individual impotence and by the urgency which disables him from lingering long over the terms of the bargain. But in the process of settling it, he has on very rare occasions been put in the position of using his power with prodigious force, so as almost to annihilate interests which seemed secure and progressive, as in the middle of the fourteenth century, and to effect a social revolution. From time to time, in a minor degree, he has been able to produce, by his discontent and the temporary cessation of his industry, great inconvenience. The power which he possessed, and the use which he made of it, suggested that the rare occasions on which he could act should be anticipated and restrained, and the Legislature at last succeeded in binding them, though he struggled vigorously, and in the end proved that his liberty was less dangerous than his servitude.

Then began a new departure. The policy of the past had done mischief to the interests which it professed to further, and the new poor law was enacted. The policy of repression had led to results which seemed to threaten the very existence of a large class of artizans and of the future of the nation, and the Factory Acts were passed. The soil of England became too narrow for its people, and employment, even under the circumstances of those restraints on employment which the Factory Acts induced, became precarious. There was danger in the air, and perhaps the Legislature became alive to the duty of considering other interests than one, and free trade in food was established.

Meanwhile the working classes were not idle, and not a few of them adopted, though still with great risks, the new freedom which was accorded them, and founded labour partnerships. These have grown ; and whatever the capitalist and some of the public may think of them, they are believed by many workmen to be a far greater and more powerful instrument for good to those who have conceived, developed, and supported them than any guarantee of law or custom. The advocates of the system have demanded as yet but little from the Legislature beyond what is essential to their free action.   It remains to be seen whether they have not been a benefit in the past, and are a principal hope in the future, not of that labour merely for whose ends they have been severally established, but of labour in general, of human progress; and lastly, whether they do not form the readiest means, perhaps the only means, by which the gravest social and political problems may be stated and solved.   I shall try to make an estimate of this question in the next and concluding chapter.

CHAPTER VIII

Changes Necessary for the Improvement of the Social State Incomplete—The
Remedies for the Present rendered more Difficult by the Errors of the
Past—Labour in Other Countries during the Past—Protection against
Foreign Competition, and its Effect on Wages—In the United States—
Fair Trade—Extension of the Functions of Government an Error—The
Meaning of Frankenstein's Demon—The Population of Large Towns,
though in a Bad State, Better than it was —Foreign Immigration—Theory
of Lodging being Provided by the State—Nationalization of Land,
Origin of the Movement for—Effects of such a Policy—Emigration of
the Young—The Agricultural Remedy—Mr. Vallis on a Peasant Occu-
pier's Earnings—Trade Unions, the Factor in Improving the Condition
of Artizans—Their Prevalence in the Fifteenth Century—Duty of the
Workman as Regards his Labour—The Economy of Waste—The Effect
of Machinery may be Mischievous if not Counteracted by Labour
Combinations—Labour Combinations and Rent, especially Ground
Rents—Domestic Servants' Wages—Overcrowded Callings often Re-
lievable by Trade Unions—Extension of Trade Unions to Women's
Work.

THE English Government, till very recent times, having been
administered by opulent landowners and successful traders,
did its best to depress the condition of those who live by labour.
Parliament has, indeed, within the last sixty years, done much in
abrogating severe and repressive laws, in giving freedom to labour,
in making the United Kingdom a free market, and thereby edu-
cating its industry, in restraining the greed which employed
immature labour, in disabling women from certain degrading
employments, in constraining employers to deal fairly with their
workmen, and in arbitrating between rapacious landlords and
defenceless tenants. It has, indeed, by no means completed its
duties to the public. It must sooner or later, the sooner the
better, sweep away the distinction between real and personal
estate, forbid the settlement of land, and release conveyances from

the grip of the attorney by establishing a cheap and compulsory registration or title. It has been reckoned that the conveyance of real estate in the United Kingdom is mulcted in law charges, exclusive of taxes, to the extent of £12,000,000 annually. I do not answer for the accuracy of the figures, or know, indeed, what are the elements from which they are derived. But I know that such charges are a present loss, which are not only without any equivalent whatever, but constantly bring about an insecurity from which properly registered titles would be free. And, again, there must be a revision of local taxation, under which landowners shall be made to bear their just share in local burdens; and to which, as I readily admit, all property should, except in the case of poor rates and roads, contribute by relieving occupancy and taxing property. But though much remains to be done, more has been done in this country than in any other to remove the legal disabilities of labour, and give it freedom of action. The result of this wisdom is manifest. The unwise delay in other needful reforms will soon be plain.

It is, indeed, impossible to do away at once with the effects of the past. The growth of society has been distorted by partial and injurious laws, and the distortion will not be removed by the removal of the causes which induced it. You cannot, as the adventurer in the Greek comedy does, take the nation, and, by some magic bath, restore it from decrepitude, disease, vice, dirt, drunkenness, and ignorance, to manliness, health, virtue, self-respect, sobriety, knowledge, forethought, and wisdom at a stroke. It will need long years of patient and disappointing labour before the marks imprinted by centuries of misrule and wrong-doing are effaced. And furthermore, the renewal, if it is to come, cannot be imposed from without. It must be developed from within. Beyond the removal of positive mischief, which it has in past times created, the Legislature can do little more than give every freedom it can for innocent energy, and check all the mischief, as far as is possible, which comes from the strong domineering over the weak. If it does too much, it enfeebles enterprise and discourages practical wisdom. If it neglects to adequately protect the weak, and thereby gives license to selfishness and fraud, it permits a trouble, for which it has assuredly to find a remedy.

Nor can the aid of well-meaning persons outside the mischief which has to be remedied do much beyond, perhaps, disclosing the disease and indicating a means of cure. If there be evil at work in the condition of those who live by wages, most of the cure must come from themselves. There is no means for it but self-help. The constitution is needed more than the medicine, and, without it, the medicine is naught. Philanthropy is superficial, intermittent, transient, partial, at best. There is infinite danger that it may become a scheme by which attention is diverted from causes which contribute to or create the mischief, and duties may be enforced vicariously. I can easily imagine a great proprietor of ground rents in the metropolis calling attention to the habitations of the poor, to the evils of overcrowding, and to the scandals which the inquiry reveals, while his own income is greatly increased by the causes which make house-rent dear in London, and decent lodging hardly attainable by thousands of labourers. It is quite possible for the indirect agents of these evils to denounce the mischief to which they are the contributors, and to claim from others the funds by which to remedy the injuries which they cause and from which they profit. When a London landowner invites the public to consider how the London poor are housed, he should simultaneously recommend that the laws and privileges which aggravate the evil should be repealed or abandoned.

Bad as the condition of labour has been in England, it has been worse in other countries. When, five centuries ago, the insurgents under Wat Tyler and his associates brought about the emancipation of the serf, the peasantry of Western Europe were thrust into gradually increasing misery. I have already commented on the beggary of the French peasant and the failure which attended his early efforts for freedom. The Peasants' War in Germany was the result of intolerable oppression. The conquest of Egypt had closed the last of the ancient routes to the East, and the traders of Italy and the Rhenish cities were impoverished. In the profits of this trade the nobles shared, and when these profits declined they strove to reimburse themselves by extortion from the peasantry. The peasants claimed to be freed not only from these new exactions, but from their ancient dues, revolted, were put down, punished severely, and driven back into more hopeless bondage.   The Thirty Years' War in the next century completed their misery.   It is noteworthy that as the Black Prince and the Captal de Buche suspended hostilities and united their forces in order to chastise the Jacquerie in France, so in 1525 the Duke of Guise, on behalf of the French king, who was then at war with Charles the Fifth, and was his prisoner, took an active part in punishing the boors in Germany.   So both the historical parties in England have been equal adepts in oppressing labour.

At the French Revolution, the people turned on their ancient oppressors and rent them, avenging the wrongs of centuries by a savage butchery.   The cruelties of the Terror were due to a reaction from the sense of accumulated wrongs, and to the dread which freed slaves feel that if they are not thorough in their work, the latter end will be worse than the beginning.   When, in his old age at Brussels, the infamous Barrère was asked to explain the mad fury into which the French Revolution rapidly developed, and the ferocity which the Mountain exhibited, he merely answered, " *Nous étions des lâches.*"   The answer is an epitome of the Terror and of its doings.

Modern governments still wrong labour by pretending to protect it against foreign competition.   What they really do is to swell the profits of the capitalist, to cripple the energies of the workman by narrowing his market, and to shorten the means of the consumer by making that dear which he wishes to purchase.   The establishment of protective duties is a con-fession that the industry cannot thrive at home, still less be successful abroad, unless the people at home pay an increased price for its use.   There is nothing done by levying such a tax on consumption, unless it be imposed on those articles which are in general demand, and therefore are the necessaries or con-veniences of the many; for the more voluntary the use of an article is, the less does it serve the ends which are proposed by the *régime* of protective duties.   It is very likely true that an industry may be developed by protection, and a foreign market found.   This is said to be the case with German iron, and that the manufacturers of this article undersell Belgian and English ironmasters.   But a moment's reflection will show that they can do so only at the expense of the German consumer, who not only pays an enhanced price for what he uses, but finds the profit which reimburses the manufacturers for what would otherwise be a loss in the foreign market.

In the United States, the process is being exhibited on the most gigantic scale. The freest people in the world, whose administrations and parliaments have been able to study and avoid the errors and crimes which older governments have committed against labour, have submitted to a tariff which clips the wages of the workman to the extent of 50 per cent., under the pretence of supplying him with variety of employment. It is a trifle that heavy duties are imposed on a few foreign luxuries, except in so far as they give a semblance of equity to those which are laid on common necessaries, on the clothing of the workman, and on his tools, and on the farmer's implements of husbandry. The motive of the impost is, of course, to increase the profits of capital; and this has hitherto been the result, and the impoverishment and dependence of labour,—a consequence as certain though not so manifest. The more remote but inevitable consequence, a bitter distrust and a growing enmity of the labourer towards the employer, has been occasionally seen in the furious outbreaks which have from time to time occurred in America, and are likely to recur whenever, as is frequent in protected trades, a great depression comes over the special industry.

From sheer folly, or from interested motives, a belief that better profits would ensue to employers, or in order to serve party ends by giving a false interpretation of economical phenomena, there are persons who are foolish or wicked enough to advocate the return to a protective policy in England under the name of fair trade. The good sense of the better educated and more experienced English workman shows him that his acceptance of this doctrine would be nugatory in articles of voluntary use, and suicidal in those of necessary use, and he has, therefore, rejected the suggestion. There are, moreover, persons who have the effrontery to invite workmen to accept and acquiesce in a tax on their food, in order that landlords may keep up their rents at the expense of the general public. Such shameless mendicancy is in keeping with the traditions of aristocratic government, which has, in the history of English finance and legislation, put the burdens of state on the many, and freed the property of the few; but when it is fully understood, it will not serve the men who advocate it, or the party which has the meanness to encourage it. Unless his nature is changed, there is nothing which the average Englishman more thoroughly distrusts than a politician who gives furtive and occasional support to a proposal which he publicly condemns.

When a Government goes beyond its proper functions, which are to maintain the public safety, to propound useful and equitable legislation, to arbitrate between interests when it is necessary, to extinguish privileges, to unite efficiency with economy in the administration of affairs, to punish fraud and violence, and to undertake those great offices for which private action, individually or collectively, is inadequate, and attempts to distribute employments among its people, to favour one class at the expense of another, to meddle with the innocent habits of its subjects, and to mould their lives after its own pattern, to coerce the open expression of opinion, and to silence criticism on its own proceedings, it makes itself, or those whose affairs it administers, responsible for all the failures of its action, and engenders the belief that if man is made unhappy, the Government has brought about the result. The English Government, from the days of the Pale till the passage of the second Irish Land Act, has attempted to create or support an aristocracy of race in Ireland, and has thereupon developed a democracy of discontent, hatred, and violence. Half the German army is engaged in protecting the German soil from an invasion of revenge, and the whole believes it is. But the other half is engaged in restraining that wild outburst of socialism which a meddling and pedantic administration has induced the German people to believe to be the only opposition which the government really recognises and fears. The huge empire of Russia is undermined by a universal conspiracy. The Austrian administration lives by setting race against race, and achieves an apparent union by nourishing implacable aversions. When the traditional purposes of a government are detested, its best intentions are distrusted.

The strange story of Frankenstein was, I make no doubt, suggested to Mary Godwin out of the opinions which she received from her father. Frankenstein had contrived to put life into a gigantic being which he had constructed, and on which he intended to bestow superhuman strength, stature, and beauty. His creation had strength and stature, but was unutterably and shockingly hideous. The maker of the monster abandoned the horrible creature, which had to shift for itself, and to learn the arts of life in solitude, as all fled with loathing from the sight of it. It possessed infinite powers of endurance, infinite capacity for learning, great determination and cunning, irresistible strength. It yearned for society, for sympathy, and for kindliness; and meeting with none of these, being rejected by all and made a loathsome outcast, after it had been called into being, it became an infuriate fiend, which pursued with implacable hate and with the most cruel wrongs the man who, being the author of its existence, was thereupon its most detested enemy. This remarkable conception was intended, it is clear, to personify the misery, the loneliness, the endurance, the strength, the revenge of that anarchic spirit which misgovernment engenders, the suddenness with which its passions seize their opportunities, and the hopelessness of the pursuit after it, when it has spent its fury for a time. Most European governments have been engaged in the work of Frankenstein, and have created the monsters with whom they have to deal.

The great cities and towns of England contain a vast population which lives, one hardly knows how, on mean and precarious wages, in dismal and unwholesome dens. Some of this poverty is merely miserable, some of it is vicious, some is criminal. The growing population of these English towns is partly of local origin; for though apparently a century ago the deaths in London exceeded the births, the increase of sanitary appliances has made London so healthy that the relations are reversed; every week the amount of the births equals the number of a large village. There is also a large immigration into London and other towns. The German population of London is fully equal to that of a first-class town in the German empire. The Irish population is probably larger than that in any Irish town, except Dublin and Belfast.

London, it is probable, also receives a considerable part of that population which has deserted the agricultural districts. Now London is the greatest manufacturing town in the world. Naturally its inhabitants are engaged in an infinite variety of occupations. But these occupations are stinted by the fact that an octroi duty on coal is levied to an amount which seems insignificant, but is sufficient to kill such manufactures as depend on a prodigal consumption of this source of power. The tax was first imposed, I believe, to supply a fund for rebuilding St. Paul's Cathedral, was continued for the use of that absurd and obsolete Corporation of the City Proper, and now forms part of the fund for the purposes of a hardly less grotesque institution—the Metropolitan Board of Works.

Evil as the condition is of destitute and criminal London, with its misery and recklessness, it is not, I am persuaded, so miserable and so hopeless as nearly all urban labour was sixty years ago. It is not, I believe, so bad as it was at the beginning of the eighteenth century, when, as one sees from Luttrell's diary, the executions at Tyburn formed a notable percentage in the weekly bills of mortality. It is not so ignorant nor so unclean as it was twenty years ago, though, as usual, the pedantry of the Education Department, in driving all children through a rigid examination, produces a distaste afterwards for books and learning, which makes the standard of proficiency a barrier towards subsequent study and learning, which is nearly as insurmountable as ignorance. In order to enable the Government officials to calculate the charge of national education in the easiest manner for themselves, they pay by results, and in consequence induce results which are very adverse to those for attaining which public money is expended.

It is a matter of great gravity whether we should welcome or even permit the perpetual immigration of a foreign element into the country. The American people, with an unlimited extent of territory, decline to allow themselves to be the recipients of European pauperism, and keep a sharp look-out on the character of the steerage passengers to the States. They suspend the rights of citizenship during a considerable period of probation. They have decided, for reasons which are very intelligible, though not very convenient to be published, not to allow their population to be polluted by the presence of a Chinese proletariat. Now it is quite certain that the English people at one time gained con· siderably by the influx of foreigners. Some of our best industries were developed before the Reformation by the inflowing Flemish artizans from the time of Henry II. onwards. Others owe, it seems, their development in England (though not without some remonstrance, as we find from an Act of 1454 directed against foreigners engaged in the silk manufacture) to the exiles whom religious bigotry and persecution drove away. Such were the workmen who fled from the Spanish Inquisition in the Low Countries, and the Bourbon Dragonnades in France. We owe, indeed, some of our best stocks in England to these migrations. No Englishman can regret, for the sake of his country, that it was an asylum for a Romilly.

But it is quite another thing, when cheap transit being provided, the great towns in England swarm with pauper foreigners. Perhaps the readiness with which this kind of population is accepted, is a survival of the experience in which the addition of the foreign element was an indisputable good; perhaps it is a convenience to those capitalists who make large profits out of degraded and impoverished labour. Working men, who understand the interests of their order, are alive to the risk which their organizations run from the competition of foreign immigrants, and with characteristic public spirit have suggested to foreign labour that it should seek to raise itself, not at the expense of other labourers, but in concert with other labourers. The advice which Mr. Broadhurst gave last autumn (1883) at the Paris conference of workmen was in the best interests of all workmen. In brief it is, Raise yourselves, not by depressing others, but by acting with them. You cannot escape, try whatever you can, from the influence of competition, any more than from the survival of the fittest. But the survival of the fittest may be the survival of the analogue to Frankenstein's demon, while the effort of all true civilisation is to improve those who are improvable, and to deal with the residuum. It is possible that the struggle for existence, unless controlled and elevated, may be the degradation of all. It nearly came to be so during the first thirty years of the present century.

Various remedies have been proposed for the immediate benefit and the permanent improvement of the working classes, especially the industrious poor in large cities. It may be expedient that I should state, in this conclusion to my inquiry, what appears to me to be the value of the several projects which have been propounded.

I am persuaded that an attempt to relieve distress, provide proper lodging, and find work for the inhabitants of large towns would in the end produce even worse evils than that condition which the expedients would seek to relieve. No one disparages kindliness and charity. For certain calamities, such as those which are relieved in hospitals, they are indispensable. For extraordinary casualties they are invaluable. But as a universal process they would be disastrous, especially if the charity is compulsory, or provided out of the funds which the Government raises by way of taxation. To adopt such an expedient would be to despair of the recuperative power of honest industry. If the London ratepayers, or even the London landlords, are to find the means by which homes are to be provided for workmen at prices which are unremunerative to those who supply the homes, and work on products for which there is no market, or an overstocked market, it needs no particular acuteness to discover that the emigration into such towns will be more rapid than ever, and the restraints on improvidence, not now over strong, will be entirely removed, and the old allowance system restored in its worst form. It seems plain, too, that in the end, what was seen to be not very remote under the old poor law will ensue, and the relief of poverty will absorb nearly all the products of labour.

The nationalisation of land is a favourite project with those who believe that socialism is the true remedy for low wages. Now I cannot believe that this project, from the extreme form which it takes in Mr. George's proposal, that the property of all landowners, great and small, should be confiscated, to the milder proposal, that after due compensation secured to existing interests, the state should constitute itself the universal landlord and appropriate for public ends all future accretions of value in land, would have been ever gravely contemplated had it not been for the policy of English landlords, who have clung to the obnoxious privileges of primogeniture and the right of settling land. The instinct of the public leads them to conclude that there is a very strong motive for the maintenance of these customs, and naturally that the motive is a selfish one. They are aware that the soil of this country is limited in extent, that what is scarce is dear, and that if what is scarce can be made artificially more scarce, it will be made more dear. That this impression is correct cannot, I think, be doubted. It is not indeed easy to discover the precise amount of additional or unnatural dearness which the application of Gregory King's Law, which formulates the effect of scarcity on the price of a necessary of life, would prove to be induced on building sites in the metropolis. But it is clearly understood that the cost is greatly enhanced, and discontent at an unfair advantage conferred by law on the owners of certain kinds of property exaggerates the impression formed as to the amount. I am at least persuaded that the socialism which desires in a more or less drastic manner to curtail the present rights of landowners will become more prevalent and more threatening as long as the invidious privileges to which I have often referred are maintained. These mischievous privileges explain the popularity of Mr. George's theory and his remedy of universal confiscation,—a confiscation which will include not only palaces and parks, mansions and farms, but every freehold cottage or homestead in which working men have invested the savings of their lives. Discontent constantly accepts ludicrous and even suicidal paradoxes.

The policy which would make the state the universal landlord, after providing for the compensation of existing interests, would be only less fatal and foolish than that which confiscated them without compensation. It would confer on the state the most gigantic functions, which would require for their administration a machinery which, were it entirely honest and thoroughly efficient, would cost more than all which the project hoped to gain, would create an enormous body of fundholders, the recipients of the rents which the government received for the use of the national estate, fundholders who would not be, by the very terms of the bargain, tied by a single responsibility to the society which paid them the dividends on the new stock, and would certainly lead to a bureaucracy which would be vexatious, inquisitorial, and corrupt. If the state is to revise its contracts with its tenants periodically, the tenant will be divested of all motives to improve his holding; if the new tenancy is to be a permanent one, the state of things which the nationalisation of land was intended to obviate will instantly recommence. But the progress of human liberty is always connected with the restraint of government interference, except when government, by arbitrating between conflicting interests, saves the weak from the tyranny of the strong, and thus secures justice, and benefits the whole community by its police. Again, the object of the wise economist, that result to which all the practical teaching of his science and all the experience of social history tend, is the distribution of wealth into as many hands as possible. A country is infinitely safer, infinitely stronger, infinitely more capable of genuine progress, in which the many are in comfort and content, than that is in which much wealth is accumulated, but the process of distribution is artificially hindered.

Another remedy is emigration or migration. Spontaneous emigration is almost invariably a loss to the community from which it proceeds. It is supposed to relieve the country of a surplus population, and thereupon to be a remedy against the danger of over-crowding. But a process which takes away the best of the working classes, as must be the case with spontaneous emigration, since only the most vigorous and enterprising are influenced by the movement, is the reverse of a gain to the country which loses them, and if their places are filled, as it seems they are, by immigrants of inferior type, and, as is generally the case with such types, of greater fecundity, the loss becomes a double one. The fact that the emigration is a benefit to the emigrant does not alter the result. Now emigration is a boon to the country from which it takes place only when it relieves society from that class of the industrious and honest workers which is certain to be over-crowded, and from which, therefore, depletion is a good to all, to the people which runs the risk of being constrained to support the excess, and far more important, to the labour which is likely to be in excess. The class which most exactly fulfils the conditions referred to, is the young of both sexes ; and it is well known that this is the class of immigrants that our colonies eagerly welcome, and are willing in their new homes to surround with every safeguard.

I am persuaded, from reason and experience, that the emigration of the young is the best remedy for hereditary pauperism. Some years ago, when I was a guardian of the poor in my own city, my Board took pains to carry out this kind of emigration, through the agency of Miss Rye, and with absolute success. Nor do I doubt that in London and other large towns, especially as education is sharpening the faculties and developing the intelligence of the young, such a system of emigration would be welcome and highly beneficial, especially if care were taken that the parent should be carefully and exactly informed of the way in which the child was going on, and the child were made to understand the duty of relieving the parent, perhaps of finding him or her a home in the new country to which he or she may have gone. The children of the poor are not undutiful or ungenerous to their parents. I am convinced from my personal knowledge that the wages of domestic servants are freely given by young women to their parents, and that the miserable earnings of agricultural labourers are constantly eked out by the wages of daughters in service. In the case of pauper children, I hold that they who have put upon others the charge of their maintenance have morally forfeited the right of determining their career ; and that in the case of criminals and persons of infamous character, they should be, in the interest of the children, deprived of parental rights at once and altogether. It is the interest of honest and industrious workmen that pauperism should be diminished as much as possible in the present and obviated in the future, and that crime should be isolated and watched. Everything which increases the cost of administering human societies, and still more everything which involves the waste of wealth, diminishes the resources available for the employment of industry.

The disastrous dissociation of agricultural skill and competent capital has led to a diminution of the rural population, and to the abandonment of tillage over a large and, it is to be feared, an increasing area of English land. The poverty of the towns has been swollen by agricultural immigration, and the necessary cultivation of the country has been injured by the lack of hands. Hence it has been proposed, and with great reason, to revive and extend the system of small holdings, so as to attract a rural population to the land before it is too late. My friend, Mr. Jesse Collings, in the House of Commons, has already procured some legislation in this direction, and the system has the warm support of Mr. Arch's practical experience. I believe that the only reason why farmers are hostile to such an arrangement is that they fear it will make the agricultural labourers too independent. It seems that it is disliked by landowners because they are wedded to the tradition of having large farm tenants and a system which is plausible in itself, and, until the recen tagricultural break-down, has been apparently successful. But at the present crisis one would think that any and every expedient which would tend to replace labour on land and attract new capital to land would be advantageous, and should be eagerly adopted. Though the individual capital of peasant holders (I am thinking of much more than miserable acre allotments of the worst land in the parish, at double the rent of the best) is small, the proportionate capital is large. I am sure, at least, that if intelligent labourers had the prospect of getting a ten or fifteen acre farm, with a decent dwelling and corresponding farm offices, the amount of capital per acre with which they would stock their holdings would soon be relatively far higher than that of the large farmer, and that the produce per acre would be far larger, especially if they betook themselves to dairy farming and ensilage, as the small fifty acre farmers of the Eastern States in America are doing, and with such marked success, on the worst land in the world. Fortunately small farms are under the protection of the Agricultural Holdings Act.

I have before me a little work, written by a national schoolmaster some fifteen years ago, and to which I then put a preface. I stated in it that "the position of the agricultural labourer in husbandry was one which pressed for a solution, and that speedily, or that the country would have to face difficulties which cannot be evaded, difficulties which, unless foreseen and provided against, may be in the highest degree serious." The crisis has come, and it is worse than I anticipated.

Mr. Samuel Vallis, in the little book to which I have referred, gives a balance-sheet of his receipts and expenditure on five acres of land cultivated by spade husbandry. He shows a gross return of £109 10s., his live stock being two cows and two pigs, his grain crops being an acre of wheat and half an acre of green peas. He puts down on the other side £3 an acre for rent,—an unconscious avowal as to the enormous rent procured for cottage farms,—£5 10s. for seeds, and £20 16s. for labour, the latter item being of course one which was necessary for the schoolmaster, but would not be incurred as a money payment by the labourer, and so shows a profit of £68 4s., which he states, almost superfluously, is more than double the the wages of the ordinary farm labourer. He steadily pursued what he calls "the soiling system" with his cows, *i.e.*, they were constantly fed under cover, and he reckons that the advantage of this over the "exposed system" is fully 25 per cent. He adds that if young agricultural labourers remained single till twenty-five, and saved half their wages, they would soon find the necessary capital for such a little holding, or, indeed, for one three times the size.

I do not doubt that it is still possible to recall a rural population to the English soil, to renew and extend the productiveness of English land, and to find abundant high-class labour, for the capitalist farmer when he reappears. It is true that the occupiers of peasant holdings might demand higher wages than they now earn. But what of that? They might illustrate anew the doctrine that low wages do not mean cheap labour, and that high wages may. It is certain that the possession of property is the best, nay the only means under which people are educated into respecting property, and that diligent labour on a small holding will lead to diligent labour on another's tenancy.

I am told that the experiment of a beneficent despotism, under which the labourer has been gifted with enough land for cow and pigs to his cottage, with the condition that he worked honestly for an employer at hire, has been tried successfully, the landowner being the arbiter as to the wages paid. The system is the revival in our own day of the old tenancy in villeinage, though with less land and on an uncertain tenure. If this system succeeds, though the intrinsic faults which belong to it were found out and commented on in the earliest agriculture, I should anticipate that a more generous tenure would be still more successful, and that the most obvious solution of the agricultural difficulty would be to win back the labourer to the land by the temptation that there is annexed to his cottage such an amount of land as would give him an interest in the soil, and by leaving him free to contract for his time and skill with the larger tenants.

In course of time it may be possible to reunite capital and agricultural skill, and bring back the labourer to the soil. It is necessary to do both, and to face the solution of the problem. At present, the parties immediately interested will not see the facts, and the public at large, which is profoundly interested in the rehabilitation of agriculture, is kept in the dark. No more deplorably unsatisfactory and incomplete account of the situation can be conceived than that contained in the report of the Duke of Richmond's commission, which is crowded with irrelevances, and destitute of true information on the real facts of the situation. So ill-informed are those who are concerned for agriculture, or pretend to be, that there are persons addressing working men who imagine that they can by bold assertions induce industry to believe that it will benefit itself by replacing taxes in the form of a sliding scale on wheat, by so restricting the foreign market, and thus rendering the wages of the workman more uncertain than they otherwise would be, and by raising the price of food, and thus diminishing their purchasing power.

The future of the artizan, factory, and urban population has yet to be discussed. For this there is but one remedy,—the extension of labour organizations on the trade union principle, but with considerable improvements in detail. If it be found that those callings alone have prospered in which labour partnerships have been developed, and those have prospered most in which the fundamental principles of such labour partnerships have been most prudently kept in mind and acted on, it stands to reason than an extension of the system to other callings, now notoriously underpaid, is the most obvious remedy for low wages and uncertain prospects. Such associations are a revival of the best traits in the mediæval guilds.

I confess that in my earlier writings, before I had studied the history of labour and its strange vicissitudes in England, I was of opinion, though with some misgivings, that the organization of a trade union was directed against the consumer through the employer, that it appropriated out of an elastic but common fund from which labour was paid (though I never agreed with Mr. Mill's wage-fund theory), an undue share, and that it aimed at establishing an aristocracy of labour, from the benefits of which the great mass of working people would be excluded. An inquiry into the history of labour has dispelled these opinions. I do not aver that the organizations of the middle ages are models for working men in modern times to imitate. They were partly concessions to artizans in towns, partly encouraged in so far as they were benefit societies; but they were much more a reaction against interested oppression. The modern labour partnership is freed from the enforced vices of the older organization, and has generally purged itself from the equally adventitious vices which were engendered by the interpretations which the courts put upon the atrocious combination and conspiracy laws.

Now the existence and development of the ancient system, described in detail in the previous pages, was accompanied by remarkable and general prosperity, for the vices of society in the fifteenth century were mainly those of the Church and the nobles. Every one throve, except the foolish people who, after wasting France, came back to England and wasted each other. The singular prosperity of the age has greatly puzzled those who have even in part recognised its character, but was easily seen, to such experienced eyes as those of Tooke, to have had no relation to the reputed value of the currency, or to the other explanations which had been given of so remarkable a phenomenon.

I can discover no other cause for this remarkable material

progress beyond the universal associations of labour. I admit
that the situation was in itself favourable to high wages. Land
was greatly distributed. The seasons must have been singularly
propitious. The country was permeated by a religious feeling
which scorned the worldliness and immoralities of the established
system, was severe, parsimonious, ardent, secret, and personal.
Unfortunately, the mass of the people either could not or would not
use what power they had to check the growing violence of the
nobles, the scandals of the Church, and the vices of the administration. They sided, it seems, with the reforming party among the
nobles, the Yorkist faction, and found, as people always find who
entrust popular interests to a noble partizan, that they were made
tools of and deluded.

It is probable, too, that the success of their private organizations, necessarily a secret, made them indifferent to such political
action as they could take. The towns, and even the villages, had
their guilds, and it is certain that these guilds were the agencies
by which the common interests of labour were protected. In a
prosperous people, legal persecution develops cautious resistance
and judicious organization. In an unprosperous one, it encourages
the growth of violent opinion and a passion for destructive
remedies. I can quite believe that the working classes of the
fifteenth century grew indifferent to politics, or found that they
could not grapple with lawless domestic feuds. I am certain that
the factions let them alone, just as I am certain that when the working classes became impoverished and powerless in the sixteenth century, the destruction of the guilds was seen by their oppressors to
be the best way of breaking up their organization. In the same
way the modern trade union has had to fight for two generations in
order to get its funds protected against fraud or embezzlement.

The evidence of the present and the example of the past appear
to prove that labour partnerships are the remedy for low wages.
They undoubtedly put the employer in a difficulty. They claim a
greater share for labour in the gross profit of industry. They
constrain him (if he is to hold his own in the struggle) to find his
remedy in the economy of waste, in the development of invention,
or in the reduction of rent. The analysis of these agencies
requires a fuller exposition of the circumstances.

The workman should seek to make his labour as efficient and fruitful as possible. The honourable desire to protect every workman in the same craft, by seeking to establish a minimum of wages, may lead to the suggestion of a minimum standard of efficiency. It is entirely essential not only to the dignity but to the strength of labour that it should do what it has to do as well as it possibly can. I am sure that the workman of the fifteenth century was as proud of the integrity of his work as he was of the agencies by which he was independent. We can, even at the present day, measure and appreciate its excellence. And in order to maintain their own character, workmen are, in my opinion, justified in denouncing incompetence, sloth, or scamping work in their own order, and in exposing fraud and dishonesty among employers. If it were possible for the employer to dispense with over-lookers, and trust his workmen, much saving would be effected, for in order to get a larger share in the joint profits of the capitalist and workmen, it is essential that the deduction from gross profits should be as little as possible. But it must, I fear, be admitted, that in the modern strife between labour and capital, the importance of securing that every care should be taken of the employer's interest by the workmen has been lost sight of, and, in consequence, that fund from which alone the condition of the workman can be bettered, the net profits of the whole industry, has been needlessly and injuriously diminished. It cannot be too strongly insisted on that employer and employed have a common interest,—the production of a maximum profit from their common industry; and that the only question which ought to arise in the partnership between them, is that of the respective shares which each should receive in the equitable distribution of the profit. But I venture on asserting that the economy of this kind of waste is the most important of all.

There are various other forms of it. The extraordinary application of natural forces to purposes of human utility is the most striking fact in the history of modern industry. The economy of waste is the discovery of the process by which the force may be used with the least friction and loss, and the success which has attended individual effort in this direction, is a commonplace in the history of industry, manufacture, and wealth. Such discoveries, secured as they are by patents, exist entirely for the benefit of the capitalist, and the profits derived from them can be appropriated in no degree by any one. In just the same way the special skill of the individual agriculturist, who cannot protect his processes by patent, remains with him as a profit-bearing agency, and cannot be appropriated by labourer or landowner till the economy is diffused among all persons engaged in the same calling. But other economies, some of which have been alluded to already, —viz., the extinction of middle profits and the moral development of industry,—immediately become the object on which labour may ground its claims to a share in the enhanced profit of the undertaking, though here again, until the economy is diffused over all the operations of a similar kind, the appropriation of the part is hindered. And perhaps the monopoly of the patentee (the natural justice of which I do not dispute, though the grant of the monopoly is constantly inequitable in fact) may help to break that immediate loss to labour which often follows for a while on the economy of productive processes, and so give time to prepare for the re-arrangement with labour, which the greater profits of the employer justify. In illustration of what I say, I may refer to the effect of sewing machines. It was calculated that this invention would materially lessen the toils, and, in the end, increase the gains of tailors and seamstresses. It has not done so, because the tailors' union is not strong enough to enable the members to claim better terms from employers, and the seamstresses have hardly any union at all. That they who have employed the labours of such artizans as I refer to have made prodigious profits, is pretty evident. I find no fault with the advantage which they have acquired, my only regret is that it has not been shared with those who have created the wealth, as it would have been under a proper organization.

The circumstances under which rent may be made to bear a larger share of public duties, in return for the enormous benefits which industry and the progress of society have conferred upon landowners, have been already in part referred to. The well-being of the mere landowner is a matter of no concern to anybody but himself. The well-being of the labourer, or of the capitalist who gives the concentration of intelligence and administrative power to the affairs of a complicated instrument of profit, or of the artizan, who conscientiously and faithfully carries out the details of work, is of interest to all. I cannot join in the chorus of exultation which comments on the virtues of a middle-man who, having saved ten or twenty millions, dies in the odours of the peerage and of sanctity. I do not care for the opulence which, beginning with questionable gifts or grants or plunder, has, through generations of fools or profligates, at last, and by the labour and even by the presence of others, contrived to take enormous tolls on enterprize, on industry, and on popu· lation, and is ever on the look-out to fleece all, if they will submit to be fleeced. To suggest that the owner of land should be deprived of his property is dishonest, and, were it carried out, would be disastrous. To value his present interest, and to appropriate the future increase of the area which he possesses, would be an enormous task, and would make government, society being a vague force of which government must be the agent, an ubiquitous function, the jobs of which would be demoralizing, the discontent with which would be dangerous, the cost of which would be enormous, and the risks of which would be formidable, Suppose in 1870 the English Government had adopted Mr. Mill's suggestion, had accepted the position of universal and immediate landlord, and had agreed to pay in perpetuity the agricultural rents which were then raised, it would have made an excellent bargain for the landowners, and an exceedingly bad one for the public. The doctrine that agricultural rent will always rise, which was at the bottom of Mr. Mill's theory of decreasing production from land, is one of the most dangerous, and I may add erroneous notions conceivable. A knowledge of the history of rent, in the third quarter, for example, of the seventeenth century, and the first quarter of the eighteenth, would have entirely dispelled a delusion which was founded on the accidental conditions under which rent was increased in the first half of the nineteenth century.

But the case is quite different with ground rents. Here the State has a right to interfere with that exceptional accretion of value which comes from other than the outlay on the land. It is easy to separate the ground value from the building value, and to tax the one on the principle which should be applied to all property, and the other on the principle which should be applied to property whose only or principal value is derived from the existence and action of others. That the reformers of local taxation should insist on the ground landlord contributing to the fund, which is necessary for the very existence of those who create his wealth, is plain ; that they should anticipate the necessity, by joint action, of lessening the exorbitant rents which their supineness induces them to pay for sites, is wise ; for in many branches of business there is clear enough evidence that trade customers will be no longer willing to pay them ; and that what is called co-operative shop-keeping, a system already in its infancy, and still exposed to the risks of inexperience, will seriously limit the future of those traders who are too slovenly or too servile to resist extortion.

The organization of labour, with a view to its sale in the aggregate, is incomparably more important, when the condition of any class is such that the wages it earns are not progressive, or are retrogressive, than it is when the demand is generally less than the supply. Persons have often stated that there has been no trade union among domestic servants, and that the wages of such persons have greatly risen by the mere operation of demand and supply. There is no doubt of the increase ; and it bears indirect testimony to the fact that the profits of the higher branches of indu.try are greater than those of the lower, and that there is more employment for domestic labour in consequence. But it is also certain that the demands made on such labour cause that it should be increasingly select. The domestic servants who satisfied the simple habits of a generation or two ago, were very inferior in tact, in manner, and in function to those which are needed in very moderate households at present. Besides, it is not quite clear that there is not an understanding among domestic servants which is just as effective as a trade union. The training of an efficient domestic servant is a long apprenticeship. Those who enter into this calling know what is expected of them, and what is the reputation which they must acquire and keep, and are very fully aware of the claims which they can make for wages. Good as the position is, and, relatively speaking, high as are the wages of peasant girls who enter into domestic service and are carefully trained in it, the calling is not in itself attractive, and young women often exchange it for a married life of much toil and little hope, for the poor earnings of dressmakers and seamstresses, and even for a ruinous freedom. The supply always tends to fall short of the demand, and those who enter the calling are fairly cognisant of the fact.

But there is no doubt whatever that many callings are, in technical language, overcrowded. I say technically, for they may not be under a better distribution of profits. I find no fault with employers for attempting to arouse the common scare of those who are threatened with the risk of having to pay higher wages, that the industry will be driven from the country, but I am not called on to believe them. The prediction is made so freely, and has so rarely been verified, that any person who hears it may be pardoned for doubting it. It is certainly not an imminent risk if the profits of the capitalist continue to be large, and there is plenty of evidence that in those callings where the labour of the employed is worst paid, the profits of employers are abnormally high, as in the case, for example, of ready-made clothes. There is plenty of evidence as to the enormous profits of most employers in the manufacture of textile fabrics in the days when factory-hands were very ill-paid. Never, I imagine, was wealth more rapidly accumulated in Lancashire and Yorkshire than it was between 1800 and 1840. It is rarely the case, however, that the liberal reward of labour is followed by a material enhancement of price. No one believes that if the London seamstresses, tailors, and match-box makers received double the wages which they do at present, there would be an appreciable difference in the price of the products sold, or any present risk that any of those industries would cease to be plied in this country.

There is some evidence that the principle of organization as applied to labour is extending even to the poorest paid workpeople. It is gratifying to see, for instance, that the process is gradually spreading among women. The first step is the modest benefit society, which provides a fund against sickness, and gradually for accidental or enforced abstinence from employment. The habit of making provision against casualties arising from the weakness of the individual's own position in relation to the risks of sickness or other contingencies, is soon extended towards making provision against the risks which attend the employment. Thence it is an easy stage to the process by which some slight barrier is made against an arbitrary lessening of wages. This step is aided by the avowed sympathy of those who are convinced that labour should be helped, or, at least, not hindered, in selling its work at the best price which it can get; and is justified in resisting, by all the means it can command, the process which would compel it to a forced sale of the only article of value which it possesses. In course of time, employers become habituated to the process under which workpeople sell their labour, on the same principle which others adopt in selling their goods, for the dealer knows the ruinous effect of a compulsory and sudden sale. And perhaps, finally, the sternest economist will come to see, not only that workpeople may adopt the principle of the capitalist in withholding goods from the market till a remunerative price is obtained, but that the process as applied to labour is ultimately as beneficial as most persons see it is when applied to trade. The market price, they tell us, must in the long run conform to the cost of production, plus the profit of the capitalist. Is this to be true of one of the factors in production only, and to be false in the case of the other?

The moralist might dwell at length and with satisfaction on the education which the principle of mutual aid gives to human nature. The rational economist knows that the best way in which the various forces which contribute to a common result can carry out their end is by the harmony of these forces. But the harmony is impossible if there be a well-founded distrust as to the equity with which the distribution of profits is effected. There will be a longing for violent remedies if law is plainly enlisted on behalf of any one interest, and to the detriment of all others. For, I repeat, the excellence of the social state does not lie in the fulness with which wealth is produced and accumulated;

but in the fact that it is so distributed as to give the largest
comfort and the widest hope to the general mass of those whose
continued efforts constitute the present industry of the nation and
the abiding prospect of its future well-being.

To the historian, however, as distinguished from the mere
annalist, the narrative of the varying fortunes which have attended
on these centuries of work and wages is immeasurably instructive.
Whatever claim other people may make to a share in the common
work of civilization, the English race may justly affirm that the
English people has instructed mankind in the machinery of
government, and in the process by which freedom may be secured
in the fullest measure to all, and the administration of public
affairs may be effectively carried on. The institutions of England
have been copied, with more or less success, by all civilised
races. They may be faulty, but they contain the best agencies
which experience has discovered and practical wisdom has
adopted.

We do not owe them to the dynasties which have ruled in
England, for the English constitution has been wrested from the
several families who have been permitted from time to time to be
at the head of affairs, and have one and all conspired against the
welfare of those who have endured them, till, more frequently
than any other people, the English have deposed them, and
driven them away. We do not owe them to statesmen and
lawyers, for they have constantly abetted their employers in those
purposes which have been so happily baffled. We do not owe
them to the English aristocracy, which has been by turns turbulent,
servile, and greedy, and is now probably the most unnecessary, as
a body, that any civilized society exhibits and endures. We do
not owe them to the Church, which has been, since the days of the
first Edward, the willing servant of statecraft, and has rarely
raised its voice against wrong-doing. Had the English people
relied on the mere machinery of its government and the character
of those who have manipulated this government, it would have
never been an example and a model of civilized organization. To
my mind, England was as its lowest degradation during the
twenty years which intervened between the destruction of the
monasteries and the restoration of the currency, when the worst

possible government was carried on, but with strict adherence to parliamentary forms.

The fact is, even in the darkest times there still was something which despotism feared or discovered that it must fear. England has never been entirely without a public opinion, which has been constantly acute, and has not infrequently been dangerous. There have always, too, been public men who could give effect to that opinion, and make it strong by marshalling it. The traditional parties have in turn thriven or become powerful,—the one by appropriating at its convenience the work of those who have interpreted and formulated popular demands; the other by putting itself at the head of all interests which are hostile to the public good, and by relying on the organization which is sure to be developed on behalf of such interests, and on apathy, ignorance, or unintelligent discontent. But by dint of patience and by watching for opportunities, the English people has developed a system which, though far from perfect, has achieved much of that which had long been the Utopia of philosophers. But the reforms which have been effected are the work of the people, and they are to be traced in that history only which is rarely written, of the stubborn perseverance with which Englishmen have criticised their own condition, have discovered that from themselves only, whoever may be the agent of the remedy, the remedy can be found, and have, under infinite discouragements, effected so much. The student of social forces will find, that in order to understand the order of things in his own time, he must take account not only of the process by which the machinery of our social condition has been made and constantly marred, but much more of the opinion and action which have developed and moulded the character of the English people.

NEW BOOKS ON LABOUR, WAGES, ETC.,

PUBLISHED BY

W. SWAN SONNENSCHEIN & CO.,

PATERNOSTER SQUARE, LONDON, E.C.

SIX CENTURIES OF WORK AND WAGES: a History of English Labour. By PROFESSOR J. E. THOROLD ROGERS, M.P., 2 vols. 8vo, 25s.

THE LAND AND THE LABOURERS: Records and Experiments in Cottage Farming and Co-operative Agriculture. By CHARLES W. STUBBS, M.A., Vicar of Stokenham. Crown 8vo, 3s. 6d.

CHRIST AND DEMOCRACY. By CHARLES W. STUBBS. M.A., Vicar of Stokenham. Crown 8vo, 3s. 6d.

REHOUSING THE INDUSTRIAL CLASSES, or Town Rookeries v. Village Communities. By the REV. HENRY SOLLY. Demy 16mo, 6d.

PRINCIPLES OF SOCIAL ECONOMY. By YVES GUYOT. Demy 8vo, 9s.

> BOOK I. Economic Science, its Nature, Objects, and Methods. BOOK II. The Constituents of Value. BOOK III. Value of Fixed and Circulating Capital. BOOK IV. The Value of Man. BOOK V. Experimental Economics. BOOK VI. The Functions of the State.

THE DILEMMAS OF LABOUR AND EDUCATION. By DR. AKIN KÁROLY. own 8vo, 3s. 6d.

W. SWAN SONNENSCHEIN & CO., Paternoster Sq , London. E.C.

OPINIONS OF THE PRESS

ON THE

SOCIAL SCIENCE SERIES.

———— ≥⟨φ⟩≤ ————

"'The Principles of State Interference' is another of Messrs. Swan Sonnenschein's Series of Handbooks on Scientific Social Subjects. It would be fitting to close our remarks on this little work with a word of commendation of the publishers of so many useful volumes by eminent writers on questions of pressing interest to a large number of the community. We have now received and read a good number of the handbooks which Messrs. Swan Sonnenschein have published in this series, and can speak in the highest terms of them. They are written by men of considerable knowledge of the subjects they have undertaken to discuss; they are concise; they give a fair estimate of the progress which recent discussion has added towards the solution of the pressing social questions of to-day, are well up to date, and are published at a price within the resources of the public to which they are likely to be of the most use."—*Westminster Review*, July, 1891.

"The excellent 'Social Science Series,' which is published at as low a price as to place it within everybody's reach."—*Review of Reviews*.

"A most useful series. . . . This impartial series welcomes both just writers and unjust."—*Manchester Guardian*.

"Concise in treatment, lucid in style and moderate in price, these books can hardly fail to do much towards spreading sound views on economic and social questions."—*Review of the Churches*.

"Convenient, well-printed, and moderately-priced volumes."—*Reynold's News paper*.

————

DOUBLE VOLUMES, Each 3s. 6d.

1. **Life of Robert Owen.**　　　　　　　　　　　　　　LLOYD JONES.
 "A worthy record of a life of noble activities."—*Manchester Examiner*.

2. **The Impossibility of Social Democracy:** a Second Part of "The Quintessence of Socialism".　　　　　　　　　　　　Dr. A. SCHÄFFLE.
 "Extremely valuable as a criticism of Social Democracy by the ablest living representative of State Socialism in Germany."—*Inter. Journal of Ethics*.

3. **The Condition of the Working Class in England in 1844.** FREDERICK ENGELS.
 "A translation of a work written in 1845, with a preface written in 1892."

4. **The Principles of Social Economy.**　　　　　　　　　YVES GUYOT.
 "An interesting and suggestive work. It is a profound treatise on social economy, and an invaluable collection of facts."—*Spectator*.

————

SWAN SONNENSCHEIN & CO., LONDON.

SOCIAL SCIENCE SERIES.

SCARLET CLOTH, EACH 2s. 6d.

SOCIAL SCIENCE SERIES—(*Continued*).

20. Common Sense about Women. T. W. HIGGINSON.
"An admirable collection of papers, advocating in the most liberal spirit the emancipation of women."—*Woman's Herald.*

21. The Unearned Increment. W. H. DAWSON.
"A concise but comprehensive volume."—*Echo.*

22. Our Destiny. LAURENCE GRONLUND.
"A very vigorous little book, dealing with the influence of Socialism on morals and religion."—*Daily Chronicle.*

23. The Working-Class Movement in America.
Dr. EDWARD and E. MARX AVELING.
"Will give a good idea of the condition of the working classes in America, and of the various organisations which they have formed."—*Scots Leader.*

24. Luxury. Prof. EMILE DE LAVELEYE.
"An eloquent plea on moral and economical grounds for simplicity of life."—*Academy.*

25. The Land and the Labourers. Rev. C. W. STUBBS, M.A.
"This admirable book should be circulated in every village in the country."—*Manchester Guardian.*

26. The Evolution of Property. PAUL LAFARGUE.
"Will prove interesting and profitable to all students of economic history."—*Scotsman.*

27. Crime and its Causes. W. DOUGLAS MORRISON.
"Can hardly fail to suggest to all readers several new and pregnant reflections on the subject."—*Anti-Jacobin.*

28. Principles of State Interference. D. G. RITCHIE, M.A.
"An interesting contribution to the controversy on the functions of the State."—*Glasgow Herald.*

29. German Socialism and F. Lassalle. W. H. DAWSON.
"As a biographical history of German Socialistic movements during this century it may be accepted as complete."—*British Weekly.*

30. The Purse and the Conscience. H. M. THOMPSON, B.A. (Cantab.).
"Shows common sense and fairness in his arguments."—*Scotsman.*

31. Origin of Property in Land. FUSTEL DE COULANGES. Edited, with an Introductory Chapter on the English Manor, by Prof. W. J. ASHLEY, M.A.
"His views are clearly stated, and are worth reading."—*Saturday Review.*

32. The English Republic. W. J. LINTON. Edited by KINETON PARKES.
"Characterised by that vigorous intellectuality which has marked his long life of literary and artistic activity."—*Glasgow Herald.*

33. The Co-Operative Movement. BEATRICE POTTER.
"Without doubt the ablest and most philosophical analysis of the Co-Operative Movement which has yet been produced."—*Speaker.*

34. Neighbourhood Guilds. Dr. STANTON COIT.
"A most suggestive little book to anyone interested in the social question."—*Pall Mall Gazette.*

35. Modern Humanists. J. M. ROBERTSON.
"Mr. Robertson's style is excellent—nay, even brilliant—and his purely literary criticisms bear the mark of much acumen."—*Times.*

36. Outlooks from the New Standpoint. E. BELFORT BAX.
"Mr. Bax is a very acute and accomplished student of history and economics."—*Daily Chronicle.*

37. Distributing Co-Operative Societies. Dr. LUIGI PIZZAMIGLIO. Edited by F. J. SNELL.
"Dr. Pizzamiglio has gathered together and grouped a wide array of facts and statistics, and they speak for themselves."—*Speaker.*

38. Collectivism and Socialism. By A. NACQUET. Edited by W. HEAFORD.
"An admirable criticism by a well-known French politician of the New Socialism of Marx and Lassalle."—*Daily Chronicle.*

SOCIAL SCIENCE SERIES—*(Continued)*.

39. The London Programme. SIDNEY WEBB, LL.B.
" Brimful of excellent ideas."—*Anti-Jacobin.*

40. The Modern State. PAUL LEROY BEAUL 7.
"A most interesting book ; well worth a place in the library of every s al
inquirer."—*N. B. Economist.*

41. The Condition of Labour. HENRY GEORGE.
" Written with striking ability, and sure to attract attention."—*Newcastle Chronicle.*

42. The Revolutionary Spirit preceding the French Revolution.
FELIX ROCQUAIN. With a Preface by Professor HUXLEY.
" The student of the French Revolution will find in it an excellent introduction to
the study of that catastrophe."—*Scotsman.*

43. The Student's Marx. EDWARD AVELING, D.Sc.
" One of the most practically useful of any in the Series."—*Glasgow Herald.*

44. A Short History of Parliament. B. C. SKOTTOWE, M.A. (Oxon.).
" Deals very carefully and completely with this side of constitutional history."—
Spectator.

45. Poverty : Its Genesis and Exodus. J. G. GODARD.
" He states the problems with great force and clearness."—*N. B. Economist.*

46. The Trade Policy of Imperial Federation. MAURICE H. HERVEY.
"An interesting contribution to the discussion."—*Publishers' Circular.*

47. The Dawn of Radicalism. J. BOWLES DALY, LL.D.
" Forms an admirable picture of an epoch more pregnant, perhaps, with political
instruction than any other in the world's history."—*Daily Telegraph.*

48. The Destitute Alien in Great Britain. ARNOLD WHITE ; MONTAGUE CRACKAN-
THORPE, Q.C. ; W. A. M'ARTHUR, M.P. ; W. H. WILKINS, &c.
" Much valuable information concerning a burning question of the day."—*Times.*

49. Illegitimacy and the Influence of Seasons on Conduct.
ALBERT LEFFINGWELL, M.D.
" We have not often seen a work based on statistics which is more continuously
interesting."—*Westminster Review.*

50. Commercial Crises of the Nineteenth Century. H. M. HYNDMAN.
" One of the best and most permanently useful volumes of the Series."—*Literary
Opinion.*

51. The State and Pensions in Old Age. J. A. SPENDER and ARTHUR ACLAND, M.P.
" A careful and cautious examination of the question."—*Times.*

52. The Fallacy of Saving. JOHN M. ROBERTSON.
" A plea for the reorganisation of our social and industrial system."—*Speaker.*

53. The Irish Peasant. ANON.
" A real contribution to the Irish Problem by a close, patient and dispassionate
investigator."—*Daily Chronicle.*

54. The Effects of Machinery on Wages. Prof. J. S. NICHOLSON, D.Sc.
" Ably reasoned, clearly stated, impartially written."—*Literary World.*

55. The Social Horizon. ANON.
" A really admirable little book, bright, clear, and unconventional."—*Daily
Chronicle.*

56. Socialism, Utopian and Scientific. FREDERICK ENGELS.
" The body of the book is still fresh and striking."—*Daily Chronicle.*

57. Land Nationalisation. A. R. WALLACE.
" The most instructive and convincing of the popular works on the subject."—
National Reformer.

58. The Ethic of Usury and Interest. Rev. W. BLISSARD.
" The work is marked by genuine ability."—*North British Agriculturalist.*

59. The Emancipation of Women. ADELE CREPAZ.
" By far the most comprehensive, luminous, and penetrating work on this question
that I have yet met with."—*Extract from Mr.* GLADSTONE'S *Preface.*

60. The Eight Hours' Question. JOHN M. ROBERTSON.
" A very cogent and sustained argument on what is at present the unpopular
side."—*Times.*

61 Drunkenness. GEORGE R. WILSON, M.B.
" Well written, carefully reasoned, free from cant, and full of sound sense."—
National Observer.

62. The New Reformation. RAMSDEN BALMFORTH.
" A striking presentation of the nascent religion, how best to realize the personal
and social ideal."—*Westminster Review.*

63. The Agricultural Labourer. T. E. KEBBEL.
" A short summary of his position, with appendices on wages, education, allot
ments, etc., etc."

64. Ferdinand Lassalle as a Social Reformer. E. BERNSTEIN.
" A worthy addition to the Social Science Series."—*North British Economist.*

www.ingramcontent.com/pod-product-compliance
Lightning Source LLC
Chambersburg PA
CBHW030821270326
41928CB00007B/833